:: **Measures of Equality**

Envisioning Cuba :: Louis A. Pérez Jr., editor

:: Measures of Equality

Social Science, Citizenship, and Race in Cuba, 1902–1940

Alejandra Bronfman

The University of North Carolina Press
Chapel Hill and London

Designed by Kimberly Bryant
Set in Monotype Garamond by Tseng Information Systems, Inc.

Manufactured in the United States of America

Portions of Chapter 1 appeared, in revised form, in "Unsettled and Nomadic: Law,
Anthropology, and Race in Early Twentieth-Century Cuba," Working Paper No. 9,
Latin American Studies Center, University of Maryland, College Park, 2002.

Portions of Chapter 2 appeared, in revised form, in "En Plena Libertad y Democracia:
Negros Brujos and the Social Question, 1904–1919," *Hispanic American Historical Review* 82,
no. 3 (2002): 549–87. Copyright © 2002 by Duke University Press. All rights reserved.
Used by permission of the publisher.

Library of Congress Cataloging-in-Publication Data
Bronfman, Alejandra Marina, 1962–
Measures of equality: social science, citizenship, and race in Cuba, 1902–1940 /
Alejandra Bronfman.
p. cm.—(Envisioning Cuba)
Includes bibliographical references and index.
ISBN 0-8078-2898-x (cloth: alk. paper)—ISBN 0-8078-5563-4 (pbk.: alk. paper)
1. Cuba—Race relations.   2. Equality—Cuba—History—20th century.   3. Social
justice—Cuba—History—20th century.   4. Cuba—Politics and government—20th
century.   5. Social sciences—Cuba—History—20th century.   6. Social scientists—
Cuba—Attitudes.   7. Sociological jurisprudence.   I. Title.   II. Series.
F1789.A1B76   2005
305.8′0097291—dc22

2004009060

cloth   08 07 06 05 04   5 4 3 2 1
paper   08 07 06 05 04   5 4 3 2 1

for Maia and Yayi

:: Contents

:: Illustrations

:: Acknowledgments

The most necessary and important expressions of gratitude must go to the staff members, archivists, and librarians who helped and guided me toward the materials without which this work would not exist. I am deeply grateful to all at the Archivo Nacional de Cuba, the Biblioteca Nacional José Martí, the Centro de Estudios de Historia y Organización de la Ciencia, the Instituto de Literatura y Lingüística, the Archivo de la Universidad de la Habana, the Archivo Provincial de Cienfuegos, the U.S. Library of Congress, the U.S. National Archives, the Schomburg Center for Research in Black Culture, the Firestone Library at Princeton University, the Latin American Collection at the University of Florida, the Hemeroteca in Madrid, and the Mudd Library at Yale University.

I have received funding from the Department of History, the Program in Latin American Studies, the Council for Regional Studies, the Council for International Studies, and the Woodrow Wilson Society of Fellows, all at Princeton University, and the Johns Hopkins Cuba Exchange Program. The Social Science Research Council provided generous support with an International Dissertation Research Grant as well as an incomparable opportunity to meet other Fellows. A research grant from the University of Florida provided funding for a final research trip, and a postdoctoral fellowship from the University of Maryland Center for Latin American Studies gave me precious writing time.

In the process of transforming this text from a dissertation into a book, I have benefited from the comments of a number of audiences, including members of the Montana State University Department of History, the Washington Area Symposium on Latin American History, and participants in "The Body and the Body Politic in Latin America Conference" at the University of Maryland. In particular I would like to thank Mary Kay Vaughan, Daryle Williams, and Stephan Palmié for taking an interest in my work. In the years since I finished the dissertation, I have been nearly as peripatetic as the objects in my first chapter. I am most grateful to the Departments of History at the University of Florida, Yale University, and the University of British Columbia for insightful comments when I presented my work, for time and resources that allowed me to complete this project, and for their warm welcomes. W. Fitzhugh Brundage, Jon Butler, and David Breen have all my respect and admiration.

I have had the good fortune to learn from many who know more about these issues than I do, especially in Cuba. Fernando Martínez Heredia, Adrian López Denis, Blancamar León Rosabal, Reinaldo Funes, Marial Iglesias, Ricardo Quiza, Oilda Hevia Lanier, Araceli García Carranza, Armando Rangel, Ana Cairo, Orlando García Martínez, Fe Iglesias, Carlos Venegas, Tomás Fernández Robaina, Manuel Rivero de la Calle, and Gregorio Sánchez have all contributed importantly to the conception and execution of this project. The Instituto de Historia in Havana, which enabled my research in Cuba, deserves my gratitude.

Likewise, the list of scholars and colleagues who have applied their intellects to my historiographic ambitions, quandaries, and muddles includes Jorge Domínguez, Fernando Coronil, Michael Zeuske, Stuart McCook, Virginia Domínguez, Alejandro de la Fuente, Ada Ferrer, Stanley Stein, Peter Johnson, Arcadio Díaz-Quiñones, Richard Pildes, Alexandra Stern, Consuelo Naranjo Orovio, Paul Gootenberg, Antonio Saborit, Jeffrey Needell, Sheryl Kroen, David Geggus, Luise White, Alejandra Osorio, Mark Thurner, Efraín Barradas, Paul Kramer, Lara Putnam, Aims McGuinness, Kathryn Burns, Marikay McCabe, Laura Engelstein, Stuart Schwartz, Gilbert Joseph, Patricia Pessar, Seth Fein, and Alexander Moon. Their interventions at key moments and their example as scholars were powerfully influential. Without the able and insightful research assistance of Matthew Bloom I would not have been able to finish this book. Barbara Weinstein has my profound gratitude for multifaceted wisdom.

My committee has demonstrated patience, generosity, and support that are difficult to adequately recognize. It has been an honor to witness the intelligence and experience of Jeremy Adelman, Rebecca Scott, Richard Turits, and Kenneth Mills as they focused on the problems in these pages.

I have been extremely fortunate to have had the advice and insight of Louis A. Pérez Jr. and Elaine Maisner to guide this project. Thanks as well to the anonymous reviewer, whose comments helped expand the scope of the book, and to Stevie Champion for incisive editing.

Some of the people who have taught me the most know little about the project at hand, and they deserve recognition. Lydia Fakundiny taught me so brilliantly about reading and writing. Roger and Dorothy Sale understood so profoundly and shared so impressively. Rachel Weil took me on and provided astute guidance. Michael Heller has brought constant warmth and friendship to a wandering life. José and Marcos Bronfman deserve a good deal of gratitude for their trust and affection. Marisa Bronfman, for whom I have such respect and admiration, has cared for me intensely. The memory of Colin Walters's sense of humor and model as a writer will endure. To Nuria Bronfman, Glenn Zacher, Max and Henry, for their example, and their love, and the home they have made for me, I cannot begin to say enough, but they know.

There are those in whose presence the boundary between work and life disappears. Reinaldo Román, Olívia Gomes da Cunha, Jessica Meyerson, and Meri Clark have read drafts, commented, listened, and shared their own work. Most crucially, however, they have set aside work for more important things. I cannot imagine continuing without their humor, understanding, intelligence, and friendship.

Alexander Dawson I thank for absolutely everything, and Maia Q, for the gift of her existence.

:: Measures of Equality

:: Introduction

Sometime during the uncertain months between 1896 and 1900 three scientists pored over the exhumed remains of General Antonio Maceo, who had died fighting in Cuba's final war for independence. In 1900 they published their findings in a short pamphlet entitled *El craneo de Maceo: Estudio antropológico* (*Maceo's Skull: An Anthropological Study*). Backed by precise statistical detail and citing the French craniometrists Paul Broca and Paul Topinard (under whose tutelage the measuring of skulls flourished as a respectable science in the nineteenth century), the three scientists claimed that their findings revealed a fortuitous racial mixture of a "white" brain capacity blended with "black" limb proportions and strength to render him a "truly superior man."[1]

General Maceo had joined Cuba's struggle for independence in 1868 and perished in battle twenty-eight years later (1896), having become one of Cuba's most respected military leaders. Maceo had taken part in a dramatic process in which a society only recently premised on slavery had attained political autonomy with a multiracial military and a nationalist ideology that transcended racial identification in its definition of a national community. His ascent through the ranks was one of many examples of the crucial participation of former slaves and descendants of slaves in the struggle against Spanish colonialism. During the course of the wars for independence (1868–98), the language of antiracism he so frequently invoked became a powerful tool on which former slaves and their descendants relied to insist on equal treatment as members of a fraternal military order.[2]

Yet the fate of Maceo's remains embodied a process that reentrenched racial inequalities with empiricist and positivist claims about the biological nature of racial differences. Although in the case of Maceo an understanding of race that linked physical proportions to mental and moral capacities reinforced his position as hero, other descendants of slaves might not have fared so well, as empiricism and positivism tended mostly to give new scientific life to old juridical and social hierarchies. *Maceo's Skull* was a product of the intersection of the exigencies of war, an increasingly influential discourse on equality, and the powerful sway of scientific positivism. As such it is a fruitful place to begin an inquiry into the history of race in twentieth-century Cuba.

Between the end of the war for independence in 1898 and the beginning of the republic in 1902, Cubans worked to come to terms with the legacies and unintended consequences of the end of colonial rule, the emancipation of slaves, and thirty years of war. In a broader sense Cubans shared the predicaments of Latin Americans everywhere, living with colonial legacies and blighted interpretations of those legacies produced almost before colonialism had become a thing of the past. Colonial relationships had shaped the economy and society, controlled politics, and inspired a search for alternative forms of governance. At the same time, the final war for independence (1895–98) marked a turning point in the United States's history as an imperial power in Cuba. Having entered the war in its closing months and ended it with the subjugation of both Cuba and Spain, the United States occupied Cuba, frustrating its hopes for national sovereignty. Cubans debated their future in the shadow of the unexpected shift from Spanish domination to North American encroachment. Even as they came to understand that the independence they had envisioned would be compromised by continuing U.S. influence, they considered the theories and practices of governance and legitimation best suited to their circumstances.[3]

As the occupation came to an end and the possibility of autonomy (however limited) loomed, political debates and social imaginings were preoccupied with the relationship between race and citizenship. The question was simple: Who was to be included? Was the answer as straightforward as some, following José Martí ("those good enough to die are good enough to vote"), claimed?[4] Or were those who worried that the descendants of slaves could drag a political community toward uncivilized backwardness or diseased impotence to prevail? Doubts about the aptitude of male Cubans of African descent for political participation lingered. Yet, in contrast to many freshly baptized democracies that had faced the same dilemma (the United States springs to mind), the new regime, however ambivalent, acknowledged the military participation of former slaves by its adoption of formal legal equality and universal manhood suffrage.[5]

Cuba acquired a new constitution in 1901. Its controversial Platt Amendment laid out a relationship of "singular intimacy" between the

United States and Cuba at the highest levels of government and diplomacy.[6] At the level of quotidian existence, however, the constitution included several articles that promised radical changes in everyday life. Article II, under the section "Individual Rights," stated simply: "All Cubans are equal before the law. The Republic does not recognize special rights or personal privileges."[7] As a liberal proclamation of equality, the article eliminated all privileges and rendered all Cubans nominally equal. As a new and significant result of republican rule, its adoption as part of the state's legal infrastructure immediately raised questions about the meaning and practice of equality.

Other innovations in the constitution indicated more specifically the meaning of equal citizenship. Article 26 stated: "All religions may be freely practiced, as well as the exercise of all sects, with no other limitation than respect of Christian morals and public order. The Church shall be separate from the State, which may not subsidize any religious group."[8] Although the explicit separation of church and state was probably the focus of many Cuban lawmakers seeking to create a secular state, the provision about public order would prove most useful to law enforcement officials and most troublesome to those whose religious practices were deemed problematic in the new republican order.

As contemporary scholars have observed, the conferring of citizenship (however qualified) generated new dilemmas and uncertainties as to the contours of political order.[9] An indication of true egalitarian sentiment to some and of resignation to political expediency to others, the inclusion of male former slaves and their descendants into the new political order nonetheless became a cornerstone of the Cuban republic.

Yet Cuba was trying to implement a republic based on liberal principles just as the world was growing suspicious of liberalism. In both Europe and the United States, liberal experiments had already given way to anxieties about "mass politics" and to endeavors to understand and reform unruly social forces with the new tools of science, quantification, and statistical analysis.[10] Other Latin American nations had engaged in liberal experiments years before the late-nineteenth-century revitalization of biological notions of race.[11] In Cuba, the political formalization of liberal ideals coincided with the ascendance of scientific theories of race.

That science proposed new ways to rank the races just as statemakers conferred legal equality on former slaves and their descendants seems paradoxical, but it was not uncommon. The elaboration of new ideologies of inequality to replace those that have fallen victim to historical circumstance has been observed by many scholars, beginning with Alexis de Tocqueville.[12] This book takes that observation as its point of departure and explores the ways Cubans negotiated conflicting notions of equality. It argues that the relatively inclusive rather than relentlessly exclusive nature of the early Cuban republic legitimated hereditarian views about the inferiority of Cubans of African descent. At the same time the context of relative inclusion allowed Cubans of color to express powerful critiques of racialist views. As a result, tensions between equality and hierarchy generated a process by which political identity and citizenship were transformed. Initial conceptions of race-transcendent, universalizing notions of citizenship gave way, by 1940, to a distinctly "black" political identity in step with a broader conception of citizenship imagined in collective, corporatist terms. This book is thus not so much about the integration of blacks and mulattoes into a political order as it is about the transformation of a political order and the terms of participation for all involved.

The promise of "racial democracy," the lynchpin in many ways of the liberal state in formation, has been a major focus of several recent studies. Understanding the goal of racial democracy as a powerful and capacious legitimizer of ideals, historians have analyzed the nineteenth-century origins of race-transcendent nationalism through the dual processes of war and emancipation, examined its implementation, and looked into the unintended consequences of its propagation.[13] Aline Helg and Alejandro de la Fuente have produced accounts of the implications of this construct in the politics of the republic. Helg has characterized the "myth of racial democracy" as specious, serving to justify actual exclusion and continuing inequality. Cubans of color who mobilized in protest were accused of racism because they relied on racial distinctions that the republic had in theory eliminated and were deemed unpatriotic because they defied national narratives of unity and harmony. Helg has argued that racial democracy, never more than a promise, was a powerful weapon in the hands of elites, who were able to silence or violently repress demands for political or social equality and to disable mobilization by Cubans of color aspiring toward meaningful participation as citizens.[14]

On the point of the power of the "myth of racial democracy" de la Fuente offers a different interpretation. He asserts that although the myth served in some instances to silence the demands of Cubans of color, it also limited the scope of white exclusionary or racist practices. In elections, for instance, the advent of universal manhood suffrage meant that all political parties had no choice but to appeal to black and mulatto voters, a significant proportion of the electorate. In addition, de la Fuente argues that Cubans of African descent were able to take advantage of whatever emancipatory potential the myth of racial democracy had to offer. He emphasizes the flexible nature of egalitarian discourses and the capacities of Cubans of color to appropriate the promise of equality and interpret that promise to their own ends.[15] Both scholars provide important interpretations of the effect of race on Cuban politics and contribute to a complex comparative debate on race, citizenship, and state formation in the Americas.[16] This book advances those debates by interrogating the category of race itself through an examination of the ways state officials, social scientists, and black and mulatto activists made, changed, and legitimated its meanings.

My approach seeks to delineate the genealogy, in the context of the Cuban republic, not just of the "myth of racial democracy" but also of theories of racial difference. At the same time, it asks how theories of racial difference engaged notions of political equality. I contend that addressing these questions will prove crucial to understanding not how race influenced politics and society, but rather how politics and society changed the meanings of race. Following Barbara Fields, I begin with the notion of race as an outcome rather than a cause: a historical product of the confluence of ideas, events, and processes. The presumption that race can be made suggests that race is neither a fixed biological category, nor a primordial attachment, nor a transhistorical phenomenon removed from space and time. Rather, it is a changing, flexible category that emerges out of particular places and times. As Fields, Thomas Holt, and Peter Wade have compellingly argued, race has a history.[17] Following this assertion, I have tried to elucidate a brief but rich moment in the history of an idea.

As the history of an idea, this project takes a broad view of what that entails. Clifford Geertz observed that "ideas — religious, moral, practical, aesthetic — must as Max Weber, among others, never tired of insisting, be carried by powerful social groups to have powerful social effects: someone must revere them, celebrate them, defend them, impose them. They have to be institutionalized in order to find not just an intellectual existence in society, but, so to speak, a material one as well."[18] Geertz might also have written that people eventually resist, invert, deflect, or reshape ideas as well.

In the transition from colony to republic, Cubans encountered the certainty of new institutional arrangements and struggled with the uncertainty of implementation as well as the potentially awkward questions of compatibility with lingering colonialist practices. Social science played an important role inasmuch as it produced (and consumed) knowledge and social categories. Yet it could not maintain complete control of the knowledge it produced. Numerous intellectuals of color—artists, journalists, political activists—explicitly engaged, contested, and redefined theories and categories that purported to define and describe them. These critical dialogues with particular racial understandings shaped the social and political aspirations of many black and mulatto intellectuals. The narrative of this book engages intellectuals, institutions, and ideas and the complex interactions among them as they both buttressed one another and came into conflict.

Social scientists and intellectuals of color concern me because they both tried to meet the challenge of the republic, that is, how to shed the vestiges of colonialism and bring about a sovereign modern nation-state by reforming racial theories and practices. They are at the center of the analysis because they thought intensely and explicitly about this problem. It would be a mistake, in this instance, to conflate "intellectuals" with "elites." The subjects of this study came from diverse backgrounds, and the class, color, and political hierarchies they negotiated never neatly lined up with one another. This book suggests a rethinking of categories such as "elite" and "popular" or "conservative" and "radical" when the meaning of race is in question. In the remainder of this introduction I offer a brief excursion into the intellectual and social roots of social science and struggles for racial equality during the transitional period preceding the republic.

Social Science and Science

The nascent field of anthropology was the focus of a modernizing project jointly undertaken by the U.S. military government and Cuban scientists. During the first occupation (1899–1902) the military government had embarked on a plan of reform and renewal of educational and scientific institutions. With the intention of reorganizing the University of Havana, Military Order 250, on December 28, 1899, created a series of new academic departments and appointed their chairs. One of the results was the institutional consolidation of anthropology, until then a diffuse and unprofessionalized, although increasingly influential, pursuit of the

The study of skulls at the Museo Antropológico Montané, Havana.

study of "man." The new Department of Anthropology and Anthropometric Exercises was to be headed by Luis Montané and supplemented with empirical materials from Havana's Museum of Anthropology—at that moment a dusty and directionless set of display cabinets.[19]

The interest in anthropology and especially anthropometry suggested that both North American and Cuban scientists were working within a paradigm that presumed biological, measurable differences among races. Anthropometry was, according to one widely cited manual, "the systematized art of measuring and taking observations on man, his skeleton, his brain, or other organs." Its utility to the state "to ascertain whether and how its human stock is progressing or regressing" was one of its most appealing qualities. Surveying, measuring, and classifying a diverse population would enable scientists to advise the government on the progress or lack thereof of different sectors of the population.[20]

Thus at its inception, social science in republican Cuba imagined a project nothing like one of race-transcendence in the interest of political equality. Rather, the study of physiognomic difference received new support from technological and intellectual innovation as well as injections of foreign capital. Equality would be measured differently in ballot boxes and in museum cabinets.

The institutional consolidation of anthropology formed part of a broader promulgation of Cuban science during the final war for independence and subsequent North American occupation. Cuban scientists noted enthusiastically that the material aid provided during the U.S. presence carried symbolic importance as well. The military government had provided support, primarily in the form of a new building, to the struggling Academy of Sciences (Academia de Ciencias Médicas, Físicas y Naturales de la Habana), which had once been the institutional center of scientific activity but most recently had faltered as much of its membership dispersed during the war.

Cuban scientists welcomed these interventions as signs that their integration into the international scientific community was imminent. In a letter to a colleague and comember of the Academy of Sciences, Dr. Tomás Coronado interpreted the occasion of Cuba's hosting the upcoming Third Panamerican Medical Congress as a sign of Cuba's acceptance into the international community. Cuban input would be important at the congress because local conditions, including "our climate, our soils, and even the degree of civilization we have achieved, modify and change the characteristics of diseases that proliferate here, in an environment so different from that of Europe." Coronado was certain that as Cuban scientists complemented "research performed simultaneously throughout the Americas," international scientific culture would flourish.[21]

According to Coronado, the war and occupation had benefited Cuban science in two ways. First, Cuban doctor Carlos Finlay's discovery of the causes and ultimately the cure of yellow fever, most prevalent among American soldiers, placed Cuba on the cutting edge of scientific progress. This enabled Coronado to argue in a Panglossian way that the war had provided an opportunity for Cuba to demonstrate its "right to freedom and sovereignty and its love of science." Indeed, he viewed U.S.-Cuban relations through rose-tinted (and perhaps quite thick) glasses: "The mere acceptance of Cuba by the United States as the host of the Third Congress," he claimed, "is an explicit acknowledgment of our independence."[22] On the eve of Governor Leonard Wood's departure from Cuba, the Academy of Sciences thanked the U.S. general for his contributions and assured him that he would leave behind a deeply grateful group of scientists.[23]

Social and political conditions in the period immediately following the war proved beneficial to the status of the professions in general and medicine in particular, as struggling former landowning families turned to professional careers in hopes of preserving their social positions.[24] The rising status of professionals was reflected in politics as they were awarded government appointments with increasing frequency. Diego Tamayo, a doctor who had participated in the constitutional convention of 1901, served as secretary of state and interior under Leonard Wood and as secretary of the interior under Tomás Estrada Palma, until political wrangling during a stevedores' strike forced him out of office. Tamayo was also president of the Academy of Sciences during Wood's tenure and was instrumental in ensuring the renovation of a convent to house the academy as well as the shipment of artifacts to the Museum of Anthropology.[25]

It was through Tamayo and others in similar positions that the state and social sciences began to engage in projects of mutual assistance and mutual legitimation. The transitional phases after the withdrawal of U.S. troops witnessed Cuban social scientists appealing to the state for approval and support. In an address to a gathering at the Academy of Science attended by Leonard Wood and Tomás Estrada Palma just five days before Estrada Palma's inauguration as the first president of Cuba, Dr. Enrique Barnet made a case for the interdependence of science and the state. Governmental authority must be used, he argued, to disinfect the population and protect it from disease. Since only a healthy citizenry could meet its social obligations and enjoy its individual rights, it was the role of law and social policy to express the public conscience and ethical values of the state through campaigns to fight disease and accompanying degeneration.[26] If, to readers steeped in Foucauldian theory, this stance seems deeply invested in social control, it is nonetheless important to note that it was rooted in an assumption of inclusion: Barnet advocated "cleansing" the entire populace so that it might more fully participate both politically and socially.

The state, through legal parameters and scientific endeavors, thus instituted new ways to order its changing polity. Yet despite scientists' enthusiasm and the realities of changing legal parameters and flourishing scientific undertakings, the Cuban state was a work in progress, its legitimacy at risk with the constant possibility (and reality) of U.S. intervention and the extent of its power uncertain. To be sure, science and social science enjoyed prestige, limited institutionalization at the University of Havana, and a measure of popular dissemination. At the same time, the state lacked the means to thoroughly enforce egalitarian measures or propagate social scientific avowals of the incapacities of some Cubans of color. Neither racial transcendence nor the science of inequality enjoyed hegemony in the early republic, either in law or in practice.[27]

An important part of the history of race, then, lies in understanding the meaning of equality to those who demanded it, for they of necessity found themselves navigating these ideological and practical tensions. As there was no consensus on the meaning of their newly acquired status, Cubans of color endeavored to formulate their own visions of how to integrate formal equality into lived experience.

Citizen Consciences

The story of access to civil rights did not begin with the onset of the republic in 1902. The demand for rights and the struggle against discrimination had begun before the end of slavery in 1886. Free people of color and former slaves had, within the constraints of a slave system, engaged in manumission, formed mutual aid and religious associations known as *cabildos* and *sociedades*, struggled to gain access to education, and signaled discontent over discrimination in public spaces. Their engagement with the colonial legal system had accelerated the process of emancipation. By the 1880s, as Spanish elites came to understand that the loyalty of people of color would be a useful asset politically, blacks and mulattoes had acquired limited political rights and obtained legal injunctions against discrimination.[28] During the Peace of Zanjón, after the Ten Years War, the Spanish colonial government had loosened its hold on civic and political life, and Cubans of color obtained a public voice in the country's numerous newspapers. Pleas for full civic status had been expressed in publications such as *La Fraternidad* and *La Igualdad*. An 1888 article in *La Fraternidad* reminded its readers that "yesterday we were slaves, today we are free, we want to participate in life, claim our rights, we want consideration and respect."[29] Journalist-politician Juan Gualberto Gómez had institutionalized struggles against discrimination through the Directorio Central de las Sociedades de Color, founded in 1892 to unify Cubans of color throughout the country. Although it was a large, heterogeneous agglomeration of sociedades, certain claims regarding citizenship became more prevalent than others.[30] Many sociedades held to a notion of citizenship based on equality but looked to education as the means of integration into political and social spheres. With the memory of slavery all too recent, they sought to dispel the stigma as much as possible and shape themselves in the image of virtuous citizens, well prepared to meet the obligations of civic culture.

If You Can Die You Can Vote

The experience of military participation afforded Cubans of color a new and distinct form of claiming the rights of citizenship. A powerful nationalist ideology now stressed valor and sacrifice in battle as the prerequisites for political inclusion. Even before the war ended, male combatants had begun to refer to themselves and their white compatriots as "citizen" (*ciudadano*). Notably, this did not mean that former black and mulatto military leaders were necessarily viewed as capable of occupying positions of leadership in a civil government. Ada Ferrer has demonstrated the ways the shift from military to civilian rule and to a regime that claimed to transcend race included complex transformations in the articulation of racism. At the highest levels of political leadership, "culture" and "civilization" often came to stand for "color" as a means of exclusion. Black general Quintín Bandera was a victim of such maneuvers, finding himself court-martialed and stripped of his command a few short years after having served as one of the most prominent leaders of the Cuban Liberational Army.[31]

Despite this dynamic, at once racist and antiracist, both elite and nonelite veterans of the wars for independence were able to invoke their status as former fighters and present citizens in making specific demands. Not only that, their participation had given them status by virtue of integrating them into clientelistic networks that formed during the wars. These networks were powerful and durable; they offered protection, access to certain goods, and by virtue of their multiracial quality created an informal venue for social mobility.[32]

In the first months of the republic, an organization known as the Comité de Acción de Veteranos y Sociedades de la Raza de Color (Committee of Veterans and Associations of the Race of Color), headed by war veteran Generoso Campos Marquetti, presented the Estrada Palma government with a series of demands intended to eliminate some of the most egregious discriminatory practices enacted during the U.S. occupation. They asked for concrete measures and received them in the promise to set aside a certain number of civil service jobs for Cubans of color. Eighty positions in the police force and twenty in the mail service were granted as a concession to the committee's demands. Against rising accusations that this group was trying to instigate a race war, Juan Gualberto Gómez offered a defense of its position, relying on the claim to just treatment as compensation for having fought in the final war for independence "so that we do not forget the sacrifices of the petitioners in the very recent revolutionary past, a time when skin color was of no importance, but quality and individual virtues were of great importance."[33] Soon afterward the committee dissolved, as some of its members entered government and others became less visible for a time. But its outlook, which combined militaristic sensibilities with demands for a share of the goods the state was capable of distributing, would inform the claims of Cuba's first and only race-based political party, the Partido Independiente de Color (PIC), in later years.

Two principal modes of imagining citizenship thus informed the actions of black and mulatto activists. One, tied to the notion of civic virtue, sought equal status through education and participation in associational life, both conceived largely as autonomous from the state. The other mode based its claims on a history of military participation and appealed more directly to the state for access to benefits of patronage. As it turned out, this mode was also more closely linked to clientelistic networks that relied on the threat of violence as one of its strategies. These competing notions of citizenship and equality emerged alongside legal and scientific discourses and practices also engaged in determining the boundaries and norms of citizenship. The chapters that follow explore the ways they converged and impinged on one another during the republic.

Chapter 1 examines the first moments of discursive convergence in the republic. Although the state had created new freedoms, it also formulated new tools with which to repress perceived threats to order. Law and social science did not necessarily coincide as they attempted to order this nascent polity, producing opposing understandings of race and citizenship. This chapter follows objects seized from police raids of African-derived religious rituals and explicates the meanings produced in distinct sites as they traveled from the houses from which they were seized to the police station, to the courthouse, and finally to the Museum of Anthropology. Although social science enjoyed a growing institutional presence, it did not offer a crystallized theory of the relationships among race, religion, and crime. A notion of inclusivity prevailed, but the proper state response to heterogeneity was still in question. Chapter 2 takes as its point of departure the sensationalist child murder case of Zoila and looks at the debates about civilization and modernity that this case (and others like it) incited.

I argue that the figure of the black delinquent became central to a number of social scientific explanations and formulations, inspiring social scientists to engage with a variegated set of international interlocutors while aiming to construct theories that would reflect and in some instances reform their own social environment. Yet this increasingly dominant notion of a vital link between race and crime was capacious enough to be used for different purposes by journalists, the courts, intellectuals, and politicians.

The narrative moves, in Chapters 3 and 4, to the ways in which a variety of black and mulatto activists and intellectuals debated their status in Cuban society. In response to circulating notions of "black criminality and barbarism" many Cubans of color acceded to the appeal of modernity, creating distance between what they viewed as their own modern secularity and the atavism of practitioners of "primitive" religions. Within these parameters, however, competing notions of citizenship collided as the PIC's reliance on military strategy proved unpalatable to influential politicians of color. Violence in 1912 precipitated the demise of military tactics as a source of power for Cubans of color. Rather than stifling all forms of black political mobilization, however, 1912 and its aftermath impelled a more decisive shift in strategy. Some black and mulatto intellectuals and activists began to pursue an alternative way to achieve equal status as citizens—through a renewed focus on autonomous associational life and tentative formulations of a collective identity. This took place against a backdrop of emerging critiques of U.S. imperialism and dependency, a context of heightened political activism, and mass mobilization. A black political identity imagined in collective rather than individualist terms began to become epistemologically and politically viable.

I then turn to the ways the science of society responded to a context of growing mass mobilization. I argue that with distinct uses of the concept of time, social science turned from a project centered on reform to one that focused on demobilization. I trace the emergence of ethnography that envisioned an ordered, exotic past as it purported to valorize Cuba's African heritage. On the other hand, the practice of eugenics aimed increasingly toward genetic purity and away from environmental reform, envisioning an ordered, Europeanized future. The branch of social science that dealt most explicitly with the present, criminology, provided the intellectual support for the institutionalization of Lombrosian connections between race and crime. Chapter 5 examines the success of each of these endeavors in attaining state support. My contention is that social science, with the exception of criminology, proved of limited value to a state interested in harnessing highly mobilized sectors of society to build political support. Chapter 6 argues that activists of color who demanded social justice and equality were equally uninterested in many promises of social science. Nevertheless, social science produced the salient categories around which new modes of political organization emerged. Although the specific claims made by social scientists fell under criticism by black activists and were understood ambivalently by the state, both the state and activists invoked racial categories in their efforts to accrue political power. Thus while the race-transcendent or culturally hybrid views of Cuban national identities held sway in literary, artistic, or touristic circles, many sectors of the state (following James Scott, *Seeing Like a State*) saw races, as well as other constituencies (women, laborers, capitalists), as distinct groups rather than as disaggregated collections of individuals or one homogeneous polity.

The final chapter explores debates about cultural and political representation. A prominent group of black intellectuals formulated claims to citizenship in dialogue with intellectual trends that rediscovered African cultures in the 1930s, but in critical dialogue that raised many questions about facile appropriation of a distant cultural history. When the prospect of constitutional reform began to dominate political life, their debates about cultural representation flowed into debates about political representation. Their demands for reform were heeded. As a result of a broad consensus regarding an expanded, interventionist state, the newly drafted constitution proposed sweeping measures to achieve social justice, including a provision that banned and criminalized racial discrimination. Though serving as the conclusion of the story I have told, the consensus that underwrote the 1940 constitution does not provide a clear end, but rather presents a moment of profound ambiguity. That it was necessary to prohibit discrimination points to the persistence of racial inequality in many spheres of everyday life. That Cubans of color mobilized against inequality and persuaded their fellow citizens to recognize the justice of their claims points to the vital presence of the *raza de color* in political life.

A WORD ABOUT terminology. Any analysis of the changing and multiply inflected meanings of race must ultimately depend on language. Wherever possible I have used the racial terminology employed by the historical actors who populate these pages. *Negro* (black) and *de color* (of color) were both used interchangeably and distinctively, as when *de color* referred to *negros* as well as *mulatos*. *Blanco* (white) signified Cubans of European descent, while *mestizo* and *mulatto* implied some form (usually indeterminate) of racial mixture. When it was impossible to quote directly, I have used "black and mulatto" and "of color" interchangeably to refer to people who would not have been considered white. I have chosen to use the term "Afro-Cuban" only when historical actors did so.

One of the transformations this book traces is the emergence of a "black" political identity. When activists who in other contexts may have used or been labeled "mulatto" chose to use "black" for reasons that will become clear, I have respected their usage. In this way I hope to underscore both the importance of language and its necessarily awkward fit with phenotype or physical features. Although my own view is that race is an intellectual, social, and political construct, the actors who inhabit this story espoused a wide range of opinions on this question.

The vessel of the embryonic Republic navigated
between the Scyla of treason and the Caribdis of
impotence, never far from catastrophe.

[Entre el Scyla de la traición y el Caribdis de la
impotencia, allá iba la nave de la embrionaria
República, expuesta a cada instante a zozobrar.]

J. BUTTARI GAUNAURD
Boceto crítico histórico (1954)

::

For both art and life depend wholly on the law
of optics, on perspective and illusion, to be blunt,
on the necessity of error.

F. NIETZSCHE
The Birth of Tragedy (1872)

1

Unsettled and Nomadic
Law, Anthropology, and Race

On May 20, 1902, the city of Havana celebrated the inauguration of the Cuban republic. After thirty years of struggle for independence against Spain, followed by two and a half years of U.S. military
government, Cuba had achieved sovereignty. Although the reality and
extent of that sovereignty were widely debated at the time, as they are
by contemporary historians, the day was devoted to festivities marking
the departure of the Americans and the beginning of autonomous rule.[1]
Even as they feared the implications of the Platt Amendment, Cubans
recognized and celebrated the acquisition of new institutions and policies
that promised long sought-after changes for many sectors of Cuban society. Most Cubans had perceived the transition from the Spanish orbit to
the North American as a move away from traditionalism and backwardness and toward modernity, but while some had celebrated this potential

transformation, others were ambivalent or deeply critical. Yet even as they witnessed this shift in spheres of influence, Cubans embarked on a nation-building project, as the nation and the state finally came to represent coterminous social and political entities. As Louis A. Pérez Jr., Marial Iglesias, and Ada Ferrer have demonstrated, Cuba underwent a complex process of nationalist construction, involving the appropriation and transformation of symbols borrowed from both the colonial and North American orders in the service of modern nationhood.[2] The imagining of a new Cuba took place through the creation of institutional structures as well as the politics of symbolism. New institutional arrangements, including the adoption of a constitution, a newly energized, U.S.-trained police force, and revitalized scientific and university communities would prove to be crucial forces in shaping the new republic.

If nationalist ideology and legal structures were predicated on a universalizing category of male citizenship, the celebrations of May 20, 1902, revealed a heterogeneous polity. While official ceremonies solemnly lowered American flags and raised Cuban ones, elsewhere in the city several groups of residents marked the occasion by gathering to play drums and dance. A swift and repressive response suggests just how problematic cultural heterogeneity was to state officials. Police officers raided at least two of these groups, arresting their members and charging them with illicit association (*asociación ilícita*). As evidence that they had assembled for unlawful purposes, the police collected a number of objects they found at the sites of the celebrations. The lists of objects were long, totaling seventy-two in one case and thirteen in another. They specified not only the drums and costumes worn by the revelers, but also such items as a small jar filled with herbs, a crucifix, a bowl, several pebbles, a plantain, three fried fish, a broom, a chicken, a bandana, five hats, and four candles.

A few days later, police captain Carlos Masso Hechavarría characterized the collection as dangerous and definitive proof that the groups were not merely random gatherings but meetings of secret societies known as *ñáñigos*, members of a shadowy cult whose practices were purported to be linked to African religions and superstitious beliefs. Descriptions of the arrested individuals were laced with an aura of violence; they were said to engage in murderous feuds with rivals and enemies.[3] The accused were convicted and sent to jail. The objects themselves traveled from the houses in which they were seized to the police station, to the courthouse, and finally to the University of Havana's Museum of Anthropology, exemplifying what James Clifford has called the "unsettled, nomadic existence of non-Western artifacts."[4]

These arrests and charges of illicit association took on a significance beyond their frequency (though they occurred somewhat regularly) in the ways that the legal apparatus and social sciences integrated them into evolving systems of knowledge. Thomas Holt contends that studying the making of race entails an examination of many levels of social action—ranging from the global to the everyday—and requires alertness to the linkages between them: "The everyday acts of name calling and acts of exclusion are minor links in a larger historical chain of events, structures, and transformations anchored in slavery and the slave trade."[5]

This chapter follows the objects seized by the police as they journeyed between religious, legal, and scientific institutions, seeking to explicate the variety of meanings the objects took on in each context. The narrative privileges the spatial progress of these items, dwelling on the ways their owners, the police, judges, and anthropologists regarded them at each site. It argues that as they circulated, the objects served as links between discursive fields and in doing so animated race-making on multiple levels, as understood by Holt. At the same time, I suggest that the notions of race generated by the nomadic objects were fragile concepts that required frequent reinforcement and were subject to disruption by a number of interlocutors. If the objects circulated, literally, on the ground, they took on meaning in the midst of and in relation to transformative "large processes," including the growing transatlantic hegemony of scientific discourses, state formation in Cuba, decolonization, and neocolonialism.[6]

Things Out of Place

Disagreement on the value and meaning of these objects reigned among different groups of Cubans of color. Many black and mulatto politicians, mindful of a modernist nationalist vision, tended to downplay, if not excoriate, African-derived religions, which many of them deemed primitive and uncivilized. None of the views of citizenship held by politicians of color included a defense of these practices. Yet evidence such as that from May 20 suggests that African-derived rituals formed a crucial part of the fabric of everyday life. Indeed, for those celebrants on the first day of the republic, religious festivities may have been an idiom expressing participation as members of the newly inaugurated polity.

Police officer Estanislao Mansip with seized *objetos* from the sites of African-derived religious celebrations. (From Rafael Roche y Monteagudo, *La policía y sus misterios en Cuba* [Havana: La Moderna Poesía, 1925])

Ritual objects seem to have played a key role in these practices. Although a full exploration of what Stephan Palmié has called "Afro-Cuban religious traditions" and described as a heterogeneous "spectrum of religious forms" including Yoruba-Cuban (sometimes referred to as *regla ocha*), Bantu-Cuban (*reglas de congo*), *regla arara* and *abakuá* (male secret societies, sometimes called *ñáñigos* by Cuban ethnographers and law enforcement officials) is beyond the scope of this chapter, it is important to indicate the role of objects within this religious complex. Although we do not have firsthand accounts by the celebrants on May 20, 1902, scholars of African-derived religious practices have observed the ways similar objects acquired their meaning through their role in rituals, as embodiments of spirits or containers those spirits occupied. According to Palmié, they were "highly complex aggregates of heterogeneous materials the conjunction of which is thought both to contain a spiritual presence and to render its power—in concretized and functionally channeled form—accessible to human manipulations."[7] Because the historical record is silent on the specific beliefs and systems at play, the precise purpose of the objects remains beyond our purview. But scholars have suggested that regardless of the particular rite in question, objects, in their "irreducible materiality," proffered power to their users.[8]

As a result of new constitutional protections and growing repression, however, these practices and the *objetos* with which they were conducted became an increasingly contentious issue in debates over race, deviance, and citizenship. Guided by a variety of imperatives, police, judges, social scientists, and intellectuals scrambled to understand what they could about this curious presence in their midst. Authorities frequently deemed the constellation of practices referred to as *brujería* (witchcraft) and *ñañiguismo*, related to, if not quite coterminous with, African-derived religions. Although the distinctions between them were never clear, "licit" religious practices were more often linked to cabildos, whereas the "illicit" ones, brujería and ñañiguismo, were thought to maintain alternative institutions, or even more dangerously to flit among and between cabildos, private homes, and public spaces. In the colonial era, both political officials and members of the respective associations drew distinctions between cabildos and sociedades, or voluntary mutual aid associations. Many sociedades had been careful to distance themselves from the African religious rituals known to be central to the practices of the cabildos. By the end of the colonial regime, however, legal stipulations forced cabildos to change their names and many of them came to be known as sociedades. This resulted in the conceptual conflation of organizations whose purposes were very different. In the context of the early twentieth century, brujería and ñañiguismo were ambiguously conceived as practices that were neither the same as associations nor completely distinct from them. As the mysterious and maligned counterparts of members of sociedades, *brujos* and ñáñigos engaged in similar (at least to the untrained eye) rituals, most notably drumming and dancing, they were also suspected of performing violent rites involving murder and cannibalism.[9]

The state controlled and monitored associations by requiring them to request permission every time they planned a ritual or meeting. Sometimes permission was granted, but with the drumming limited to a few hours in the afternoon. Other times, officials forbade these events, not on (nonexistent) legal grounds or even because rituals or celebrations were intrinsically harmful, but because of what they might reveal about the city's level of progress toward civilization.[10] One such request made during the U.S. military occupation (1899–1902) reached the American governor. In it, Cornelio Delgado, president of the African Lucumí Association, asked the governor to review his application, denied by Mayor

Alejandro Rodríguez of Havana, for permission to "use their drums." The governor deferred to the mayor, who again refused his consent, arguing that "spectacles of the kind are improper at this stage of civilization, and reflect on the dignity and culture of a city, and are detrimental to order, under whatever aspect they are considered."[11] He was probably drawing from a municipal ordinance, passed in 1900, that prohibited African drumming for any reason.

This ordinance was part of efforts, beginning in the late nineteenth century, to control expressions of culture perceived as African or African-derived—among them, public processions known as *agrupaciones* or *comparsas* and private gatherings such as the one held on May 20, 1902. Associated both with Día de Reyes slave processions and pre-Lenten carnivals, the comparsas were conducted by Afro-Cuban ensembles who paraded usually with musical instruments, extravagant costumes, and vibrant dancing. As Robin Moore notes, during the first U.S. occupation and the early years of the republic, comparsas were ambiguously integrated into Havana's legal and political fabric. Though banned by municipal ordinances, they were tolerated unofficially and occasionally appropriated by Liberal politicians who were appealing to working-class Cubans of color. They were more definitively prohibited in 1913, only to emerge again in 1937 in a transformed context and as the source of further controversy.[12]

The early ordinances banning comparsas did so under the rubric of forbidding the public appearance of "symbols, allegories and objects that detract from the seriousness and level of civilization of the inhabitants of this country."[13] This complaint marked a shift in the kinds of objections to such rituals made in colonial times. Under the Spanish, religious rituals had been treated ambivalently: the state had allowed them but endeavored to carefully control them, for it believed that gatherings of any kind were potential seats of rebellion. Colonial officials had been less worried about image—that is, the extent to which rituals indicated a lack of civilization—than about Cubans using these meetings to plan anticolonial uprisings. After the war ended, however, the concern about rebellion waned as it was increasingly replaced by anxieties over the degree of primitiveness represented by these practices.

State-sponsored descriptions of African-derived practices, especially their obscure and purportedly more sinister incarnations (brujería and ñañiguismo), referred to them as vestiges from the former era, marks left by Spanish colonialism and slavery. One police captain testified that "this association has been persecuted and punished by law since time immemorial."[14] Another described ñáñigos as a "long-standing secret and illicit society that was the governors' constant nightmare in the colonial era."[15] Brujería was characterized similarly as an "African fetishism or cult that was imported to Cuba by enslaved blacks."[16] Ironically, although they were portrayed as vestiges of the past, it was a more recent legal change that both created protections for these practices and provided the means with which to repress them more effectively.

Classification, Criminalization

The legal system in place in 1902 was a hybrid consequence of Cuba's particular brand of colonialism and neocolonialism. Until 1899, law in Cuba had emanated from Spain. When the Americans arrived, they initially planned a complete overhaul of the legal system. Instead, once they realized how overwhelming a task that would be, especially since there was no single collection of all royal decrees and laws, they decided to amend existing statutes as necessary when problems arose. Thus some laws persisted whereas others changed radically. The penal code of Spain, written in 1870, was extended to Cuba in 1879 and remained in place until 1936, surviving two U.S. occupations and the volatile politics of the republic.[17] In it, an illicit association was defined as an association that "by its purpose or circumstance is contrary to public morals."[18] According to this code, ñañiguismo, but not brujería, fell under its jurisdiction.

A series of constitutions promulgated during the colonial period had created freedoms, however limited, that protected non-Christian religious practices. As a result of particular times when liberalism was dominant in Spanish lawmaking bodies, Cubans had been granted a number of civil rights during the course of the nineteenth century. In 1881 Cuba adopted Spain's constitution of 1876. This document, written by opponents of enforced religious unity, retained Catholicism as the official state religion but for the first time allowed the private practice of other faiths.[19] Thus article 26 of the 1901 constitution declared the right of all creeds to practice freely. Yet it stipulated that "all religions and cults enjoy freedom of worship, as long as they respect Christian morals and public order."[20] Despite the difficulties involved in the rehabilitation of a bedraggled state, the Americans did manage to accomplish "the quiet severance of church and state" in Cuba.[21]

The relationship among ñañiguismo, brujería, and the law was complex. Since brujería was not a crime, it was technically impossible to arrest anyone for practicing it. Ñañiguismo was easier to prosecute, as it was deemed illegal by the penal code of 1876. However, the freedom of religion loophole created with the constitution of 1901 meant that anyone charged with illicit association could claim innocence and protection by arguing that they were engaged in a religious practice. Paradoxically, although the changing legal climate promoted greater freedoms, it also formulated new ways to transgress the law. If article 26 loosened previous restrictions on non-Catholic faiths, it also defined these newly liberalized religious practices as potential disruptions of public order. The definitions were slippery and the consequences indeterminate.

A sizable gap opened between the (uncertain) letter of the law and the aims of law enforcers. Police Chief Sánchez Martínez's guidelines for his force reveal one strategy for negotiating legal complexities. He confirmed that African cults, or brujería, had become more difficult to restrain or regulate because of the constitution's twenty-sixth article granting religious freedom. That, and in Martínez's eyes, the unfortunate absence of a law explicitly directed at "uncivilized" rituals and ceremonies meant that policemen were forced to limit themselves to charging brujos for holding large disruptive gatherings or having "objects and artifacts pertaining to their cult" in their possession. Yet even the possession of objects was not technically illegal. Martínez's instructions reveal that despite this setback he had found a way to convict brujos for possession of objects. The solution lay in sanitation regulations, which stated that "it is forbidden to accumulate or deposit in any house, room, cellar, patio or other locale trash, leftovers, bones, or any other materials likely to decompose and which might bother the neighbors or emit unpleasant odors." Attention to public health, one of the most notable legacies of the U.S. occupation, provided the missing justification. The code's definition of offenses against public health included the manufacture and circulation of substances injurious to people, the dissemination of "chemicals capable of causing great destruction, the alteration of food or beverage such that it becomes toxic, and the sale of contaminated food and beverages." Finally, it was unlawful for anyone to "throw into a spring, cistern, or river the water of which is used for drinking purposes, any object which should make the water injurious to health."[22] Decaying material, then, would finally provide the stuff from which convictions could be assured.[23]

Although colonial officials had invoked the notion of public order in nineteenth-century campaigns against prostitution, vagrancy, and street disturbances, they had not linked it explicitly to religious practices. In the new, more tolerant context, these practices fell under the rubric of public order. The possession of suspect objects, as threats to public health, was an even more concrete way to obtain a conviction. Even so, the objects in question were sometimes presented as evidence without any reference to their role in marring public health. Illicit association became the catchall accusation against those thought to be engaging in sinister practices. Because some of those practices fell outside the official definition, however, the charges were always ambiguous. At the same time, this shift in legal discourse introduced a distinct meaning of race. If the political lexicon of inclusive nationhood had attributed loyalty and gratitude to Cubans of color, especially those who had fought in the wars for independence, in this instance a legal lexicon attributed disloyalty and rejection of a modern secular nationalist project to those who engaged in African-derived religious practices (even as it grudgingly granted their right to engage in those practices). Grafted onto an understanding that former slaves and their descendants had earned their place as an integral part of the nation, anxiety about the presence of Cubans of African descent as an obstacle to its progress complicated the theory and practice of inclusion.

The ways those arrested proceeded to defend themselves reflected the ambiguity of the charges. But it also revealed a familiarity with legal discourse and an awareness of the potential for manipulating a changing legal system. The accused claimed that perhaps they had been dancing, which they might have defended as innocently celebrating, but not while wearing ñáñigo suits, which would have undoubtedly led to a conviction of illicit association. When they claimed ignorance about the objects in question, or maintained that the objects were utilized in the dances, they seemed aware of the suspicion objects would arouse if they were thought to "detract from the seriousness and level of civilization of the inhabitants of this country." One person, looking to exonerate his actions by implicating a lax police force, admitted that he and his companions had been dancing attired in ñáñigo suits, but they had also done so the day before without any reaction from the police, who had watched from a nearby street corner. The owner of the house where the dancing occurred opted for what he must have thought the most reliable strategy, invoking his patriotism: they were "celebrating the flag." (It was after all, the inaugural day of the republic.) Granted, they did not have permission for the gathering, but the sticks, brooms, and chicken were nothing more than decorations, he asserted, distancing himself from African-based rituals, still under a haze of suspicion even though they had been legalized by the new constitution.[24]

In *On Longing*, Susan Stewart analyzes the relationship of a narrative to its objects: an object cannot be understood without the narrative that explicates its identity.[25] In the case of the arrested groups, the meaning of the objects was one of the main points of contention in determining the nature of the offense. The outcome of the trials and the criminalization of a set of practices depended on the multiple narratives of drums, clothing, brooms, shells, and bits of food as everyday possessions, sacred objects, carriers of magic, mere decoration, or threats to public health. Whether conceived of as sacred objects invested with awesome powers, evidence of nefarious activities, the prosaic stuff of everyday, or a combination of all three, these objects left the police offices and circulated among legal and scientific institutions.

Police Ethnographers

It is perhaps not coincidental that the intensified campaign against all things deemed uncivilized occurred alongside the expansion of the state. Wartime economic conditions had decimated many among the national property-holding elite, opening up the country to increased foreign investment. The reciprocity treaty hindered the development of new industry and the diversification of the economy. Massive immigration drove unemployment up and wages down. As a result, one of the few sources of income and employment was the state: "Public administration in general and politics in particular, early acquired a special economic significance. State revenues early became the principal source of economic solvency for the generation of 1895. Public office, patronage appointments, and civil service jobs became ends: political and electoral competition were the means."[26] In addition, an expanded electorate meant that elected officials had to dole out jobs to a larger clientele. As one official said: "Two factors contribute to this. One is bureau mania, the epidemic functionarism, which pertains to the Spanish race in all its varieties, the other is the general state of poverty prevailing in this country."[27] Included in this overall swelling of the state was the police force, its growing ranks joining those of other public agencies.

The police were crucial mediators of convoluted law. The Detective Bureau, a special division of Havana's police department, infiltrated groups it suspected of questionable practices, attending their gatherings and collecting information about their activities. One such report, written in December 1900, narrated a number of rituals in vivid detail. The detective skeptically described the ceremonies of "several forms of brujería."[28] Patronized "by the colored people and those of the lower classes," the witches or brujos discerned clients' problems and then performed rites to alleviate them. Most commonly the brujos were consulted about "problems of love" or "problems with enemies." The writer's sense that these practitioners were charlatans and their practices nothing more than lucrative schemes informed his descriptions of the ways brujos and their partners attracted patrons and took their money. Despite his cynicism he observed the rituals closely, noting, for example, that the brujo "spreads a small carpet rug upon the floor, placing upon it pictures with the images of several saints, a lighted candle and other articles. . . . He then takes a rosary bead made of small white shells and wood and after praying a few moments throws it also upon the rug. . . . The heads of these fowls are placed at the feet of the images already referred to, together with various scraps of food, stones stained with blood and some small white shells. This is called La Comida de Santa Bárbara."[29]

These detectives could be called the country's earliest ethnographers of the hybrid religious practices of Cubans of color, moving from armchair research to participant observation earlier than any Cuban anthropologist. Latter-day extirpators of error and misbehavior, the police produced detailed information to inform and justify their enforcement of often vaguely defined laws. Knowledge about the rituals enabled them to recognize otherwise meaningless detritus, such as bowls, drums, hats, pebbles, and shells, as objects of brujería. Yet this knowledge was not uniformly absorbed by all police investigators, as revealed by the way they treated these objects over the course of several years. Court records show a recurrent uncertainty as to how to deal with the alternately sacred and burdensome objects. In one case, a judge reported to the rector of the university the successful transfer of objects from courthouse to museum, except for the "uncured goat skin, plantain, white yams, corn, and other items that are difficult to preserve, as contrary to hygienic practice"; these had to be thrown out because they were rotting and the smell was becoming unbearable.[30]

Police and law enforcement officials were able and willing to ascribe certain characteristics to objects of brujería, but evidently they saw the utility of turning to scientific authority for confirmation or further investigation. What they meant in republican Cuba was still unsettled. They continued to circulate from the courts, their identities not precisely determined. Out of that circulation emerged a concept of race that associated crime, physiological traits, and cultural artifacts.

The Objects of Anthropology

The courts sent the confiscated objects to the Museum of Anthropology at the request of Luis Montané, professor of anthropology, director of the museum, and dean of the University of Havana's Faculty of Arts and Sciences. Not long after the hearing of the individuals arrested for possessing the objects, the rector of the university initiated the transfer with a letter to the presiding judge communicating Montané's request. On at least two occasions between 1902 and 1903 the museum received a number of such objects. The first shipment included drums, a lantern, candlesticks, ñáñigo suits, sticks, feather dusters, bundles of fabric, maracas, brooms, knives, an iron ashtray, and a crucifix. The next shipment included one suit, drums, sticks with leather, a *vara* (a staff possessed by *abakuá* titleholders), a crucifix, and bundles of ritual herbs.[31] Afterward Montané and the rector both professed gratitude to the judge, who had so quickly complied with their requests.[32]

This leg of the objects' journey suggests optimism about the relatively new discipline of anthropology, or "the study of man." Recently granted a place in the state, its potential had been noted for years. In a speech to the Cuban Anthropological Society fifteen years earlier, Arístides Mestre, who would later head the university's Department of Anthropology, direct the museum, and write extensively on anthropology and archaeology, identified the promise and purpose of anthropology. Drawing from classical and Enlightenment sources such as Georges Buffon, Johann Blumenbach, and Aristotle, as well as from French craniometrist Paul Broca, Mestre argued that the study of politics, as a modern positivist science, ought to intersect the study of "man." If politics was concerned with the laws of collective behavior, it must direct attention to the study of "peoples, of both their physical characteristics and their customs, in other words, with ethnography."[33] Mestre's basic unit of analysis was race and the principal concept heredity, which, if properly understood with regard to natural selection and biological laws, could be applied to the analysis of politics.

Ultimately, he asserted, the brilliance of a nation rested entirely on the races that constituted it. Cuba's history had created a particularly interesting case: because colonization had introduced a number of races, it was an ideal laboratory in which to study racial mixture. He acknowledged that since some of the races introduced were inferior, anthropology would prove useful in addressing, as he put it, "the delicate problem of criminality." In the end his theories of race, heredity, and degeneration were a (not untypical) combination of Darwinian and Lamarckian claims about evolution and physiological change. If his European training shaped a theoretical viewpoint in which, as George Stocking has written, "in the mixed Darwinian/Lamarckian context of late nineteenth-century biological thought these cultural evolutionary sequences took on a racialist character," his position as a Cuban scientist allowed him to throw more races into the experimental data set.[34] Mestre held both that a race had specific physical and psychic characteristics and that climate, disease, and even food could affect those characteristics in inheritable ways. Straddling different paradigms, he maintained that races were capable of both degeneration and progress.[35] The task was to understand "man" and "race" by means of a set of approaches, bundled under the rubric of anthropology but including ethnography, history, archaeology, statistics, and analysis of religions. While Mestre was studying Cuba's race problem he also intended to contribute to the honing of anthropological theory, a field dominated by European scientists. Moreover, his proposals allowed him to study exotic races without traveling farther than the marginal neighborhoods of Havana or, at most, its nearby plantations.

A Cacophonous Collection

As the flirtation between state and science progressed, scientists remained attached to a bundled conception of anthropology. The *Anales* of the Academy of Sciences included an essay by Dr. Jorge Le-Roy y Cassá discussing the effects of climatological change and promulgating the new techniques of anthropometry, a report by a naturalist on local archaeological findings speculating on the features of Cuba's vanished Indian culture, a philosophical essay on E. H. Haeckel, the German zoologist who developed recapitulation theory, and a debate between two lawyers over Lombrosian theories of innate criminality.[36] A capacious conception of anthropology together with the belief that it intersected with a number of disciplines allowed for the coexistence of an array of different (yet all "scientific") understandings of race and its significance in social and political life.

When the opportunity arose, Montané continued this project and added to it the latest theories from Europe. The only trained anthropologist on the island, Montané promulgated a cacophonous approach to the "study of man." Montané was born in Cuba but had spent most of his childhood and youth in France. Educated as a physician in Paris, he became interested in anthropology and studied with Paul Broca, who had made craniometry "a rigorous and respectable science" in late-nineteenth-century France.[37] Returning to his native land in 1874, he presided over the founding of the Cuban Anthropological Society in 1877.[38] Montané forged ties with European and American anthropologists, participating in U.S.-initiated archaeological expeditions in search of Indians and representing Cuba at several international conferences.[39] As a professor at the University of Havana he taught both physical and juridical anthropology and supported Mestre's teaching of "philosophical" anthropology, which included visits to mental hospitals and prisons.[40]

As soon as he became responsible for the museum's holdings, Montané began to collect. One of the first things he did as curator was to write to the university rector requesting that the medical school send both normal and deformed skulls, so that his students would have the materials with which to study anthropometry. As his mentor Paul Broca practiced it, the measuring of body parts, especially skulls, was intended to confirm the polygenetic belief that races were distinct species. The introduction of Darwinist evolutionism had not eliminated polygenist thought but rather altered it so that it complied more or less with the demands of evolutionary theory. Thus Broca's aim, according to his colleague Paul Topinard, was to use his assumption that brain size was directly correlated to intelligence to "determine the relative position of the races in the human series."[41]

In 1903 Montané received the brain of an executed murderer, sent by the president of the Audiencia de Santa Clara, along with a note asserting the scientific value of the brain. Also included were a long description of the crime, an explanation of the process of conviction and sentencing to death by hanging, and a detailed analysis of the convict's behavior just before dying. The author repeated his suggestion, already presented to the secretary of state and justice, that the Museum of Anthropology ought to be the repository of all skulls and brains of criminals who had died in prison. That these contributions were deemed valuable at all is a reflection of the introduction of the theory, formulated primarily by Italian anthropologist and criminologist Césare Lombroso, linking evolutionary stages to criminality with claims of the physical and therefore measurable manifestations of those characteristics. Lombroso's theory of atavistic criminality explained the existence of what he called "born criminals" by positing that mistakes of nature could reverse evolutionary progress and produce "evolutionary throwbacks in our midst."[42] Criminals, who behaved like the savages they were, were fortunately visible to society through physical markers that revealed their dangerous nature. Criminal brains would prove useful, then, for identifying more precisely those features that signaled atavism and degeneration.[43]

Lombroso linked race to criminality under cover of evolutionary thought. Ranking races according to their level of civilization, he held that the atavistic savages of the evolutionary past had not quite disappeared in the modern world, persisting as what he called "inferior peoples." Committed to morphology as the indicator of criminality, Lombroso mapped the propensity to crime onto entire races.[44] Since Montané taught Lombrosian theory to his anthropology students at the university, the donated brains would have proven convenient for illustrative purposes.

The museum also held artifacts from archaeological excavations. During the late nineteenth and early twentieth centuries archaeologists had conducted a number of expeditions in search of traces of the island's original inhabitants. The discourse directing the "search for the extinguished Indian" was very different from the emerging discourse linking race and crime. It was more reminiscent of an older, gentler ethnological tradition, dominant before the discipline's seduction by positivism and "the allure of numbers."[45] Cubans imagined the Indian with a nostalgic view of vanished purity and integrity more resonant of Jean-Jacques Rousseau or Bartolomé de Las Casas than Herbert Spencer or Lombroso.[46] Nonetheless, at this time the museum focused on peripatetic drums, shells, stones, and garments and the insights they might provide on the new republic's most exotic and problematic, not to mention still living, inhabitants.

The objects finally came to rest in the Museum of Anthropology. Historians of anthropology have followed the journeys and classifications of other artifacts as they oscillated between the scientific and aesthetic, moving from anthropological museum to art museum, exhibited "in context" or as "masterpieces."[47] Yet few have observed objects passing through a stage as criminal evidence before becoming cultural artifacts. The trajectory of the objects taken during the arrests of ñáñigos reveals their importance both in the production of knowledge about the world of unorthodox religious practices and in the institutionalization and legitimation of anthropology and science. In addition, the objects as artifacts/evidence informed an emerging concept of race, the local version of a transatlantic trend in which "the racial hierarchy of nineteenth-century polygenism and the cultural hierarchy of the eighteenth-century historians became part and parcel of one scheme of universal organic evolution."[48] The objects' trajectory through the courts and metonymic relationship to their former owners rendered them the overdetermined material evidence of this reconfigured evolutionary scheme. Torn from their context as the ritual stuff of an alternative belief system, they were inserted into theoretical schemes and material display cases and understood to lend empirical weight to the imbrication of race, crime, and evolution.

It was this convergence of circumstances and ideas that constituted Cubans of African descent as objects of study. From the outset the notion of criminality inflected the study of "man," and so the links between race and crime came to be understood in hereditarian terms. The traveling objects served to embody those links: based on the accepted if benighted logic of the day, they were proof that many Cubans did engage in these rituals, that the rituals were based on African practices, that Africa was the source of atavistic races, and that these races were prone to criminality. Therefore, Cubans of African descent were likely to be inclined toward crime. Although those initially arrested were not all Cubans of color, social scientific knowledge about the phenomenon of ñañiguismo tended to erase or underplay participation by white Cubans, underscoring even further the links between race and crime. Since anthropology or "the study of man" was bundled, it was not considered unorthodox to use cultural artifacts to support a hereditarian notion of race. Rather than separate theories, they were thought to complement one another and were used as such. During this period links between race and crime were not necessarily gendered, but in later years a series of sensationalist crimes would engender a much more fixed notion of a male brujo.[49]

If proximity and familiarity with the cultures on display enabled this overdetermined formulation of a racial scheme, it was precisely those qualities that destabilized fixed categories of "primitive" and "civilized" on which the scheme was based. Because they inhabited the same city, it was difficult to situate brujos and ñáñigos, as represented by their seized and peripatetic possessions, in a primitive past.[50] Not only were these groups and associations a visible and vocal presence in the social life of Havana, but also the boundaries between elite politics and uncivilized disturbances were never clear. The Liberal Party, for example, was known to have cultivated relationships with African sociedades, which embellished Liberals' populist appeals during election campaigns with their music and dances. If on the one hand these "criminals" were objects of study for Cuban social scientists, on the other hand they were fellow citizens, neighbors, and members of the same clientelistic networks. In other colonial contexts the study of "primitives" has been simplified by their absence in daily life. By contrast, in Cuba they occupied an ambiguous position, rendering the categories less useful than in other contexts.

Nor was the boundary between the nascent science of anthropology and its objects of study clear. Fernando Guerra, secretary of the Afro-Cuban association Sociedad de Protección Mutua y Recreo del Culto Africano Lucumí, "Santa Bárbara," sent a letter to the provincial governor of Havana, with copies to the governor's secretary, the president of the republic, and the director of the museum. "On this date," he wrote, "I present to you the drawings of drums used to produce the music [that] the cult of Santa Bárbara uses in its civic and religious festivals."[51] Taking matters into his own hands, Guerra rendered potentially suspect objects legitimate in official eyes through his deft descriptions. As a mediator between a religion that understood itself very differently from official descriptions and the state that produced those (mis)understandings, his translation was intended to deflect persecution.

By the same token, the purpose of the objects' confinement was never entirely clear in official eyes. Word of the museum's new acquisitions reached the highest levels of government. In August the secretary of state and justice conveyed to the Supreme Court the thoughts of Tomás Estrada Palma, president of the republic, on the matter of the objects' future. He noted that it would be beneficial in a number of different ways for the items to remain at the museum: first, they would serve as examples for analogous cases; second, they could be displayed "como cosas curiosas"—as curiosities. Finally, he argued that the requirement of article 61 of the penal code that objects of illicit commerce be "rendered useless," in other words, not be used again, could be accomplished by keeping them at the museum.[52]

New legal structures and the growing status of science offered new modalities in which to shape racial theories and practices. Yet if one tried to read from the above statement or the museum's variegated collection the purpose of anthropology in the eyes of the state, one would see a rather undisciplined discipline. In effect, the collection called into question the kinds of distinctions drawn by museums in other contexts. Rather than creating a clear line between the "national body" and the "uncivilized other," this museum displayed the uncivilized other as part of the national body itself. Not only was there a lack of clarity between categories (national and other), there was also a great deal of messiness within categories. The multiplicity of understandings underscores Stocking's argument that "in spite of the all-embracing etymological singularity of the term anthropology, the diverse discourses that may be historically subsumed by it have only in certain moments and places been fused into anything approximating a unified science of mankind."[53] Anthropology cannot be described as a totalizing agent of the state, ordering a coherent past and displaying that past to the public. Rather, shaped as it was by Broca's French school, older ethnological concerns with culture grafted onto new Lombrosian concerns about criminality, and a nostalgic archaeological pursuit of Indians, it is perhaps more convincing to say that it engaged in "feverish imagining" of its past and its present.[54]

Conclusion

This chapter has examined the making of race in a period of transition. Just as state and citizen were reconfigured to allow for a relative expansion of rights and opportunities to express political voice, the unorthodox versions of citizenship came to be more zealously policed. As a result of legal transitions, ritual objects whose original meaning and purpose derived from a complex set of religious practices served as evidence that those who used them were committing crimes against public health. Paradoxically, provisions about rights to religious practice meant that African-derived religions were immune from prosecution even as law enforcers and state officials imagined them to be a blight on progress and civilization. The heightened legitimacy of positivistic science provided new tools with which to encase and redefine threatening practices. Out of this legal, political, and scientific conjunction was elaborated a set of understandings of race in which Cubans of African descent, especially those presumed to be linked to African-derived cultural practices, were deemed deviant, unfit for citizenship, and thus occupying an ambiguous position in a national scheme. These understandings ran counter to both colonial and official nationalist ideologies. As colonial subjects, Cubans of African descent had been either slaves or freed workers whose religious practices were of little interest to the ruling elite. In nationalist discourse, male Cubans of color had achieved the status of citizen, however ambivalently predicated on a promise of their good behavior. In the newly independent republic, Cubans of color seemed to come under more intense scrutiny, a scrutiny that produced contradictory notions of African-derived religions and their practitioners as at once powerful, threatening, incoherent, and fascinating. Ultimately, the objects of ritual and their owners refused clear categorizations. The final emphasis must remain on the transitional nature of the early republic, as law and anthropology shifted with competing currents and the objects on which they focused never stood still.

Liberty, equality, fraternity . . . scientifically
absurd: determinism denies liberty, biology
denies equality, and the principle of survival of
the fittest, according to which all living beings
exist, denies fraternity.

[Liberté, egalité, fraternité . . . scientifiquement
absurde: Le determinisme nie la liberté, la biolo-
gie nie l'egalité, et le principe de la lutte pour la
vie, auquel sont soumis tous les êtres vivants, nie
la fraternité.]

JOSÉ INGENIEROS
*La legislación du travail dans
la république argentine* (1906)

2
Social Science
and the Negro Brujo

On November 14, 1904, *El Mundo*, Havana's conservative
daily, reported the "mysterious disappearance of Zoila," a four-year-old
white girl, from her home in El Gabriel, a small town outside of Havana.[1]
Over the course of a year the newspaper devoted a great deal of space
to the story. Eduardo Varela Zequeira, who reported the story and who
would eventually build a career based on his coverage of racial issues,
surmised that the child had been a victim of brujería. El Gabriel's increasingly alarmed and vocal residents demonstrated before the courthouse
and police station, demanding a search of every household in the vicinity
until the brujos were apprehended.

Suspicion settled on Pablo and Juana Tabares, a black couple living
together, and on Domingo Bocourt, a former slave known for his participation in African-derived healing and religious practices. They were

detained briefly but released after questioning for lack of evidence. The same month a parallel case involving the death of Celia, another young girl, and the arrest of a man of African descent named Tin-Tan also occupied the front pages of the newspapers. About two weeks after Zoila's disappearance, the police found a body. A gruesome description of its alleged condition communicated in graphic detail the barbaric nature of the crime. A large portion of the torso and extremities were missing skin and flesh. Yet the feet were intact and still covered by shoes and socks. The heart had been extracted, according to forensic doctors, with a sharp instrument. After a lengthy investigation in which the number of accused grew to a dozen, the following story began to emerge. Bocourt was said to be the leader of a group of brujos who gathered regularly to enact rituals and healings. Juana Tabares, whose children suffered from ill health, had sought Bocourt's help, and because his remedy required the blood of a white child, he was said to have demanded that someone in the group kill one and bring him the corpse. At this point investigators had failed to pin down the actual murderer, although they suspected Victor Molina and another man of African descent, but they had confirmed (or so they claimed) the instigating role of brujería.

By January 1905 Bocourt and Victor Molina had received the death penalty for murder. They were executed amid a great deal of attention from the press in 1906. After the execution, their brains were sent to Professor Luis Montané at the University of Havana to be put on display at the Museo Antropológico Montané (renamed after him in 1903). There, they took their places alongside ñáñigo suits, ritual objects, and archaeological findings, adding to the collection of "criminal brains" examined by students of anthropology for morphological evidence of violent tendencies.

The Zoila case was the first of a series of sensational brujería scares that shook early republican Cuba. As this example suggests, the unfolding of events reverberated, beyond the families and towns most immediately affected, into courts of law and elite intellectual spheres. In the courts, both prosecutors and defendants exploited the contradictions arising from a changing legal system. Long investigations and trials tested the elusive boundaries among brujería, illicit association, and delinquency against changing notions of legal responsibility and new codifications of rights to freedom of religion and association. Social scientists drawing from anthropology, criminology, and sociology (disciplines also characterized by elusive boundaries at the time) took it upon themselves to understand and explain the presence of what they perceived as aberrant practices among Cubans mostly of African descent. As such, these recurrent events and their repercussions reveal much about changing racial discourses in the first two decades of the Cuban republic.

The time and place in which the scares occurred bewildered observers. Brujería and its codified counterpart ñañiguismo emerged as inherent but inexplicable features of a recently inaugurated inclusionary republic. As *El Día* noted: "Until after the triumph of the revolution blacks raised white children without eating or abusing them. The war has ended. . . . Cuba has been liberated from Spanish tutelage, legal equality and rights of all citizens have been recognized, and those people have begun to drink the blood of white girls, and even to martyrize their own daughters, under the impression that they are the tainted members of the family. Where is progress, then, where is civilization?"[2]

Mingling irony with incredulity, the author of this commentary pointed to the accusations against Cubans of color as curious manifestations of Cuba's experience of modernity and formal political democratization. The coexistence of a vibrant religious and social life of former slaves and their descendants along with an expanding political base created a context different from any in Europe or the Americas.[3] At stake was proving to the rest of the world (and themselves) Cuban capacity for self-understanding and self-rule. Would the nascent republic survive independence from Spain and its adoption of universal manhood suffrage with the United States looking over its shoulder, ready to invoke the Platt Amendment at the first sign of "instability"? Cuban uncertainties about new political contours may have lent the campaigns against brujería an added urgency.

During the first two decades of the republic, Cubans of color continued to claim their place, not without conflict, as citizens. As Alejandro de la Fuente has shown, elections, both local and national, became intense contests over black and mulatto constituencies. Cubans of color themselves were elected as representatives of both parties, and although skeptics expressed doubts about the extent to which they represented "genuine black interests," their inclusion in public life marked a significant change. In addition to formal political participation, blacks and mulattoes benefited from educational campaigns and voiced their views in a number of arenas, including the proliferating press, both in mainstream and exclusively black newspapers. Neither contemporaries nor historians argue that Cubans of color achieved complete inclusion and equality, but an

"Until after the triumph of the revolution blacks raised white children without eating or abusing them." (*El Día*, September 6, 1918; 1900 photo courtesy of Cuban Heritage Collection, University of Miami Libraries, Coral Gables, Florida)

egalitarian nationalist ideology gave them a powerful tool with which to fight ongoing battles about desegregating public spaces and obtaining increased access to civil service positions.[4]

In light of these changes the presence of brujería and ñañiguismo seemed particularly vexing, especially since brujería had never before been associated with murder and cannibalism.[5] Many Cubans perceived these practices, which were cast as a manifestation of the "problem of race," as obstacles to the kind of republic they envisioned. As such, they inspired intense scrutiny and thought on the causes and remedies of the perceived civilizational malaise, taking on a significance that magnified their actual prevalence.

Rather than seeing these incidents as reflective of Cuban society as a whole (a somewhat misleading approach), this chapter instead focuses more precisely on racial discourses in three different contexts: the press, the courts, and social scientific arenas. Although these settings remain, for the purposes of clarity, distinct, I suggest that the process of constructing the brujo involved considerable seepage and overlap among them. The chapter thus seeks to elucidate the ways in which a series of mysterious crimes served as a catalyst for the brujo to be rendered an object of social scientific scrutiny, both boldly constructed and undermined in the press and contested through appeals to the law. Indeed, as Stephan Palmié has observed, the brujo and scientific knowledge constituted one another in the burst of discursive productivity that characterized the early republic.[6] Narratives emphasizing the primitive or criminal nature of Cubans of African descent received sustenance from the changing conditions of an increasingly inclusive polity.

Reading the Brujo

The discussions that formed around the problem of black criminality easily slid into ongoing debates about Cuba's viability as a democracy, often expressed in racialized terms. Politicians and intellectuals on different sides of the ideological divide frequently conceived of problems and solutions based on the hereditary characteristics of the nation's inhabitants. Both Francisco Figueras, a politician whose writings, according to Aline Helg, "made a deep impression on Creole intellectuals and literate audiences and became a reference for other writers,"[7] and Francisco Carrera y Justiz, whose course on municipal government became one of the most enduring at the University of Havana, published essays using race as the primary interpretive tool to diagnose the "social problem." Figueras's two most influential works, *Cuba y su evolución colonial* (*Cuba's Colonial Evolution*) (1907) and *La intervención y su política* (*The Politics of the Intervention*) (1906), argued that Cubans were racially incapable of forming an independent republic. From Spaniards they had inherited a propensity for "education based on feelings" and an attachment to slavery. Africans had contributed lasciviousness and lack of foresight to the national character. In *La intervención y su política*, Figueras asserted that this backward and corrupt connection had fostered the 1906 rebellion—as much a racial revolt as a political one. The subsequent necessity for a U.S. occupation to establish peace and stability proved that Cubans were not ready for self-rule, that universal suffrage had been a mistake, that racial and cultural heterogeneity was a drawback, and that the solution was "pacific penetration" by American culture.[8]

Carrera y Justiz also envisioned a racial conflict as the root of Cuba's problems, but he translated the global and historical battle between the Anglo-Saxon and Latin races to the Cuban context. More optimistically than Figueras, he tracked the gradual but inevitable takeover of the Anglo-Saxon races with their superior rationality and state-building abilities. Yet, somewhat contradictorily, he argued that the Latin race could be fortified to struggle more effectively. This fortification was to take place at the level of municipal government, where a measure of autonomy allowed for the acquisition and honing of governing skills. In any case, whether due to total domination by Anglos or successful Latin resistance, his predictions posited enhanced racial vitality.[9]

The notion of race as the source of social ills shaped the ideas of an observer whose analysis diverged sharply from those of Figueras and Carrera y Justiz. For black commentator Dr. Emilio Céspedes Casado, addressing Havana's Booker T. Washington Society in 1906, Cuba's social problems derived from "unhealthy fomentation" between the races. The solution lay in education and social sanitation. Relying on the increasingly persuasive alignment of race and civilization, while at the same time inverting diagnoses that sought a North American cure, he blamed the U.S. intervention for Cuba's degenerating condition: "The odious Intervention introduced, along with its civilization, its barbarism and its narcissism."[10] A wide array of visions of Cuba's future shared an assumption that racial vitality provided the key to the preservation of autonomy and self-government.

The intense journalistic attention to a series of violent crimes poured amorphous anxieties about race defined as Latin, African, or Anglo-Saxon, pure or mixed, degenerating or regenerating, into the figure of the black criminal. Reinaldo Román's research on this subject has uncovered well over three dozen cases reported in the press between 1904 and 1943. If Céspedes tried to convince his listeners that barbarism had been imported from the United States, the press campaigns that brought brujería and ñañiguismo to a larger reading public construed them as a national problem.[11]

As the first, the Zoila case set the tone for many that followed. The reporting was endlessly thorough, detailed, and repetitive. Long daily articles, always on the front page, summarized facts and speculations previously recounted and offered new evidence regardless of its relevance. Interviews with the family and acquaintances of the little girl filled columns when fresh information was unavailable. The stories also provided visual "evidence," including photographs of the family, of the discovered shoes, of the accused and their companions. When the trial began, its proceedings were diligently reported. By the time of the execution, readers were completely familiar with each stage of the case. As Román has argued, out of the interactions between journalistic and popular discourses about witchcraft emerged a genre of brujería stories and a new social type, the brujo. Regardless of the variations, the stories generally involved one or more black men, in some way associated with African-derived religious practices, attacking and/or murdering white children, usually girls, in order to collect their blood for ritual purposes. The accused brujo, depicted in stock fashion as a remorseless murderer driven by savage instincts, was proof of Varela Zequeira's observation that "amidst full liberty and democracy, these barbaric citizens are initiating cannibalistic practices."[12]

The gendering of the brujo as male marks a departure from earlier European and North American witchcraft scares, of which women were nearly always the target. Yet in the context of recently granted citizenship and universal male suffrage to black men, it is not so surprising that men of African descent drew upon themselves the attention and anxieties of those seeking to prove Cuban aptitude for democracy. Undoubtedly overdetermined, and encompassing other factors such as the importance of male sugar workers in Cuba's economy, the image of the black brujo desexualized the African male, thus denying any evidence of miscegenation, and made him instead an instrument of violence, in which nationalists found, according to Stephan Palmié, further evidence of the sins of the colonial fathers.[13]

One possible approach to the question of how widely these journalistic narratives were disseminated (always a thorny issue in examinations of print culture) involves looking at the role of literacy and printed materials in Cuban life. Some evidence suggests an attentive readership, a growing literacy rate, and an increasing volume of newsprint produced in the early years of the republic. Newspapers had been part of public life since the early eighteenth century, with the first printing press established in 1720. In the nineteenth century newspapers had proliferated despite (or perhaps because of) ongoing battles with Spanish censors. Many sectors, such as workers, black associations, and mutal aid societies, published their own newspapers and periodicals. During the wars for independence newspapers had proved a crucial way for exiles and supporters of the movement to communicate with one another.

In the early republic, the availability and appeal of newspapers grew as a result of changing material conditions. A tariff agreement resulted in the increased importation of paper for periodicals. Developments in technology made it easier to print photographs, perhaps rendering newspapers more attractive to readers. Between 1899 and 1907 the literacy rate rose by 13.4 percent.[14] Moreover, since relatively few books were published at the time, the choices of reading material were limited.[15] At least two major Havana newspapers, *El Mundo* and *Diario de la Marina*, reported the brujería scares.

Varela Zequeira must have assumed that he had captured a readership hungry not only for details but for analysis as well, for along with his diligent reporting of the facts, he explained the source of the problem.[16] The murder was not an isolated instance of racial antagonism but rather a symptom of a deeply rooted historical and sociological malady, deriving from slavery, the original sin tainting Cuba's colonial past. Although he vacillated in his assessment of brujos' authenticity as religious leaders, claiming at times that they were nothing more than perverse and manipulative con men, he believed that an ignorant multitude, which was willing to believe in and practice brujería, was at the heart of the problem. "Slavery was a great sin," he wrote. "It left us our ignorant, nearly savage masses. The murder of Zoila was not meant as a punishment for whites, but it is one of the fruits borne by the tree so fatally sown by our predecessors. I refuse to see, nor do I want anyone to see, in the assassination of Zoila a proof of racial hatreds."[17]

Although Cuba had managed to eradicate many signs of its slaveholding, colonial past, Zequeira argued, this vestige lingered and was growing more threatening by the fact of its continuation into the present and its dissemination to masses recently included as citizens: "Brujería, with its sinister practices has unsettled the entire republic, and what was perceived before as a ridiculous or absurd religion is now perceived as a terrible threat against our peace of mind. Brujería has reached alarming proportions. The rites and practices of brujos signal, at the very least, a threat to hygiene and a threat to morality."[18] More than a singular event, Zoila signified corruption and pointed to the fragility of the republic.

The day of Bocourt and Molina's execution, Fernando Ortiz, a young man who would soon rise in intellectual circles, published his response to Zequeira's interpretation. In an article in *El Mundo*, Ortiz gave his view of the causes of the crime. Cubans looking for a clear condemnation of Bocourt and a commendation of the way the Cuban justice system had handled the crime would be disappointed. Ortiz situated himself above politics, with science; he sought scientific truth rather than moral judgment. It was a shame, he declared, that the brujo was going to be executed, because he would have been a valuable scientific specimen. Not only had he committed one of the most ferocious crimes known to Cubans, but also his African origins and his prominent role as a priest in the "barbaric cult, with a well-defined theology and an extensive, indisputable, if not fully solidified organizational structure," were significant characteristics that would have yielded much empirical evidence for the understudied phenomenon of brujería.[19]

Nonetheless, Ortiz offered a few criminological insights: first of all, since Bocourt was a fervent believer of his religion, his had been a crime motivated by altruism and goodwill. "When he convinced the others to assassinate Zoila," he wrote, "he did so believing that his act, although recognized as a crime, was perfectly moral and even altruistic, according to the ethical criteria he had brought from Africa and had clung to, due to an arrested moral development, something which is quite common amongst the inferior levels of our society." In marked contrast to Zequeira's imputation of inexplicable savagery, Ortiz claimed to uncover the logic and ethics of Bocourt's actions. If he had ordered the murder, knowing that he risked punishment by the authorities, he had done so because the intensity of his belief left him no choice. "If Bocú insisted on the necessity of the white child's blood, it was because his primitive sorcery and the tradition of his ancestors dictated it, and due to his own conviction in his beliefs and a sense of honor, he couldn't escape the primitive and antisocial aspects of his fanaticism."[20]

Religious relativism informed Ortiz's account of the events: it was a matter of understanding a different but potentially valid set of religious beliefs. He outlined briefly the mythological and theological bases for beliefs that had required, in the end, the shedding of a white child's blood. But his relativism did not extend to entire civilizations. It was precisely the possibility of civilizational evolution that was the source of the problem. Because Cuba was more advanced civilizationally than Africa, African religions were untenable in the Cuban context. A brujo was simply out of place in Cuba: "a respected person in Africa, who perhaps led his tribe according to the moral criteria compatible with their level of civilization, and a delinquent in Cuba for his inability to submit to the ethical norms that this society has established under the influence of its own social and ethnic components over the course of time." It was, ultimately, a problem of translation: "It would be more appropriate to say that in the course of being taken from Africa to Cuba, it was society itself that jumped forward, leaving him and his compatriots in the deepest savagery, in the first stages of psychic evolution . . . they are savages brought to a civilized country."[21]

Ortiz relied on established European and Latin American anthropologists and criminologists, including Armand Corre, Nina Rodrigues, Girard de Rialle, and E. B. Tylor, to validate his theory of the altruistic brujo. The ideas of Italian criminologist Césare Lombroso, with whom Ortiz had studied in Italy, figured prominently in the Cuban's evaluation of the kind of crime disturbing the new republic. Ortiz believed that two of Lombroso's explanations of crime and criminal typologies were applicable to Cuba. Lombroso held, on the one hand, that criminals were atavistic throwbacks to a primitive state, and as such they had underdeveloped or underevolved moral sentiments. They committed crimes because their sense of morality simply did not fit that of the more civilized society around them. On the other hand, entire races that were less evolved could be prone to crime and delinquency. This was true, for example, of the gypsies, which he deemed a race. Ortiz drew from both claims and combined the theory of atavism with the notion of delinquent races. It was not that these individuals had been thrust backward by an accident of birth, but rather that they had been transferred to an environment pushed forward by the accident of progress.[22]

In contrast to Zequeira, Ortiz was more optimistic about the state of Cuban civilization. Although brujería still posed a very real threat, he maintained, it had only become a problem because of its dissonance with Cuba's generally civilized condition. The emphasis, for Ortiz, was on the disorientation of criminals rather than on the fragility of the republic. His rendition of the problem erased the contradiction between claims about Cuba's modernity and the brujos' presence as a manifestation of backwardness. They were not opposing forces but rather proofs of one another's existence. It was only because Cuba had made so much progress that brujería seemed so out of place. Only the tools of modern science could provide a clear view of the problem.[23]

Yet the brujos' presence required investigation and self-scrutiny: How was it that these savages still existed in such a civilized society? What must Cubans do to ensure that this kind of parasitism did not continue to reproduce itself? First, they must study the problem objectively and scientifically, and then they must respond, following the recommendations of Enrico Ferri, another Italian criminologist, not with repressive measures but through prevention. "Let us not be so primitive," he wrote, "as to be satisfied with the meaningless death of Bocú, but rather let us consider the criminal brujería that is corrupting our society with objective observation and cold serenity, and let us understand that repressive measures will not do enough to eliminate such a complex phenomenon, and that we ought to adopt wide-ranging, methodical and long-term preventive measures, of the type that Ferri called 'penal substitutes.'"[24]

The press, having constructed the notion of the demonic brujo, provided the space in which Ortiz could reinterpret the problem. He had transformed the worrisome proliferation of ritual murder and cannibalism into evidence of Cuban progress. In addition, his work contributed to European science. At the end of his article, Ortiz announced that Bocourt was such an ideal specimen of what his mentor called a "criminal nato," or born criminal, that the Italian criminologist had requested a photograph for his reknowned Archivio di Psichiatria (Archives of Psychiatry) in Turin. In a neatly self-promoting move, Ortiz had created a long-lasting mandate for himself and anyone who cared to join him in the pursuit of "objective observation," as well as a market for his soon-to-be-published study of what he called "criminal ethnology."

Los negros brujos

In 1906 Fernando Ortiz was a relatively unknown lawyer. He had studied at the University of Havana between 1896 and 1898 and traveled to Spain afterward, returning to Cuba in 1902. In 1903 he had received a degree in civil law; his thesis was entitled "On the Reorganization of the Police as Necessary to the Administration of Criminal Justice."[25] By 1904 he was in Genoa, Italy, serving as Cuban consul. He had published a few brief articles introducing the field of criminology to Cuban readers in *Azul y Rojo*, a journal directed by the well-known intellectual Raimundo Cabrera, who later became his father-in-law.[26] Although Ortiz was out of the country when the Zoila case obsessed the press and the public, he seems to have followed it from afar. Not long after the story broke, he had apparently begun the research on which he would base *La hampa afro-cubana: Los negros brujos (apuntes para un estudio de etnología criminal)* (1906) (hereafter cited as *Los negros brujos*), the book that became the canonical disquisition of the Cuban *hampa*, or underworld.[27]

The book is an expanded version of the article Ortiz published the day of Bocourt and Molina's execution, formulating as its principal task the scientific study of the causes and manifestations of the Cuban nexus between race, religion, and crime. Yet, beyond the argument, the book's significance lies in its novelty of form and genre. In between Europe and Cuba, criminology and ethnology, textual and empirical bases of knowledge, *Los negros brujos* was a new kind of book for Cuban readers, turning a sensational series of events into the raw materials of a learned, original, and (in the author's eyes) redemptive social analysis that placed Cuba on the map of modern nations plagued by similar ills. At the same time it launched Ortiz's remarkable career as a translator of people, practices, ideas, and texts.

In a book crammed with footnotes citing European intellectual heavyweights such as E. B. Tylor, A. B. Ellis, James Frazer, Emile Durkheim, and the recently published Marcel Mauss on magic, as well as references to Spanish criminologist Rafael Salillas on lowlife ("la mala vida") in Madrid and Napoli, Ortiz marshaled evidence both to draw parallels to the European phenomenon of brujería and to make a case for Cuban exceptionalism. As social scientists were beginning to discover, flourishing lowlife was a phenomenon that disrupted many European capitals. Because of the country's ethnic makeup, however, Cuba's lowlife was unique. Europeans did not need to account for the effects of importing African slaves into the mix.

Even while the book is based on the effect of race on criminality and delinquency, it rests on several different and potentially contradictory notions of race. The first chapter, which examines the emergence of Cuba's underworld, concludes with a fluid conception of race and its effect on cultural change: "Ethnicity is the fundamental factor," Ortiz theorized,

> and it not only produced delinquent milieus particular to each race, in addition, by contributing their specific vices to 'low life' in general, a common criminal milieu was created out of the fusion of diverse psychologies, a layer which constituted and constitutes the nucleus of our delinquent strata . . . due to the mutual influence each race exercised upon the other, the black race acquired an impulse toward progress, which continues to develop . . . and the white race has Africanized its criminal class.[28]

But the descriptions and analyses that occupy most of the book drop this fluid notion for a catalog of inherited traditional practices and psychological characteristics not responsive to external influences. In some ways the conflict between these different notions of race stems from the problem of time and where to place Africans within it. Were they to be viewed through a historical lens as participants in the stream of change, beginning with their presence in Cuba in the sixteenth century, or were they to be placed, after the fashion of much early-twentieth-century ethnography, in a timeless vacuum, existing in the present but perpetually primitive?[29]

A mixed methodology produced a number of different conclusions. Although Lombroso and his hereditary, morphological criminal anthropology is the proclaimed godfather of the book, Ortiz filled his chapters, not with the expected physiognomic descriptions and comparisons but with detailed descriptions of brujos' belief system, of their rituals, of clothing and objects used, of their social organization, of their place in society, and of their language, including specific words, incantations, names and nicknames.

Ortiz did invoke Lombroso and his theory of the criminal as a "throwback" to a primitive state to explain recent and particularly violent manifestations of brujería as the acts of a few aberrant criminals not at all representative of a cultural milieu. Thus he wrote in one section that the Zoila case was an exception in the history of Cuban brujería: "Recently all of Cuban society was upset by a horrible crime: by the assassination of a white girl, committed by brujos . . . because in reality, a similar case had not occurred, or at least had not been heard of, since the time of slavery."[30] Elsewhere, his reliance on more "cultural" explanations led to a view of brujería as a long-standing, widespread problem: "The crime has surprised us, more because it has exposed the cancerous fanaticism that corrupts ignorant masses of our nation than for the criminality revealed by its individual authors."[31]

Once he had introduced this array of interpretations, Ortiz altered his voice from synthesizer of ethnological and sociological material to reporter of contemporary, local phenomenon. An entire chapter lists excerpts from newspaper clippings that report incidents of brujería between 1902 and 1906. Notably, given the overwhelming dominance of stories on child murders after 1906, these pages ascribe a wide range of behaviors to brujería. The excerpts detail healing and ritual practices, describe many gatherings from which telling objects were seized, and in one case recount the extraction of a black cat from a woman's belly. Only one of these accounts involved the abduction of a child (apart from Zoila's, some of which is reproduced in the chapter), and it was one of the least persuasively reported. This suggests that the later obsession with child murders did indeed emerge in the twentieth century and that the case of Zoila was perhaps the template for many others.

Several themes unify the book. A critique of Spain underlies the discussion of religion. Throughout, Ortiz insists on parallels and interrelationships between the animist religious system he attributes to the brujos and the superstitious practices of Spanish Catholics. Not only are the differences between Catholicism and animistic religions a matter of degree rather than type, but also the history of slavery in Cuba entailed an interaction between African and Catholic religions. Thus the emergent practices and their tendency toward criminality ought to be seen as a syncretic mix.[32]

His proposals for the elimination of brujería, imbued with faith in science and modernization, are also tinged with a critique of Spanish backwardness (as well as the more obvious African primitiveness). First, following the precepts of positivist criminology, the brujo must be studied as a type. Merely focusing on the crime—the approach of classical criminology—would deliver only a partial solution. Yet what precisely Ortiz's solution entails is never clear. The book closes with a deep ambiguity. Powerful rhetoric obfuscates poorly developed proposals for "the defensive battle" ahead:

> The first step in the defensive battle against brujería must be to eliminate the brujos, isolate them from their followers, like those stricken with yellow fever, because brujería is essentially contagious.

. . . Once those charlatans have disappeared, once their celebrations, dances and savage rites are gone, their temples destroyed, their impotent gods confiscated, all the tentacles of brujería that tie its believers to the barbaric underbelly of our society severed, then those believers will be able to begin to relieve their not-yet-de-Africanized minds from the weight of chaotic superstition and rise to more elevated levels of culture.[33]

Los negros brujos was a transatlantic endeavor, materially as well as substantively. The production of knowledge in this instance involved the literal transportation of sources and ideas. Since Ortiz was in Italy when the Zoila case broke and while he wrote the book, he relied on informants and correspondents for information. Along with the newspaper clippings sent to him in Europe as the case unfolded, his files contain correspondence, received just as he was drafting *Los negros brujos*, with detailed reports of brujería. Written by Emiliano Gato, police chief of the small Cuban town of Palos, and Miguel Talleda, police officer from the town of Abreus, these letters provide descriptions of rituals, translations of words and phrases, and accounts of local incidents.[34] Ortiz thus relied on the police, who, continuing the tradition begun by the Havana Detective Bureau in 1900,[35] of close observation and description, translated practice into text for an emerging social scientific view of "the problem of race." The police reports would become an important source not just for social science, but for legal decisions as well.[36] Ortiz molded his informants' reports with theoretical tools acquired in Europe and produced a newly packaged vision of Cuban lowlife. His thorough and reassuringly scientific text, first published in Madrid, traveled back to Cuba, where it was consumed and digested by an eager public.

From July to November, reviews of *Los negros brujos* appeared in major Havana newspapers across political and ideological spectrums. Though their assessments varied, most authors insisted that their criticisms should not detract from the importance of the contribution Ortiz had made. They shared an acceptance of his premises that combined despair with optimism as to Cuba's place in the world. They also charted and contributed to Ortiz's rise to prominence in public life.

In *El Mundo*, M. Muñoz-Bustamante dubbed Ortiz "The Main *Brujo* of the Republic," noting with admiration his linguistic skills, his qualifications as lawyer and sociologist, the amount of work involved in producing so well grounded a book, and the attention the book and author had received from Lombroso. All these elements had been brought together for Cuba's benefit: "A psychologist like Dr. Ortiz put his finger on the sore and quickly found the source of superstition and criminality. It is true that we did not have extraordinary delinquents, but we did have in brujos and ñáñigos two centers of abominable machinations, two sites of conspiracy against progress. From this Dr. Ortiz derived his subject for this book."[37]

A review by Ruy Díaz in *El Comercio* began with praise but used a considerable amount of space to criticize Ortiz, taking issue mostly with his research methods: in reference to Ortiz's use of "street rumors" and articles taken from *La Discusión*, Díaz complained that "many of his observations are based on data compiled with unforgivable superficiality." Even so, these were quibbles among professionals and should not "subtract a bit of glory from the learned youngster."[38] An anonymous reviewer for *Diario de la Familia* admitted that he had not read the book but nonetheless commended the author, whose stature as an intellectual, he asserted, so exceeded the average that usual words of praise would not suffice: "We must find new adjectives for men of Dr. Ortiz's moral and intellectual stature."[39] In *La Discusión*, Jesús Castellanos expressed ambivalence about Ortiz's findings, even as he insisted on their importance as "a central contribution to modern anthropology" and on Ortiz's role as a public intellectual.[40]

A final review in *La Unión Española*, by José Aguirre, took issue on partisan and consequently pro-Spanish grounds. Challenging Ortiz's critique of Spanish religious and slaveholding practices, Aguirre argued that the colonial administration was better able to control ñañiguismo and brujería, and that brujería had reemerged so pervasively because of the new regime's inability to control the populace. This position renders more understandable the insistence of Ortiz and other Liberals that the Cuban republic was a modern, progressive polity. On the other hand, Aguirre maintained that Ortiz "has already contributed and will continue to contribute incalculable services to our society, exposing those repulsive social wounds, so that they can be cauterized according to the prescriptions of modern science."[41] The growing hegemony of science as the anodyne to social ills is evident here, especially in light of Aguirre's and Ortiz's disagreement on the sources of those maladies.

News of the book's publication traveled back to Europe, where Lombroso, who had already contributed a laudatory preface, and Max Nordau, the author of *Degeneration*, reviewed it favorably. Sociologist and criminologist Alfredo Nicéforo, a professor at the University of Brussels, cited evidence from the book in his article on human sacrifice appearing in a Trieste daily, *Il Picolo della Sera*. Soon afterward, *Avanti*, a criminology journal directed by Enrico Ferri, published his review of *Los negros brujos* entitled "Triumph of a Cuban." Translated in *El Mundo* in October 1906, it emphasized to Cuban readers Ortiz's growing status abroad and the importance of his contribution to the European study of "superstitious masses."[42]

Of Rights and Rituals

Despite its endurance in the press and its influence in the social sciences, brujería did not fare so well in the courts. Between 1904 and 1923, according to Ernesto Chávez Alvarez, eight cases of men of African descent accused of murdering white children (including Zoila) were prosecuted, each of them reported sensationally in the press. In three of the cases, "el niño Onelio" (1915), "el niño Marcelino" (1919), and "la niña Cuca" (1922), the suspects were released upon discovery of plots to frame them. In three more, the charges were dropped for lack of evidence. The accused in the seventh case, "la niña Cecilia" (1919), were killed by the military amid a lynching attempt. Zoila's, then, was the only case in which the accused were found guilty and executed.[43]

Since there was no law against brujería, attempts at conviction were thwarted by claims about rights or simply the requirements of evidence, indicating a measure of autonomy of the legal sphere despite the pervasiveness of social scientific discourses.[44] The example of three other cases in which the defendants were accused of brujería (under the rubric of illicit association) suggests an inconsistency in the power of ritual objects as irrefutable grounds for conviction. In 1906 a woman was accused of "rendering another's faculties useless" after police received an anonymous letter accusing her of practicing brujería. In 1915 Paulina Alsina and eleven others were apprehended with their objects (*piezas de convicción*) and accused of illicit association. In 1916 twenty-four individuals from Regla were taken into custody on similar charges. All were dismissed for lack of evidence.[45]

Constitutional rights were central in the 1919 trial of Narcisa Allones Montalvo, Belén González, and Vicenta de la Paz for illicit association. In this case the prestige of science was challenged by the logic of the constitution. Both Fernando Ortiz and Luis Montané appeared as expert witnesses for the prosecution "to provide information as to the purpose the confiscated objects serve in rituals of brujería." Invoking the freedoms of "religion and cults," defense lawyer Angel Larrinaga rejected the claim that possession of the objects in itself was a crime. As the trial records end before the final hearing, the outcome remains unknown.[46]

A rare instance in which the records are complete through inquiry and appeals affords a glimpse at the ways the social sciences and the legal system interacted. A case against Quirino Montalvo Marty, Diego Ozeguera Rodríguez, Faustino Pino, and Manuel Rente González (all "black" according to the court records) for illicit association in 1913 reveals continuing battles over the legal definition of ñañiguismo and the theoretical relationships between race and crime. It also clearly demonstrates the perceived importance and role of ethnographic knowledge gathered by law enforcement officials.[47] In what by that time must have been routine procedure, the police gathered objects when they seized the four men. The objects included "a bell named Encárnica, four wooden and two metal candlesticks, four complete *diablito* suits of different colors, three hats for those suits stamped with the symbol of said association, a pair of shoes, a large drum, named Bongo, another named Ecué, another of the order, another bearing the name of Eribo, and two more whose names are unknown." Despite the suspects' not-guilty pleas, these items were enough evidence for the judge conducting the preliminary hearing to determine that the accused ought to be detained and tried.[48]

But the judge wanted to know the relationship of the objects to each other and to the accused. He ordered the secret police to conduct an investigation to ascertain whether the accused were indeed ñáñigos, to what association they belonged, and whether its practices and rituals, especially those "not considered scientific," included healing.[49]

The initial findings of detectives Amador Prío Rivas and Juan González, assistants to Lieutenant Inchaustegui, must have disappointed the judge, for they underscored the absence of real grounds for conviction. Prío Rivas stated that although it was a known fact that there were at least fifteen ñáñigo organizations in Havana, their vows of secrecy made it almost impossible to gather any information about them. He could only state that he had discovered that one of the accused, Diego Ozeguera, did indeed live at the address he had given and that the other suspects had met there on several occasions. He noted that when one of their members had been killed, ñáñigos customarily gathered at the house of the deceased and conducted "barbaric ceremonies" that concluded with vows of vengeance and silence. These ongoing feuds were rampant in Havana, he claimed, especially recently when ñañiguismo had been reorganized by "those people addicted to its institutions." It was precisely due to their vows of secrecy that the police were constantly frustrated. With this Rivas created a nonfalsifiable proposition that denied the accused the possibility of self-defense and afforded the police a slippery but potentially powerful tool.[50]

For detective Juan González, it seemed enough to point out that all members of the association were "black," doing so twice, as he denied that they engaged in healing practices and could only state with assurance that they played dominoes at the gatherings, undoubtedly, in his eyes, a pretext for other activities.[51] In his summary of the case thus far, Judge Ponce declared that the men had been arrested as a result of an investigation ordered by the chief of the National Police, that they were accused of "various crimes" for the moment unnamed because of the ñáñigo vow of silence, and that they would remain in custody and await trial for illicit association: "Several crimes have gone unpunished, or rather, uninvestigated, for it is the duty of a member of a group of ñáñigos to withhold information about any crime . . . that these events reveal the criminal qualities of illicit association suggests good reason to deem those accused responsible for the acts."[52]

The question of what the offenders had actually done became the principal issue for both defense and prosecution. Pedro Herrera Sotolongo, a lawyer defending Quirino Montalvo y Martí, claimed his client's innocence on the grounds that "the presumption of guilt is not punishable." He insisted that the law against illicit association was an outdated relic of colonial times: "The crimes attributed to secret societies in the colonial era were real political crimes which had to be attributed to someone."[53]

In Prío Rivas's report, he admitted that he had failed to "investigate the issues as laid out in said order" as they had been defined. Refusing to give up simply because he could not specify what the accused had done, he used the opportunity to submit a report about "practices, beliefs, ceremonies and aims" of the ñáñigos, foreshadowing the Ortiz of a decade later who would seek to describe the very same things. He characterized his subject as "wrapped in the most impenetrable mystery" until recently, when it was forced into the public eye as a result of "the tolerance of said groups due to political issues." The credibility and authenticity of his material, he asserted, as if to stave off accusations of its fabrication, derived from interviews with "persons intimately related to said association." Placing the origins of ñañiguismo in the regime of Tacón, a notoriously repressive Capitán General who ruled Cuba from 1834 to 1838, the policeman traced the history of early associations, linking the most intense conflicts between different groups of ñáñigos with changes in the racial makeup of the associations. All of the original groups had been of African descent, and it was when the first white groups organized that they began the homicidal feuding for which ñáñigos were most infamous in contemporary times. Prío Rivas rendered a detailed account of the initiation ceremony and burial rites, including the phrases used during these rituals, some of which are translated (although the original language is never provided), followed by a reiteration of his nonfalsifiable theory of the vow of silence, this time buttressed by concrete information on how these vows were made and under what circumstances. He closed with a critique of the constitutional freedoms that had allowed ñañiguismo to flourish after being nearly wiped out under the final Spanish administration, as well as of José Miguel Gómez's permissive liberal regime that also failed to condemn ñañiguismo, if not encouraging it outright. Thus he managed to mingle a historical, ethnographic, and political account of the practice, even as he underscored the secrecy that surrounded it, constructing himself as an irrefutable authority at the court's disposal.[54]

The case records also include a report submitted by Luis Sánchez, subinspector of the secret police, that deals more directly with the relationship between race and crime. It begins, unlike Prío Rivas's, by naming the members of the association under investigation and providing as many facts about them as possible. Foremost is their identification as "black," followed by the observation that many were stevedores. But for Sánchez their racial identification was ultimately the most incriminating piece of evidence: "Most of these individuals are or have been stevedores and are friendly amongst themselves, so that they are joined by ties of race, of ñañiguismo, in short, by all that is illicit."[55]

The accumulated information in these reports proved incriminating enough to send the case to the Audiencia (*sala tercera de lo criminal*) for an oral hearing with a recommendation of imprisonment for one year, eight months, and twenty-one days. An apparently skillful defense—Juan Latapier (who had represented Domingo Bocourt and was Cuba's first nonwhite lawyer) represented Manuel Rente González, Herrera Sotolongo represented Quirino Montalvo Marty and Diego Ozeguera Rodríguez, and Antonio García Hernández represented Faustino Pino—resulted in a reduced sentence. The four defendants were convicted of illicit association as stated in articles 186 and 187 of the penal code. But since the investigation had failed to reveal the names of the directors and founders of the association, the court could only convict them for participating as members of their association, thus reducing the sentence to four months.

Perhaps the success (however limited) of the defense impelled Herrera Sotolongo to attempt an appeal. Herrera framed his motion with an eye to exploiting the conflicts between a Spanish penal code adopted in the colonial era and a Cuban constitution granting individual rights. He argued that the 1901 constitution's provisions guaranteeing freedom of association and freedom of religion ought to override two of the laws used to convict: Article 849 ("article regulating criteria for conviction") and the decree issued by the governor general in 1876. Although his appeal was technically procedural, the language with which he stated his case reveals that he was aiming at the moral implications of the law against association:

> From this may be deduced two things: either that the association is illicit for pursuing ends contrary to public morals, or it is illicit because they gather in order to commit crimes. We argue that neither of these reasons holds . . . ñáñigos, though they may dress in diablito garb and dance to the sound of their drums, are not bad people . . . it is true, these ñáñigos gather for their dances and their religious ceremonies. There is no crime in their activities. There is no clear description, in the sentence, of the ways in which they offend public morals and society at large. With regards to the most grave offense, that they gather in order to DEFEND THEMSELVES, and to seek vengeance for the offenses committed against them, this is not only a puerile accusation, it is in effect not a crime, because defending oneself against aggression is not considered criminal behavior.[56]

The appeal was denied on the grounds that the conviction had been based solely on the law against illicit association in the penal code, not article 849 or the governor's decree, as Herrera had suggested. Although the appeal failed, the lawyer was able to use the questions raised by the adoption of the 1901 constitution to make his plea heard, not only for the primacy of rights, but also for the unfairness and bias of the definition of illicit association. That the judge settled the case while ignoring the question of the rights to freedom of religion and association indicates that changing legal definitions of permissible religious and associational practices opened significant ambiguities potentially exploitable by both sides. Years before, in defense of Domingo Bocourt, Juan Latapier had also appealed to the Supreme Court. Latapier's appeals had been based on claims that brujos were not in possession of their faculties and therefore should not be held responsible for their crimes. The use of that argument suggests the rapidity with which Latapier integrated recent criminological debates over free will and responsibility into the Cuban context. But the introduction of a new theory of criminal responsibility backfired, perhaps, for Latapier's clients received harsher penalties as a result of the appeals.[57]

Intellectuals Energized

The troubles of brujería's prosecutors in the courts did not dampen social scientific enthusiasm for investigating its implications. The problem of delinquency seems in fact to have encouraged Cuban intellectuals to take broad steps to resolve the dilemmas of modernity. Ortiz's success at collecting ideas and materials from different parts of the world in order to shed light on a problem perceived as uniquely Cuban preceded, and probably provided the impetus for, a burst of intellectual activity focused on what was referred to as "the social question." His engagement with a number of social scientific currents of thought from Europe and Latin America (while defying Spanish intellectual dominance) and his intimations of hope for the future of the Cuban republic must have appealed to Cuban men of science and letters, already poised for their ascent to prominence. Both as members of academe and as contributors and editors of a number of new journals, these men pursued the questions Ortiz had raised about race, science, and social reform. Within this context a strong belief in the application of positivist and scientific approaches to social problems took hold.

The University of Havana provided one home for the emerging field of criminal anthropology. After the Department of Anthropology was established in 1900, Luis Montané taught two versions of a course on anthropology. Revealing the fluidity and expansiveness characteristic of the "science of man" at the time, as well as his own cosmopolitan approach to learning, Montané drew from a number of traditions in constructing his course syllabi.

His first course on criminal anthropology for the law school focused on the application of anthropology to penal law. The prominence of measurement and analysis of the skull and brain in the course description points to the influence of what Stephen J. Gould has called "the allure of numbers."[58] Leading his students through the complexities of "craneology: notions of craneo-cerebral topography; craneometry: cranial capacity measured over time by way of different contemporary races; craneography: pathological and ethnic deformities," he impressed on them the importance of measurable manifestations of criminality. He also included a section on anthropometric exercises, taking advantage of the instruments for skull and bone measurement donated by the Americans when they established the department. Assigned texts were exclusively in French, in accordance with his training. Students initially read French anthropologists Paul Broca, Paul Topinard, and Armand Quatrefages, although by the second year they had begun to study the work of Italian criminologist Césare Lombroso as well. The program for students in the School of the Sciences and Pedagogy had a more evolutionary focus. Montané covered the "evolution of civilizations," the prehistories of the Americas in general and Cuba in particular, and the "formation and classification of human races, with an examination of ethnic characteristics."[59]

By 1906 a university reform formalized the distinction between anthropology for law students and for students of the arts and sciences, creating a professorship of juridical anthropology and one of general anthropology.[60] The changes in juridical anthropology favored a more positivist approach, with new sections on anthropometric and dactiloscopic identification and the application of those methods to the law. Subsections on "civil status from the medico-legal point of view" reveal a striking mix of medical, psychiatric, ethnographic, and legal categories: "Birth: evolution of the human family. Pregnancy. Sex. Monstrous births. Marriage. Puberty. Divorce. Consanguinuity. Dementia. Impotence. On Death: evolution of the cult of the dead. Questions related to cremation." Law students also took field trips to Havana's prison and mental asylum so they might better understand Lombrosian doctrine, as well as study the individual characteristics of delinquents.[61]

Montané, recently returned from the 1906 Congress on Criminal Anthropology in Turin, Italy, exposed students to debates in the literature. By adding the works of Gabriel de Tardé, Juan Vucetich, Alexandre Lacassagne, Lombroso, and Ferri to the reading list, he presented the discussion of criminal responsibility preoccupying the French school, represented among others by Lacassagne, who challenged Lombroso's notion of the "born criminal" with his emphasis on the sociological origins of crime.[62] These debates received a good deal of attention in Europe and would come to play a role in the Cuban judicial system. At stake was the extent to which criminals could be held responsible for their actions, gauged by contrasting characterizations of humans responding to free will or bound by determinism. In the Cuban context, this was a question often posed of accused brujos and ñáñigos.

The content of this course remained the same until at least 1940. For the duration of Montané's tenure, until he retired in 1919, the only differences were additions in the techniques of policing, from hands-on skills like dealing with cadavers to lectures on the psychology of criminals. When Arístides Mestre took over the professorship after Montané's departure, he retained most of the curriculum. Mestre did alter it slightly, however, adding a section on "brujería, ñañiguismo y criminalidad" and thereby institutionalizing the tropes that had been circulating in the press and various publications since 1906. In an address to the Sixth Latin American Medical Congress in 1923, later published in the University of Havana's *Revista de Facultad de Letras y Ciencias*, Mestre laid out his thoughts on the persistence of what he called "Afro-Cuban criminality." He reiterated most of Ortiz's ideas, insisting on the continuing relevance of his analysis. A child murder reported only the previous year demonstrated the persistence of the problem originally brought to light with the death of Zoila. Although Mestre described Afro-Cuban religiosity with more sophistication than Varela Zequeira, his conclusions were similar: "What I have described of the Afro-Cuban brujo, who with good reason has been considered one of the most repugnant and harmful social types in Cuba, illustrates the criminological problem to which his superstitions gave rise."[63]

Outside of the university, prominent Liberal intellectuals including Ortiz, Diego Tamayo, Raimundo Cabrera, Enrique Garrido, and Orestes Ferrara sponsored and contributed to several new journals, founded mostly between 1906 and 1909. Together, *Reforma Social*, *Derecho y Sociología*, *Vida Nueva*, *Azul y Rojo*, *Cuba y América*, and *Revista Bimestre Cubana* created forums in which the social sciences were called upon to diagnose and heal social problems. The ambition with which they conceived of their task is evident in the subtitle of *Derecho y Sociología* (Law and Sociology): it stated that the journal would include articles on "jurisprudence, anthropology, biology, history, philosophy, ethics, political economy, and sociology." Indeed, all of the journals did address such a wide range of topics that they defy categorization. Yet an examination of their contents reveals a recurrent set of broader themes: delinquency, public health, the role of the state in reform, and the modernity of Cuba compared with Europe, the United States, and Latin America. They also indicate a concern for keeping abreast of intellectual activity in those places, including articles by Argentine sociologist José Ingenieros, Mexican educator José Vasconcelos, and Uruguayan essayist Enrique Rodó, and reporting the proceedings of various international scientific congresses.

The editors of these journals worked principally in the fields of law and medicine, though, as evident in *Derecho y Sociología*'s subtitle, they delved into other social sciences as deemed necessary. The history of book publication in this period also suggests a burgeoning interest and growing readership in law and medicine. Between 1917 and 1924, from a total of 731 books published, although 197 were works of poetry, 139 volumes were on law, 132 on medicine, and 110 on Cuban history.[64] Lawyers and doctors, some of them already political leaders, formed part of the intellectual elite as well. This group seemed to monopolize the task of interpreting Cuba's social and demographic changes. In 1914, during Conservative Mario Menocal's regime, Orestes Ferrara, Ortiz, and Dr. Jorge Le Roy y Cassá were called upon to compile statistics for an unofficial census to be published between the censuses of 1909 and 1917.[65]

These intellectuals shared similar concerns with reformist progressives ascendant in the United States and Europe. As Daniel Rodgers has argued, the concept of progressivism itself has been notoriously capacious and therefore elusive. He does provide some guideposts, however, signaling the concepts of "antimonopolism," "social bonds," and "social efficiency" as key components linking a wide variety of reformist projects. The early twentieth century witnessed intellectuals addressing problems created by democratization and industrialization in these terms, both in the United States and in Europe. In the United States, as Gary Gerstle has contended, political liberals believed that greater democratic participation could be achieved through a cultural politics of assimilation and education. In Europe, Daniel Pick has demonstrated that Lombroso himself operated within a liberal reformist paradigm, and that his theories were invoked during the period of Italian unification in order to find a way to shape and orient new citizens.[66] Latin American intellectuals faced with similar problems began dialogues on the notions of social reform and scientific rationalization of society.[67]

The languages of social bonds and social efficiency resonated with the concerns of these intellectuals. Often steeped in medical terminology as well, their writings in journals conveyed a sense of responsibility for healing the body social. In the midst of electoral and economic crises, Diego Tamayo, physician and editor of Havana's *Vida Nueva* (*Journal of Hygiene and Social Science*), wrote in 1921 that "many of the syndromes that disturb our country could be addressed from within our profession, and therefore, we feel obligated to study them, so as to understand the pathologies and propose those remedies we determine to be most effective."[68] Tamayo and his colleagues founded medical clinics for the poor, worried about prostitution and venereal disease, and sponsored eugenics and homiculture projects.

The fascination with race and crime continued to be a notable feature of many journals. The work of Israel Castellanos, frequently published in *Vida Nueva*, which he eventually edited, indicates one of the directions in which they pointed. One of the most prolific criminologists writing on race, as well as one of the most difficult to categorize, Castellanos sustained a dialogue with Lombrosian positivism and hereditarian criminal anthropology long after Ortiz turned away from them. His book, *Brujería y ñañiguismo desde su punto de vista médico-legal* (*Brujería and Ñañiguismo from a Medico-Legal Perspective*), published in 1916, demonstrates, like Mestre's speech, the tenacity with which anxieties about African-derived religious and cultural practices invaded the Cuban social sciences.

Castellanos aimed to strengthen the hereditary link between race and crime. The young student, a year away from receiving his bachelor of arts degree at the University of Havana when his book was published, gave new life to Lombrosian theories even as their power was fading in legal contexts and in some intellectual circles. Castellanos was an autodidact, reading Lombroso, Ferri, and Garofalo on his own before being taken under the wing of Spanish criminologist Dr. Salvador Velázquez de Castro, director of Granada's *Gaceta Médica del Sur*, and Diego Tamayo. Castellanos's early publications in both the *Gaceta* and *Vida Nueva* had clearly made a favorable impression on the members of Havana's Academy of Sciences (Academia de Ciencias Médicas, Físicas y Naturales), for his 1916 book won a prize as the best publication of the year. In the same year he was commissioned by the secretary of health to carry out anthropological studies in the reformatory for men in Guanajuay as well as in the Reformatory of Aldecea.[69]

Castellanos complicated the relationships among race, crime, and evolution that Ortiz had mapped out fairly simply. If the main impetus of Ortiz's book was to show that brujos committed crimes out of a misunderstanding of their moral context stemming from their displacement from Africa to Cuba, Castellanos drew moral and social distinctions between two forms of what he understood as black delinquency. If the notion of intentional malice was stripped from the definition of brujos, whom he accepted as altruistic misfits, it was brought in through the back door to describe ñáñigos, in his view "born criminals." The major difference from which everything else derived was that a brujo "is characterized by his religiosity," whereas a ñáñigo "lacks that quality." Whereas the actions of brujos were well intentioned even if driven by superstition and misguided religious beliefs, the actions of ñáñigos were purely criminal, driven only by their thirst for homicidal revenge, the organizing principle of their societies.[70]

Even though their categorization principally as members of social groups rather than races might have made it difficult for Castellanos to map out their physical characteristics, he did not find that to be the case. In a far more Lombrosian vein than Ortiz, he insisted that ñáñigos, whatever race, shared the sloping forehead, protruding jaw, and jumpy, elusive gaze characteristic of the "born criminal."[71] His book dropped the ethnographic paradigm for a more statistical approach. The Cuban data supporting his claims were the product of scientific studies conducted in controlled environments by scientists trained in criminological methodologies. Gone were informants with firsthand reports. When he referred to current events, he presented brujos as specimens, rather than historical actors, accompanied by photographs and measurements.

Yet even Castellanos could not quite keep his data within the biological framework of the theoretical paradigms on which he drew. To begin with, he complained that the information simply did not exist to test many Lombrosian theories. He was forced to admit that although he was convinced that studies would reveal atavistic stigmata of criminals marking the skulls and bodies of ñáñigos, he could not provide examples because the data were so scarce. Despite his apparent mistrust for anything but statistical data, at times his analysis veered off into the "cultural." For instance, his book contains a discussion of tattoos, as a sign, both physical and moral, of the ñáñigo psyche.[72]

Castellanos's career in government was long and influential. In 1921 he became director of the National Bureau of Identification. In 1928 he created and became director of the Laboratorio de Antropología Penitenciaria (Laboratory of Penitentiary Anthropology), dedicated to keeping anthropometric records of inmates. Among his publications were *La talla de los delincuentes en Cuba* (*The Height of Cuban Delinquents*) (1926), *El peso corporal de los delincuentes en Cuba* (*The Weight of Cuban Delinquents*) (1928), and *El pelo en los Cubanos* (*Cuban Hair*) (1933), all of which received prizes from the Academy of Sciences. Also in 1929 his *La delincuencia femenina en Cuba* (*Female Delinquency in Cuba*) was awarded the Lombroso prize from the Archivo di antropología criminale, psichiatria e medicina legale (Archive of Criminal Anthropology, Psychiatry, and Legal Medicine) in Turin. As ensuing chapters show, his publications and work in these institutions created the energy and amassed the resources for the continued application of criminal anthropology to law enforcement strategies, sustaining and legitimizing a link between race and crime in one sphere of public life well into the fourth decade of the twentieth century.

Conclusion

The deaths of Zoila and Bocourt in a moment of Republican fragility precipitated the creation of enduring links between the *science of race* and the *science of crime* in early-twentieth-century Cuba. By looking at the ways these ideas circulated in the press, in printed material for lay and scientific readers, and in legal contexts, I have tried to render concretely some of the dynamics at play in the making of race. Neither solely imported from elsewhere nor crafted in hermetic elite circles, race was constituted and contested by numerous sectors of society. Because these racial discourses were elaborated within the context of increasing political inclusion and democratization, they were at once powerfully persuasive and fundamentally ambiguous. Their appeal to intellectuals and social scientists eager to contribute to European and North American debates about modernity and social ills spurred an intense interest in the application of positivist truths to the Cuban case.

Narratives of brujería and ñañiguismo initially presented most vociferously in the press came to occupy privileged positions in public debates and social science as the most distinctive manifestations of the Cuban "racial problem." At the same time, the adoption of formal legal equality and a bill of rights that defended freedoms of religion and association mitigated, in courts of law, the hegemony of racial discourses premised on the primitivism and inherent criminality of people of African descent. The social scientific discourse on brujería thus failed to construct as impervious an intellectual edifice as its authors might have desired. Competing visions of republican progress worked to simultaneously support and undermine links among race, crime, and unorthodox religious practices.

That the observed phenomena took place in Cuba rather than in a distant land raises a further question. How did Cubans of color respond to and participate in these constructions and speculations? How did their own notions of citizenship and republican modernity engage the figure of the brujo and the implications it carried of epidemic barbarity? As demonstrated in the next chapter, for many black and mulatto activists, politicians, and intellectuals, issues of the science of blackness were deeply entangled with issues of the politics of blackness.

Progress, I understand, is necessarily ugly.

W. E. B. DU BOIS
The Souls of the Black Folk (1903)

3

Barbarism and Its Discontents

The early republic's limited sovereignty gave rise to what Jorge Domínguez has called the "politics of pluralization." Groups opposed to the central government quickly learned to use the continuing threat of U.S. intervention to their advantage to strengthen their position and support, turning to armed insurrection as a way to draw the United States into domestic struggles. Thus one of the consequences of a fragile state was the emergence of multiple sources of political influence.[1] In the aftermath of the 1905 elections, for example, a frustrated Liberal Party led by José Miguel Gómez challenged Tomás Estrada Palma's claim to victory with accusations of fraudulent elections, backing its accusations with an armed uprising. The ensuing U.S. intervention and three-year occupation ended with the Liberals in power and the state's autonomy and legitimacy very much in question.

Cubans of color found themselves negotiating the contradictions and changing circumstances within this context of political fragmentation at the highest level. Against a jumbled backdrop of new rights, new restrictions, and imputations of backwardness and savagery supported by the power of science and the state, they considered old strategies and new languages in their pursuit of equality. Of necessity, they drew from continuities from the colonial era as well as changes wrought in the struggle for independence. It should be no surprise, then, that they spoke with a multiplicity of voices.

Those who had mobilized against racial discrimination before the war continued their efforts during the republic. Central figures such as Juan Gualberto Gómez and Martín Morúa Delgado took their places in high politics, with Gómez serving as representative to Congress from the province of Havana for many years and Morúa Delgado serving as senator until his death in 1910. As they and other black and mulatto politicians debated the merits of different forms of mobilization for greater access to civil and political rights, their strategies ultimately coalesced around two distinct models of citizenship. One model, as practiced by Gómez and others before the war, what I will call "civil citizenship," envisioned political integration for Cubans of color as a process involving education and the acquisition of civic virtue.[2] The other model, voiced by the Partido Independiente de Color (PIC), eschewed a vision of deferred citizenship, preferring instead to assert that military participation justified immediate inclusion in the state's political infrastructure. As Alejandro de la Fuente has argued, leaders of the PIC viewed "autonomous political mobilization as the only way for blacks to get their share as citizens of a republic that they had fought so hard to create."[3] When political success meant access to jobs and patronage networks, the PIC's language and strategies, as we shall see, linked the issue of jobs to broader issues of political inclusion and participation.[4]

The major difference between these stances, in both theory and practice, had a great deal to do with the role of blacks and mulattoes in the wars for independence. Led by war veterans Evaristo Estenoz and Pedro Ivonet, the PIC represented one (if the most clamorous) perceived solution to the problem of continuing inequality. The first and only race-based political party in Cuba, it was composed of veterans of the wars for independence as well as some veterans of the recent Liberal rebellion in 1906 and made the greater integration of Cubans of color into state patronage networks one of its most prominent demands. As many historians have observed, the PIC's efforts ended tragically. Although the party was banned in 1910, its leaders, demanding reinstatement as a legitimate party, mobilized an uprising in May 1912. After almost two months during which armed bands in Oriente and Santa Clara, Cuba's easternmost and central provinces, roamed the countryside, setting fire to sugarcane fields and intercepting telegraph and railroad lines, the rebellion culminated in one of the bleakest incidents in the history of the Cuban republic. In Oriente, site of the most intense activity, government troops and vigilante groups that had formed to aid in the repression assassinated Estenoz and Ivonet and massacred untold numbers of alleged participants.[5]

If the drama of the PIC understandably drew a great deal of attention, it was precisely during this period that other black and mulatto politicians and journalists invoked an entirely different set of justifications and created alternative institutions to those of the PIC. Since many participants on both sides invoked a race-transcendent nationalist ideology to justify their actions, historians have focused on the conflict itself and the extent to which it acted to debilitate the "myth of racial democracy." But it is important as well to look beyond the PIC and the state.

This chapter will argue that the crisis in 1912 involved a dispute over competing claims of citizenship elaborated by activists and politicians of color. It focuses specifically on irreconcilable divisions among those groups as they engaged in public debate during this period. The increasingly tangible specter of "barbarity" haunted visions of citizenship as well as justifications for violence. Although the violent end of the PIC signaled the effective termination of one mobilizing strategy, other strategies and notions of citizenship survived—frayed, perhaps, but not eliminated.

Good Promises and Bad Habits

In the title of his biography of Rafael Serra y Montalvo, Pedro Deschamps Chapeaux indicates that Serra "struggled tirelessly for our independence." In everyday usage, such a description would likely refer to someone who had fought in the wars for independence. Yet Serra, who lived during the period spanning Cuba's anticolonial struggles (1858–1909), never fought in a war, experiencing the years of military struggle from the vantage point of New York City. Nonetheless, as Deschamps Chapeaux suggests, he participated extensively in the ideological struggles not only for independence but also for racial equality. Serra's views were publicized through his work as a journalist and collected, toward the end of his life, in a book of essays entitled *Para blancos y negros: Ensayos políticos, sociales y económicos* (*For Whites and Blacks: Essays on Politics, Society, and Economics*) (1907). The essays are worth lingering over, for they offer a rare lengthy discussion of social and political issues by a Cuban of color deeply involved in the transition from colony to republic. Through an examination of his life trajectory, political activities, and the texts he produced, a genealogy of the distinct notion of civil citizenship emerges.

Born in Havana in 1858, Serra was the legitimate son of Rafael and Marcelina, neither of whom were slaves at the time. His parents baptized him and sent him to school, where he learned the catechism but was forbidden, like all students of color, to study history, drawing, grammar, and geography. At age thirteen, in the middle of the Ten Years War, he became an apprentice in a cigar factory. Just after the war he married María Gertrudis de Heredia, a free black woman. He came of age and began his professional and political life during the Peace of Zanjón, when he moved to Matanzas and founded a free school as well as an educational association, or *sociedad de instrucción*, and a newspaper, both named *Armonía* (*Harmony*).[6] During this period, as the Spanish colonial government loosened its hold on civil and political life, Serra's actions reflected a time when Cubans of color entered the public sphere with numerous publications and were granted limited civil rights.[7] Serra's entry into politics during colonial rule was significant in shaping the strategies and justifications he saw as necessary to "model citizen consciences."[8] His was a liberal notion of citizenship, premised on equality but also on a sense that citizens had obligations that could be met only if they began their civic lives with adequate education and preparation. The purpose of his newspaper was to be "*harmony* in the first instance, and as its name indicates, holds as its primary purpose the creation of harmony between all races and social classes . . . and in order to obtain such admirable ends, we have resolved to undertake all possible efforts to develop popular education, the basis of morality and instruction of the masses and the ensuring of public peace."[9]

After the Guerra Chiquita ("Little War," 1879–80), Serra traveled to Key West with Martín Morúa Delgado, whom he had met during his years in Matanzas. After a brief stay in Key West, Serra joined José Martí in New York City to work on behalf of Cuban independence. Between 1888 and 1890 Serra organized a sociedad named La Liga, which aimed, much like the one he had helped to found in Matanzas, to re-create the practices he believed would foster civic virtue among citizens of color. Indeed, he used almost the same words to describe its purpose: "It rests on the benevolent principle of harmonizing all the ethnic elements of our country through the elevation of character of those who are morally, intellectually and economically disadvantaged."[10] Serra lived in New York for twenty-two years, working with La Liga and running several newspapers. Crucially, when Martí returned to Cuba in 1895, he persuaded Serra to remain in New York and continue their battle on the civil front. Serra did so, working, as Martí had done, to construct a viable nation in the service of a place he had not seen for many years. He only returned to Cuba in 1902, once Estrada Palma was elected president.[11]

Serra's continued work on behalf of civil rights and social and economic equity rested on presumptions quite unlike those that derived justifications for equality and access to resources from black and mulatto participation in the wars for independence. The claim to citizenship based on participation in the wars had proved compelling even to those, such as the military and political elite, who might be most reluctant to grant it. Serra may well have underestimated the complex transformative power of a multiracial army, since he had not fought in any of the wars. At the same time, however, his status as a noncombatant may have allowed him greater insight into the limitations of relying so heavily on military participation to justify political inclusion. His model for equal citizenship was based not on the achievements of the "good and grateful insurgent" as described by Ada Ferrer, but instead on the reality of a conscience that was moral, virtuous, and educated.[12] Serra privileged social scientific and philosophical arguments in defense of this model. When he did invoke a historical argument, he placed the participation of former slaves and their descendants in the wars within a broader context of their engagement in a prolonged struggle for rights that began during the Spanish regime.

One of Serra's fundamental claims was that all human beings were equal. As previous chapters have shown, this view was under siege in Cuba as well as in Europe and the Americas, as some branches of social science developed racial theories that reinstated old hierarchies with new forms of evidence. In defense of his egalitarian views, Serra supported critiques of racialist thinking. In one essay, for instance, he applauded the publication in France of *Le préjugé des races* (*Racial Prejudice*) (1905), by Juan Tinot, which argued that anthropological and anthropometric theories about superior and inferior races were false. Tinot's book challenged all racialist claims about brain capacity, cephalic indexes, and innate inferiority. Just as Domingo Bocourt was being condemned to death and the Montané Museum of Anthropology was preparing to receive his brain, Serra brought this criticism of atavism and degeneration to the attention of his readers. In one deft essay he challenged the methods and conclusions of his contemporaries in social science.[13]

Serra defended inclusive citizenship and universal suffrage through his critiques of traditional politics based on hereditarian principles. Again, this was broader than the justification based on participation in the wars. Suffrage should be universal, according to Serra, because exclusive and hereditarian political rights had become obsolete with the ascendance of democratic principles. "We should choose equal rights for all men, through an understanding that democratic suffrage ought to triumph over exclusive and hereditary rights as under a monarchy." In fact, the wars, for Serra, were not ennobling but potentially corrupting, the legacies of which needed repairing rather than celebrating. Of the U.S. Civil War, he observed: "Once the redemptive war against slaveholders in the South was over, the most urgent task for that prescient nation was a vigorous battle against the corruption any war leaves in its wake."[14]

When he did turn to a historical argument, Serra envisioned the pursuit of equality as grounded in a prewar set of practices and understandings. Thus the recent war was not, for him, the only event worth analyzing, but rather one of a series of contests in which Cubans of color had engaged since the Peace of Zanjón. His genealogy of the struggle for rights began "in Spanish times," when a defensive elite had "openly opposed the enjoyment of civil rights which the monarchy had granted to blacks." That initial political opening and its subsequent closing had been the first of several instances in which people of color had been asked to suppress their demands for equality in the name of unity. War and occupation had used the same logic: Cubans of color had traded their right to complain for the promise of future equality. Serra downplayed the centrality of war, as he situated both the acquisition of formal rights and struggles for their true recognition in the colonial era.[15]

Serra maintained that virtuous citizens and a virtuous nation would constitute one another. This nation of "citizen consciences" and the practices that citizenship entailed, had been conceived in 1878, long before the Cuban state existed as an autonomous entity. He offered concrete examples of a citizenry including, but not limited to, the deserving insurgent. The text of *Para blancos y negros* includes numerous photographs of exemplary citizens. Many of them are women, among them school-teachers like Serra's own daughter Consuelo, who received a degree in education in the United States, or Ursula Coimbra de Valverde, a "distinguished pianist, capable teacher, and wielder of a colorful and eloquent pen."[16] The transformation from insurgent to citizen is evident in the photograph of Quintín Bandera on page ninety-five of the text. The picture suggests a "civilized" setting—Bandera appears to have posed for a studio portrait and is dressed in formal black tie. As Ada Ferrer has argued, Bandera had earlier been singled out precisely because he was deemed "uncivilized" by military leadership after the war: although he had been a respected military leader, in peacetime the military elite determined that he lacked gentlemanly qualities and ostracized him.[17] In Serra's rendition he is redeemed, not as a military leader but as a "civil" citizen, in formal, cultured garb. Thus Serra's visions of citizenship extended to women and shifted the focus to civic institutions, transcending the gendered, military boundaries of the suffrage qualifications adopted by the 1901 constitution.

Yet even as he crafted a hopeful vision of a revitalized nation inhabited by virtuous citizens, Serra expressed concern over the concrete ways the Cuban state was beginning to coalesce. Soon after Martí's death, Enrique José Varona created the Sociedad de estudios jurídicos y económicos (Society of Legal and Economic Studies) to establish the foundation for republican institutions. Serra was very critical of this society's exclusivist views on suffrage and embarked on a publicity campaign to expose its antidemocratic positions. Under this and other pressures, the society lasted only two months. After that initial experience, Serra remained suspicious of those engaged in state-building during the transitional period. While still in New York, during the first U.S. occupation, he worried about the emerging political leadership in an open letter to the director of the publication *El Pueblo Libre*: "Those in power believe the nation to be a physical extension of the state, free from external domination, but they still want to conserve all the inequality that they themselves used to rationalize the war against Spain. I believe the nation ought to strive for the legitimate satisfaction of all."[18]

After Serra returned to Cuba in 1902, his dissatisfaction with emergent state institutions grew. His critique of political parties reveals the tension in his observations between an idealized nation and an inadequate state. He believed that political parties were ill-disposed to abide by the principles of equality and justice and unconcerned about the creation of a "unique and vigorous national conscience," mostly because the "un-savory ambitions" of party members derailed them from more principled goals. At times he seemed to argue that the state acted to stifle the organic growth of the nation: "Our political parties do not seem interested in the creation of a unified, vigorous national conscience."[19] Political parties, for Serra, fostered corrupt self-interest rather than virtuous citizenship.

This critique of political parties developed through repeated disap-pointments with the way politics was conducted. Serra, a longtime ob-server and elected official, noted that "they have perfect knowledge of their good promises, as well as of their bad habits of never abiding by them." He spoke from outside of José Miguel Gómez's Liberal network, a patronage system that solidified during the war and included many Cu-bans of color. *Para blancos y negros* gives some oblique but pointed critiques of blacks and mulattoes who participated in the 1906 Liberal rebellion. Estrada Palma could hardly be blamed for continuing exclusions, the au-thor contended, and the Liberal Party would not provide solutions. Serra was elected on Estrada Palma's Moderate Party ticket in 1904 but lost the post as a result of the 1906 rebellion and the downfall of Estrada Palma's government. He was reelected in 1908 as a representative from Santiago de Cuba on the Conservative Party (the successor of the Moder-ate Party) ticket, but by that time he had begun the final year of his life. More analysis is needed of the clientelistic structures that were subordi-nate to Gómez's, but Serra's dissatisfaction suggests that as an outsider his opportunities and those of others outside clientelistic networks were much diminished.[20]

Out of a faith in the citizenry and suspicion of state-supported parties and patronage networks grew a defense of autonomous institutions. Serra endorsed the reinvigoration of institutions that were more autonomous from the state than dependent on it, such as private schools, social and cultural associations, and newspapers. On returning to Cuba he founded the newspaper *El Nuevo Criollo* and continued his advocacy of education and civil liberties, including just treatment by the judicial system and as-sociational freedom. He proposed bills to reform the criminal courts and to support education. His defense of black and mulatto associations in-sisted on their respectability and legitimacy. In an essay in *Para blancos y negros* he denounced the mistreatment of Santiago's black and mulatto societies in the hands of overzealous police: a "pronounced and bitter dis-gust" pervaded the class of color as a result of this constant harassment. Contrary to the peaceful aims of that group, the police committed violent and unjustified assaults on Santiago's societies of color in an attempt to repress "prohibited games." This was not only unjust—it also dishonored respectable societies.[21] Serra's emphasis remained on the autonomy and dignity of these institutions rather than the extent to which they benefited from resources distributed by the state. In keeping with this approach, he often urged Cubans of color to be as economically independent as possible.

In his writing and political activities Serra constructed a model for claiming equality based on the civil citizen who engaged in associational life, valued education, and participated in activities informed by a vigorous sense of nation yet autonomous from the state. Rather than serving as a source of legitimacy and beneficence, the state operated, according to Serra, with deception and corruption. The source of legitimacy lay rather in nonstate institutions, unified against both Spanish and North American incursion and committed to equality and justice. Serra's proposals aimed to open spaces and create a broader context in which to practice citizenship.

War, Status, and Citizenship

Serra's model of citizenship did not appeal to those who believed in making more direct claims on the state. In the aftermath of war, veterans enjoyed heightened social and political status. "This period," according to one historian, "can be considered veterans' peak years, when they acted as a well-organized and active force which intervened in the nation's most important issues."[22] The links made in the wars for independence between soldier status and citizen status prevailed in the early years of the republic.[23]

Also to the advantage of many veterans, clientelistic networks that had formed during the wars were at the heart of republican politics. The aftermath of war wrought changes in the national economy. Incursions of foreign capital led to diminished Cuban control over production and property. Combined with high levels of unemployment, this meant that state administration and public office became one of the few sources of employment for Cubans. Since access to political power meant access to jobs, elections became opportunities to distribute benefits among clients in patronage networks.[24]

Beyond the specifics of who participated in those networks, evidence suggests that the *style* of working through clientelism, which combined access to state patronage with a looming threat of violence, was a powerful and effective political tool in the early republic. José Miguel Gómez's Liberal network promised state resources to war veterans and in some instances delivered. The 1906 rebellion revealed the enduring power of these networks and their belligerent strategies. A number of black and mulatto veterans, dissatisfied with continuing exclusions after the Liberal rebellion, drew from this combination of circumstances as they created their own political party, the PIC. Although their explicitly race-based claim differed from the frequently cross-racial nature of many clientelistic networks, the PIC relied on the political style that had proved successful until that moment. As a race-based party that demanded state resources, this model of claiming the rights of citizenship received a great deal of attention and a measure of legitimacy.

The PIC's platform set out a long list of demands, including:

1. Greater representation in the diplomatic corps
2. Jury trials
3. Abolition of the death penalty
4. Schools (envisioned as "boat-schools") for delinquents
5. Free primary, secondary, and university education to be administered by the state
6. The monitoring of both private and state education, and state responsibility for the uniform education of all Cubans
7. Naval and military schools
8. Inclusion of the "Ethiopian race" in military service, and in administrative, legislative, and judicial branches so that all races are represented in the service of the state
9. Eight-hour workdays
10. A government commission to mediate conflicts between workers and management
11. Agrarian reform

In contrast to Serra's mistrust of political parties and his wariness of the state, the PIC platform centered on state action. This was partly symbolic, as in the plea for diplomatic representation, but also substantial, as in the call for increased black presence in the administrative, judicial, and military branches of government. While both Serra and the PIC privileged education, their differences indicate a broader disagreement over boundaries between the state and civil society. Whereas Serra and others wanted control over the schools in order to implement their particular version of civil citizenship, the PIC demanded state intervention at all levels, including in private schools. In the PIC's version, citizenship itself seems to have been less dependent on the notion of virtue requiring education and awareness of obligations. Rather, the PIC called for immediate access to state resources, based on claims of status that had already been achieved.[25]

More than that, the way in which they had formed suggested a continuing appeal to practices and networks established during the war. Since the core of the PIC was a group of veterans who had participated in the uprising of 1906 and had been disappointed with the outcome, the tools they relied on to bring about political change were ones that had proved successful historically: persistent military networks, the exploitation of political division as a way to create the possibility of U.S. intervention and thus serve as leverage, and a publicly belligerent presence. In 1910 Estenoz announced in *Previsión*: "Any man of color who does not instantly kill a cowardly aggressor who may attack him in a public place is a miserable male specimen who dishonors his country and his race."[26] To be sure, they may have believed this stance to be the only viable strategy with which to confront what they considered recent betrayals. But this bellicose attitude, whether intended as an accurate reflection of their goals or as a bid for attention, certainly projected a very different image than that of Serra's civil citizens.

From the beginning, criticism and uncertainty arose from many sectors. Along with Serra's critique of Cubans of color who had participated in the 1906 rebellion, Juan Gualberto Gómez and Morúa Delgado took issue with the PIC's tactics. In basic agreement with several of their demands, such as the eight-hour day and equity in employment practices, they quarreled with the racial exclusivity of the proposed party. Some groups of rural workers, less worried about matters of ideological consistency, perceived the elitist makeup and urban focus of the PIC's leaders as unlikely to address their particular concerns. Whatever the reason, the elections of 1908 failed to elect a PIC candidate. In 1910 Morúa Delgado dealt the party a blow by proposing an amendment that rendered it unconstitutional, based as it was on racial identity. Party cohesion suffered a greater setback after an extensive round of arrests sent many members to jail. This provoked a split within the party as members disagreed over tactics and objectives.[27]

Although some of their proposals were familiar and welcome, PIC tactics seemed to have alienated potential sources of support. Unprecedented as a form of political mobilization, the PIC provoked confusion as well as criticism. In a fragile state rife with splintering groups and fleeting factions, it was unclear how to understand or respond to this permutation of party politics. On the eve of the uprising, then, Cubans of color had expressed serious reservations as well as support for the party. They had also built alternative networks and created different paths from those proposed by the PIC for voicing their positions and working toward equality. When violence erupted, responses in the media and in official circles reflected conflicting assessments of the PIC.

Defining the Danger

When the PIC initiated its armed rebellion on May 20, 1912, the newspapers called it a *brote*: an outbreak, the beginning or appearance of something new. Although some headlines and the hindsight of its bloody termination suggest a consensus that the uprising was a "race war" from the onset, many initial reactions hesitated to use that label. Despite the insistence of some journalists—using words like *convulsión*, *rebelión* and *sublevación de racistas*—that PIC leaders aspired to reenact Haiti's revolution of 1791, various editorials offered more ambiguous interpretations. Reluctant to characterize the conflict as one centered on race, a commentary in *El Mundo* ascribed cynical political motives to the rebels, whom it represented as nothing more than petty malcontents. What they really wanted, it argued, was access to patronage networks and jobs without having to work for them. "In Spanish America there are no revolutions made in the name of social or political ideals . . . the only thing there has been or can be are convulsions. Their aim is well known: control over government, the treasury and public offices."[28] Moreover, the editorial blamed the Cuban government for its inability to maintain order and declared that under a U.S. regime an uprising of such proportions would have been inconceivable. Rather than invoking the danger of a "race war," *El Mundo* was far more concerned with the possibility of U.S. intervention.

Observers disagreed not only about motivations, but about facts as well. Alongside stories of armed men on horseback disrupting railroad lines and terrorizing local populations were assertions that the violence and terror were much exaggerated. No one seemed to know how many "rebels" (*alzados*) there were, nor precisely how to distinguish them from "ordinary" suspicious or marginal characters: when a policeman disappeared, reporters wondered if he had become one of "them." Some rumors associated brujería and *espiritismo* (spiritism) with the rebels in Oriente.[29]

In the first few days, caution and emphasis on unity accompanied factual disputes and portentous speculations. The newspaper *El Popular*, a self-described "defender of the laboring classes and of national/patriotic freedoms," echoed the position of some mainstream commentaries, noting the Morúa Amendment's just and reasonable goal to prevent the escalation of divisive racial politics and marshaling both scientific and historical evidence to call racial hierarchies into question. It was possible, then, to censure the rebels' strategy while acknowledging that they had legitimate grievances. At the same time *El Popular* fought a tendency to demonize leaders of the rebellion. The portrait of Pedro Ivonet characterized him as an honest, intelligent man deserving of sympathy and respect both for having fought with General Antonio Maceo·in the 1895–98 war for independence and for being an exemplary husband and father.[30]

The day after the armed protests began, the secretary of justice called for restraint with regard to accusations and arrests of Cubans of color. It would not be acceptable, he said, to apprehend those merely suspected of conspiracy. Law enforcers must have absolute proof before acting. The majority of blacks, who were not involved, ought to be treated respectfully: they should not be given any justification for accusing the government of an unjust response.[31]

President José Miguel Gómez's reaction revealed a need to negotiate between conflicting interests. Much of his popular base included black and mulatto supporters, including veterans of the 1895–98 war for independence and the 1906 Liberal rebellion; he could not afford to alienate them with an overly bellicose response. But the anxious vigilance of the U.S. government and both North American and Cuban sugar magnates meant that Gómez also had to assure those interests that he was capable of maintaining order and preventing extensive destruction of cane fields and property.[32] To initiate an all-out attack against the rebels was to concede to his critics that he was unable to manage opposition and dissent. He responded to descriptions of lawless rebels pushing the nation toward a chaotic demise by balancing an acknowledgment of the threat with assurances that he was able to control it. The leadership of the PIC had added to the threat of U.S. intervention with their requests for recognition by the United States. By repeating the strategy of the rebels in 1906 they had added an international dimension to a local crisis, calling into question the legitimacy of the Cuban government even further.[33] With the threat of

La actualidad palpitante

PRECAUCIONES DE DON JEREMIAS

"Let's not speak of that (the portrait) right now, because if by any chance the
Evarista party triumphs, it will be very convenient to have her for an ancestor."
(*La Política Cómica*, 1912)

a U.S. invasion looming, Gómez's legitimacy, both at home and abroad,
depended on achieving this balance.

As alarmists insisted on raising the specter of a race war, critical voices
spoke out against mass arrests and the indiscriminate expansion of the
category of "rebel" to encompass all blacks. In caricatures and mordant
if unsubtle cartoons, Havana's journal of political satire, *La Política Cómica*, directed barbs at the hypocrisy of Cubans vilifying all people of
color: a portrait of a black grandmother, it suggested, hung on the walls
of many, even the most elite, Cuban households. And many recognized
the contingency of political fortunes. In one cartoon, a husband and wife
are removing all black items from their house—an umbrella, ink, all of
their black clothing. When the wife asks whether the portrait should go
as well, the husband equivocates: "Let's not speak of that (the portrait)
right now, because if by any chance the Evarista party triumphs, it will
be very convenient to have her for an ancestor."

For all of its snide commentary, the magazine assessed the matter with
a measure of sincerity as it echoed the secretary of justice's plea for rea-

son: "The zeal with which all good Cubans, both white and black, are combating the disturbances caused by the Independientes de Color is admirable, but the suspicions, the searches, and other police practices can easily result in lamentable errors and abuses. Be aware that it is but one small step from the sublime to the ridiculous."[34] In the weeks that followed, inflammatory reporting persisted in the mainstream press, and responses to it intensified as vigilante groups formed and families fled the countryside seeking security in the city. That many in positions of power interpreted the rebellion in Manichean terms and used it as an excuse to give free rein to prejudice is undoubtedly true. Yet many refused to believe that Cuba had been overtaken by a race war in which most people of color were either conspiring with or fully supportive of the PIC's strategy. The uprising created significant disagreement over the interpretation of events, rather than a polity divided along racial lines.[35] Given the more subdued approach of individuals like Serra, as well as the reality of black and mulatto participation in many spheres of life, many white Cubans witnessed and acknowledged far more heterogeneity than evidence of conspiracy.[36] In the early stages of the uprising at least, the general acceptance of the notion of black civility slowed the momentum toward a unanimous declaration of race war.

As if he understood what was at stake in the use of the language of civility, Estenoz tried to fashion himself and his movement in its image. Ten days after the uprising began, he characterized his actions as driven by the continuing concern for peace and equality. His demand for the abrogation of the Morúa Amendment was founded, he argued, "not [on] racist ends but rather the logical and natural ambition of the Cuban black to be equal to his white brother, in the interest of social peace and in the interest of Cuba's reputation."[37]

But the turn to armed rebellion had alienated some politicians of color, who refused to accept Estenoz's claim as leader of the entire "race of color" toward civilization and progress. Discussions in the legislature suggest delicate maneuvering in a potentially explosive climate. Senators Ramiro Cuesta and Nicolás Guillén (father of the well-known poet) carved out a rhetorical space critical of both the PIC and the status quo, juggling loyalties as representatives, whether assumed or imputed, of "Cubans of color" and as members of the governing class. Distancing himself from the PIC with subtle insults and open condemnation, Cuesta insisted that "these are not Cubans of color, merely a group of malcontents." But it was a matter of degree and means, rather than a radical disagreement with the PIC's grievances: "We are not perfectly satisfied, we have witnessed days full of sadness, and even have cause to complain, but those complaints will never be numerous enough or serious enough to place Cuba's freedom and independence at risk."[38] His stance reveals a greater concern over the possibility of U.S. intervention and an emphasis on national unity as the only way to maintain sovereignty and to work toward greater equality.

Similarly, Guillén, invoking the architect of Cuba's race-transcendent nationalist ideology, José Martí, supported the view that the rebels were racist and that the uprising would lead to the disintegration of Cuban society. This was not a rebellion of all Cubans of color, but rather the actions of "less cultured Cubans of color, a few who have thrown themselves into this sad adventure, and who have made the rest of us struggle with the task of maintaining the Cuban nation, her civilization, her strength, her progress."[39]

Estenoz and his rebels also failed to persuade many ordinary Cubans of color that an armed revolt was justifiable. A few weeks after the uprising began six hundred residents of Camagüey, a city in central Cuba, refused to support what they considered to be reprehensible conduct. Invoking liberty, progress, and justice, they condemned the behavior of the rebels and deemed it a threat to the republic and the nation. It was fanatical and racist, they argued, and it would stigmatize not only those guilty of actually conspiring against the government, but also all other blacks, who as "victims of the intense pain of the anathemized and persecuted pariah, will wander to the ends of the earth, dragging an existence that will be no more than this: abjection in the form of flesh, repugnant misery, vileness, disgusting scourge, pestilence."[40] Whether opportunistic, specious, or genuine, the effect of their rhetoric was to challenge the coupling of civilization with whiteness and barbarism with blackness. If the republic was splitting, it was not dividing in two but rather fracturing into complex patterns determined by increasingly distinct hierarchies of "race" and "civilization."

In effect, all parties involved used the language of civility and its implications of citizenship to stake out their positions. To invoke civility was to invoke aspirations that could include national autonomy, individual equality, and peaceful negotiation of political disagreements. The absence of civility, or the threat of barbarism, had acquired a specific meaning in early republican Cuba. The cumulative effect of brujería scares, cannibalism trials, and the interest of social science in these phenomena had created a powerful image of a racialized, gendered "savage" whose presence in the republic posed a problem for everyone, including Cubans of color who were determined not to be included in that category. This image, supported by scientific, legalistic, and journalistic knowledge, readily served as an explanation in moments of crisis. Events would prove how quickly a hint of sexual violence could call up that image.

In early June rumors that rebels had raped and killed a white school-teacher eliminated many deliberations over the nature of the conflict. In debates within the national legislative body over the suspension of constitutional guarantees, news of the alleged rape and death revived the figure of the barbaric black man, now more sexualized than in typical brujería scares, threatening white Cuban women. Judicious caution and subtle politicking faded in the face of dramatic defenses of the codes of honor and civilization now perceived to be under attack. "Can Cubans protect the honor of its women," wrote one commentator, "against the black individuals who have begun to defile it? If they can, Cuba's Christian, European civilization will be saved. If not, Cuba will be an uninhabitable and hellish place, a terrifying replica of equatorial Africa."[41]

President José Miguel Gómez shed his apparent concern to maintain the balance between his popular base, his anti-imperialist critics, and the owners of sugar estates, especially in Oriente, who demanded swift reprisals. He too now cast the conflict as a battle against barbarism: "It is not permissible that in the twentieth century, in a country as civilized as ours, a society like ours, that has the reputation of being respected and respectable, our moral and material peace be disturbed yet again by these manifestations of savage ferocity enacted by those who have placed themselves, especially in the eastern province, outside of the realm of civilization."[42]

Although subsequent reports stated that the schoolteacher had not died, suggesting that all accounts of atrocities had been exaggerated, violence intensified after this incident. Riots broke out in Havana as news of government troops killing rebels appeared more and more frequently in the press. On Saturday, June 8, 1912, residents of the town of Regla tried to lynch one of their neighbors, a black man who had fired his gun at a white man in response to his assertion that all black men were conspiring against the government. In Havana, police invoked familiar connections among race, religion, and crime in attempts to neutralize potential sources of disorder. In one of many examples of heightened persecution during this period, police captain Francisco Pacheco turned over to the courts "an infinity" of objects (the usual suspects: drums, costumes, shells, stones, images, necklaces, bowls, etc.) associated with brujería and ñañiguismo. There were so many, in fact, that he requested the use of the police station's larger truck to transport them all.[43]

This time politicians of color appealed directly to the public rather than merely to peers and colleagues. They published a manifesto in *El Mundo* that proposed to "define, limit and combat" the uprising, suggesting that they believed the struggle over language and meaning was crucial and not yet settled. Their first move was to align themselves with history, justice, and reason. Not only had they fought for these ideals and helped to achieve them, but also they were benefiting from their implementation in the form of legal equality and suffrage. Furthermore, they argued that the PIC might have benefited as well, as discussions to abrogate the Morúa Amendment had been under way and would in all likelihood have been approved.[44]

The signers of the manifesto marked a sharp distinction between themselves and the PIC. They did so in part by challenging the idea that Cubans of color formed a homogeneous and cohesive group with shared goals. In their effort to define the events they were living through, the authors portrayed the rebels as misguided and out of touch with all but a small minority of Cubans of color. Emphasizing the multiple and fractious political stances and convictions of blacks and mulattoes, they cited statistical evidence to show that the PIC enjoyed only one-half of 1 percent of voter support. As such, the party could be understood to represent merely its own dangerous interests. Invoking popular support, the authors and cosigners of the document claimed to represent a majority of Cubans of color as they emphatically stated their opposition to the PIC's strategy: "The time has come to say this: that the race of color is not with but rather against the rebellion."[45]

It could be argued that this was a strategic move on the part of politicians interested in saving themselves. Whatever the motivation, their response had the effect of publicly articulating divisions among Cubans of color and publicly disavowing the notion that they ascribed to a single collective identity. If some Cubans of color did not support the movement, it was not because they had somehow "betrayed" their race, but rather because other allegiances prevailed. The number of signers of this document and their diverse, often conflicting political allegiances point to the coexistence of multiple black political identities. In stark terms, there was no "race" to betray. Race was at this moment a weak way to organize political identity.

The list of signers included Nicolás Guillén, from Camagüey; Francisco Audivert, from Oriente; Generoso Campos Marquetti, from Havana; Luis Valdés Carrero, from Havana; Alberto Castellanos, from Oriente; former general Agustín Cebreco, from Oriente; Ramiro Cuesta, from Matanzas; Manuel Delgado, from Santa Clara; Lino D'Ou, from Oriente; Juan Felipe Risquet, from Matanzas; Hermenegildo Ponvert, from Santa Clara; and Juan Gualberto Gómez. This group included members of both Liberal and Conservative Parties, senators and representatives. Many had fought in the wars for independence, and some had participated in the 1906 rebellion; others, such as Agustín Cebreco, opposed the 1906 rebellion and had attempted to negotiate a peaceful solution.[46] Of this heterogeneous group, then, there were those for whom participation in the war had meant a great deal and from which they had benefited. But at this point they rejected the armed pursuit of political goals. Perhaps they were persuaded to practice politics in a different manner. Or perhaps they foresaw the danger involved in Estenoz's tactics.

Among the signers of the manifesto were outspoken critics of the government's lack of attention to issues of racial equality. Lino D'Ou, for example, had called for greater representation of Cubans of color in public jobs and for the prohibition of discrimination in "any party, association, or political, educational, religious, social, or recreational institution." Alongside this more radical voice were Conservatives like Juan Felipe Risquet, who believed that education was the key to positions of equality. Risquet placed much emphasis on applauding the accomplishments of educated blacks and mulattoes, implicitly placing on them the responsibility for "advancement" rather than blaming unyielding ideological or institutional structures.[47]

Black and mulatto politicians thus found themselves on both sides of the "civilizing line" and claimed the right to participate in drawing that line. Rather than reinforcing clear divisions between "black" and "white," circumstances in the early republic had fragmented racial meanings. The terms in which the rebellion was cast could encourage Cubans of color to choose "civilization" over "race consciousness" and create an "uncivilized" (racialized) scapegoat. If, as Louis Pérez argues, race war rhetoric resulted in dividing a multiracial peasant class and unifying the white elite, then it also underscored divisions among Cubans of color.[48]

Conclusion

By the middle of June 1912 too many factors worked against the rebels. In the press, malevolent clarity replaced most initial uncertainty. Black and mulatto politicians chose to publicly disassociate themselves from a movement that appeared increasingly doomed. The landing of U.S. marines in Guantánamo exacerbated tensions, as President Gómez's need to appear in control became more urgent. Accounts of the violence that occurred vary. By the end of June General Monteagudo, in charge of Cuban troops in Oriente, referred to what his men were doing as a "veritable butchery."[49] From what historians have been able to gather from other sources, it was a horrific interlude, as black men were decapitated, hung from trees, and shot as they attempted to flee Cuban troops.[50] Most shocking to contemporary witnesses was the public nature of these killings: accounts tell of bodies hanging from trees and piles of ears exhibited as trophies by government forces.

The reliability of some of these firsthand reports is questionable, suggesting the power of rumor and the limits of historiography with regard to instances of extreme violence. By the end of June, with the PIC leaders among the many dead, officials announced the end of the rebellion. Certainly part of this story remains shrouded by what Thomas Holt has called "the sheer incomprehensibility of racist phenomena."[51] The crisis of 1912 nonetheless reveals the variety of claims to citizenship in early republican Cuba and allows us to consider the nature of their differential appeals. Competing models of the relationships among nation, state, and citizen were at stake: the PIC had developed in the visible realm of electoral and party politics and failed dramatically, while Serra's views took root more quietly and appear to have lost their grasp for a time. With Serra's death, followed by the grim unraveling of PIC attempts to obtain a share of resources and the fragmentation of black political mobilization, Serra's model of civic virtue receded to the background, or at least out of historians' field of vision. But shifting social, intellectual, and political forces would soon create the conditions for the reconstitution of black political activism, even in the shadow of terror.

"It is the anti-Semite who makes the Jew" writes
Sartre, and this means, first, that the Jew does not
make himself and, second, that he must make
himself an (authentic) Jew. The same thing is true
of the black man: he did not choose blackness,
now he must choose blackness.

MICHAEL WALZER
Obligations: Essays on Disobedience,
War, and Citizenship (1970)

Contested Histories
Public Memory and Collective Identities

Speaking to supporters soon after his election to Congress
as a Liberal representative from the province of Havana in 1914, Juan
Gualberto Gómez worried about the state of public memory: "We are
abandoning the remembrance of those great events in our history that
ushered in independence, because we are losing the religion of memory,
because we are turning our backs on the past." His biographer tells us
that at this point in time Gómez was reproachful of revolutionary leaders
who, as he saw it, sullied heroic and morally redemptive memories of
revolution as well as their own reputations with their corrupt and self-
ish political tactics.[1] Gómez astutely observed a nation foundering in a
wave of forgetfulness, but it was not a unified amnesia. Instead, different
groups were at that moment engaged in different projects of remembering and forgetting. He could have been referring to the white elite that

in his eyes had reneged on its promise of racial equality and mutual re-spect for all Cubans. Or, under the sway of lingering memories of 1912, he could have been alluding to leaders of the Partido Independiente de Color (PIC) who had resorted to violence, thereby betraying a past of interracial cooperation and legitimized venues of political participation. The con-flicts of little more than a decade of autonomous rule had undermined the "religion of remembrance" and, with it, the political health of the Cuban polity.

In the years following 1912 many activists of color seeking to extend the practices of citizenship faced a delicate set of dilemmas in interpret-ing and remembering the recent past. Dissemination of the notion of the "black barbarian" and its invocation as justification for antiblack vio-lence complicated efforts to construct Cubans of color as virtuous citi-zens. Although Cubans of color themselves participated in the discursive construction of the "black barbarian," they struggled with the legacies of that entanglement with hegemonic discourses. Blackness was too easily identified with irrationality, immorality, shadowy and secretive violent practices, and, most recently, overt antistate violence. How were they to continue to insist on equality and the rights of citizenship in light of the specter of barbarism, which they themselves found repellent?

This chapter examines the ways in which, in the aftermath of 1912, members of associations, Afro-Cuban religious leaders, journalists, and other Cubans of color forged and, importantly, made public, a series of viable historical memories. In the context of associational reforms, de-bates in the press, and protests against antiblack violence, their writings reveal an ongoing engagement with concepts of race and evolving defi-nitions of the meanings of citizenship and equality. Coinciding with the emergence of a broader "culture of mobilization" in Cuba, these formu-lations lay the groundwork for the crystallization of black political iden-tities.[2]

Rebuilding and Remembering

Juan Gualberto Gómez's critique of Cuban society extended to socie-dades de color, whose presence in public life had greatly diminished in re-cent years. At a gathering of these associations in 1915 he chastised them for their fragmentation and lack of unity. They may have retreated as a self-protective response in the aftermath of 1912, but as a long-term strategy retreat would prove fatal to the organizations and detrimental to all Cubans of color. Gómez insisted, probably as much for the benefit of state officials as for his audience, that black and mulatto associations had a legitimate role in Cuban public life, especially since Spanish associations were proliferating. Looking back to the functions of associations that he and others like Rafael Serra y Montalvo had envisioned since the colonial era, he asserted that in the face of continuing exclusion from white societies, Cubans of color were entitled to organize and assemble on their own to provide aid, access to health care, education, and libraries to their members. In calling the sociedades de color to action, he rendered the revival of associational life a sacred task: "We have several small parishes, yet we have refused to unite our energies to build a great cathedral, where we ought to kneel before the god of progress and civilization."[3] It was time to overcome the recent disarray and reinsert themselves into the civic life of Cuban society.

Soon afterward, new associations emerged and long-standing ones initiated new projects. The Club Atenas, which would become a major center of debate over race and citizenship, was founded in 1917.[4] The well-established Unión Fraternal answered Gómez's exhortations with a program of reforms intended to rejuvenate the association. Founded in 1890, the Unión Fraternal was one of Havana's more prominent associations. The proposed reforms reinforced its organization's traditional goals insofar as they emphasized the aspirations of an educated black and mulatto elite, but they also reflected new ambitions in their gestures toward cross-class unity. The leadership announced the creation of a literary section for accomplished writers and journalists to exchange their work and ideas, as well as a scientific section that would organize conferences pertaining to their areas of expertise and study "those problems and social phenomena that affect the community." If the problem of black incivility persisted, they might at least study it to better combat it. In this vein, the stated goals of the reforms reached out to a "more democratic base" through programs directed at poorer, less educated Cubans of color. There were specific proposals to establish a night school for illiterate adults and a "university of the people" that would offer free instruction; to serve poor children meals at school and provide them with clothing; and to build a *casa de beneficencia* to care for pregnant women, orphans, and the elderly. Together, these proposals indicate a sense of responsibility toward poorer Cubans of color that, if somewhat paternalistic, nonetheless explicitly acknowledged the existence of what they referred to as the *colectividad*, or community. Walking a careful political line, members of the Unión Fraternal emphasized that these projects were to be undertaken "with moral and educational intentions and [be] completely devoid of politics or aspirations of personal gain."[5]

If these moves suggest a nascent aspiration toward a collective identity, the contours of that identity emerged in greater relief with the elaboration of a social memory for the association itself. In 1918 its leaders announced an essay contest on members' renditions of the history of the Unión Fraternal. The contest produced remarkable results. Five long essays, although they varied in style and content and clearly reflected the writers' varying educational levels (some had more misspellings and grammatical errors), articulated a vision of Cubans of color as citizens, full participants in modern urban life, and in control of the knowledge that would guarantee their affirmation of citizenship with the legitimacy of science.

Re-creating a history of the Unión Fraternal meant for many of the essayists integrating the history of the association with a general history of Cubans of African descent. They did this self-consciously, recognizing that the creation of a collective memory needed to be in their hands: "Gathering the facts, summarizing them, organizing them, and arranging them into a definitive narrative is of utmost importance. . . . We must make history." This would be the culmination of a series of achievements in which they had been active participants rather than passive observers: "The tasks of education, of emancipation, of revolution, of conquering equality are the products of our brains, of our hands, of our blood, and of our perseverance."[6]

To be sure, many of these histories were teleological narratives moving toward the recent triumphs of the Unión Fraternal, but what distinguished them were the milestones their authors deemed crucial to the narratives. The key dates did not, for the most part, coincide with military or political events but instead traced the history of black and mulatto access to associational life. Thus 1892, the year of the reorganization and expansion of the Directorio Central de las Sociedades Negras de Cuba, figured prominently in all of the essays, but 1886, the official end of slavery, was mentioned only once or twice. Similarly, civil rights granted by the colonial Spanish regime—those of limited suffrage but rights to association—received much more attention than the acquisition of universal manhood suffrage under the constitution of 1901.[7]

The wars for independence occupied an ambivalent place in these narratives. The essays echoed Serra's desire to construct a vision of citizenship that was not entirely dependent on participation in the wars. The authors could not ignore the wars entirely, but they did not integrate Cubans of color into nationalist accounts of multiracial brotherhood, unity, and the overthrow of colonial despotism. Rather, their story of the wars contributed to a broader picture of the acquisition of citizenship by Cubans of African descent. Thus allusions to the battles in 1895–98 stressed how they led to unity among members of the Unión Fraternal who had fallen victim to factional bickering. In addition, they recalled participation not just as soldiers but in a wide range of roles, including personnel recruitment; procurement of clothing, weapons, and supplies for soldiers and the wounded; and assistance with delivering secret correspondence between military chiefs. The narratives assigned the role of servant, to which many black and mulatto recruits were initially relegated, the same importance as the highest level of command.[8]

Strikingly, the authors of these essays forgot as effectively as they remembered. In contrast to references to the wars for independence, which were specific and detailed despite their ambivalence, there was no mention of the conflict of 1912, the enormously divisive event that had dominated the headlines only six years earlier. If some of the Unión Fraternal's members, such as Juan Gualberto Gómez, had been outspoken at the time, they were silent now. One of the narratives followed the association from the late 1880s through the wars for independence, then skipped from the end of the wars to the attempts to unify all sociedades in 1916. The only possible allusion to 1912 was indirect: In reference to continuing hesitations to unite many atomized societies, one essayist cited fear as a significant deterrent. "No," the author complained, "they are not interested in uniting, they prefer to continue as in primitive times, lest . . . they suffer the consequences of those who appear to belong to a society of dissidents." These accounts of the development of civil citizenship had room for neither the uprising nor the repression of 1912.[9]

This forgetting coincided precisely with José Miguel Gómez's campaign for reelection in 1920, during which both Conservatives and Gómez's Liberal opponents led by Dr. Francisco Zayas y Alfonso attacked him by invoking the events of 1912. According to Alejandro de la Fuente, Zayas, who had been vice president during the armed rebellion and subsequent repression, especially needed to distance himself from the crisis. He thus suggested that the repression had been entirely Gómez's doing, depicting him, in one headline, as "The Eternal Demagogue, the One

Who Machine-Gunned the Colored Race in Oriente." This was not the first campaign to revive the memory of 1912 in attacks on José Miguel Gómez and his status quo. His opponents had recalled the massive slaughter as early as September 1912 and continued to do so in the 1916 elections.[10] That the repression was addressed in public debate yet remained absent from the essays indicates continuing ambivalence about its role in narratives so concerned with collective black identities. We can only speculate as to the discursive dangers surrounding this issue. If the essayists emphasized the notion of a race-based identity, thus challenging dominant "race-transcendent" paradigms, they would be hard pressed to critique the PIC's own defense of a racial identity as divisive. On the other hand, their assertions of apolitical aims made it difficult to critique the state's role in the massacre of thousands of Cubans of color in 1912. Backed as they were into a rhetorical corner, they may have chosen silence as the most appealing option.

Marking the rejuvenation of their race ("labor that will be a source of pride for all Cubans and principally for our race") by demarcating physical space on which to erect a building for the association emerged as one of the most important concerns of all the essayists. A new building promised to ensure the creation of "a new social life," proving to other Cubans the social and intellectual progress of the race. A building would render the sociedad visible and present as part of the city—Unión Fraternal's members would, taking advantage of one of the benefits of citizenship, partake of urban life. The insistence on a visible, physical presence in the city called into question the frequently invoked geography of "black barbarism," so often situated in rural settings or in hidden urban spaces, either behind closed doors or in dark alleyways or enclosed patios, all of which were deemed inimical to the clean, well-lighted spaces demanded by modernity. Indeed, in a manner evocative of Virginia Woolf's *A Room of One's Own*, these writers attributed autonomy, independence, and recognition to their acquisition of a home for the sociedad: "We witnessed a transcendent event in the history of [its] existence: the inauguration of our building." Furthermore, its walls would create more distance between themselves and undesirable aspects of African-derived cultural practices: "The existence of attractive social and cultural activities has produced its natural effect: the rumba, the tango, and the cabildo have moved to the category of the forgotten, the legendary—or at least their erotic, vulgar, and violent characteristics." The creation of an autonomous space was not meant to preserve African traditions and customs, for which the membership had little use. Rather, it was meant to place as much distance between the Unión Fraternal and those customs as possible.[11]

Finally, the essayists explicitly critiqued theories of black inferiority and savagery, such as those articulated by Fernando Ortiz, Varela Zequeira, or Israel Castellanos, with sophisticated attacks on scientific racism. "It is not scientific to accept degradation. It is not acceptable to believe in innate incapacity. We also do not believe in atavism." Citing both scientists and the Bible to refute theories of inequality, the author of one essay insisted that claims of Afro-Cuban inferiority were false. In keeping with the racialist thinking of the day, however, he outlined his own views about an ethnic hierarchy in which "el negro de Cuba" occupied a rather lofty position. Caribbean blacks should not be equated with Africans, who held a much lower position; rather, the proper analogy was that of Anglo-Saxons to Turks. Another writer, who apparently had less access to scientific scholarship, stated only that Cubans of color had been successful in journalism, politics, and law because "their brains are well-organized."[12]

Together these essays contributed to a tentative exploration of the importance of a collective identity for Cubans of color. Writing against the image of black barbarism, they reconstructed a civil, moral identity using memory, physical space, and scientific knowledge to crystallize their vision of an educated, participant citizenry that deserved a place in the polity. The recrudescence of associational life thus turned from direct challenges to the state and engagement in party politics to focus on the autonomy and strength of the members' own institutions. Although their membership generally comprised the educated, socioeconomically advantaged sector, the Unión Fraternal and other associations began to position themselves as caretakers and spokesmen for disadvantaged Cubans of color, those at whom accusations of black incivility could be hurled more easily. If they enjoyed a measure of success with their emphasis on education and secularism and their overt critiques of "suspect" cultural and religious practices, they did not manage to silence potent, persistent discourses on barbarism.

Let Us Also Make It Known

After 1912 African-derived religious groups also took their place among black associations seeking to strengthen their standing and insert themselves into public life. As the most vulnerable to ongoing imputations of atavism, their strategies demonstrate the extent of the struggle over representation and citizenship. Fernando Guerra drew from the contradictions surrounding memory and identity to articulate a remarkable framework in defense of his association. As secretary and later president of the religious and mutual aid society, Sociedad de Protección Mutua y Recreo del Culto Africano Lucumí, "Santa Bárbara," he crafted a rhetorical style that integrated a respect for constitutional rights and legal institutions without sacrificing a defiant defense of his African-based religion and his right to protest brujería scares. He declared that African traditions and modern citizenship were not only compatible but also mutually interdependent.

In a July 1913 circular addressed to the president of the republic, the secretaries of interior and justice, the mayor of Havana, and the general public, Guerra endowed the members of his association with the capacity to move between categories often thought incommensurable. The practices of Lucumí did not interfere with Catholicism, and acknowledgment of African heritage did not imply disregard of modern citizenship:

> We declare that we are native Cubans, advanced in age, who from infancy have practiced the Lucumí religion, without neglecting the Catholic religion, that we have never nor will never deny that our ancestors were African, that we respect freedom of religion and the laws of the republic. . . . There is a need that the rights that the Constitution has granted to all inhabitants of the Republic be guaranteed by the forces of law, and wherever it appears that Cubans with unjust intentions try to interfere with the sincere democratic sentiment of the Cuban people, who support liberty, not a corrupt bureaucracy, pushing it toward a new slavery, let us beware of the microbes infecting this social body. Let us think about and study the progress of nations without hatreds and resentments.[13]

But the democratic aspirations of members of his association were continually threatened by accusations of brujería. Guerra distinguished his own association, rooted in traditional practices and protected by modern freedoms, from brujería, which he deemed a recent, malicious invention: "CONSIDERING that a number of Cubans who study politics propose, with their fantastic theories about brujería, to create, with their moral systems, a new form of slavery."[14] Whether or not it existed beyond the imaginations of propagandists, a point on which he was ambiguous, he clearly asserted the distance between brujería and his own practices:

Let us also make it known to the authorities of the Republic that the rites of the African Lucumí religion, the playing of drums in its religious ceremonies, are not at all analogous to other rites and practices of African origin. . . . We would also like to request a meeting with those from the press who know what brujería is and what the Lucumí religion is; that way government officials will know the difference between the two; the problem of brujería will never go away, but despite the fact that our ancestors are African, we do not practice brujería, nor do we use the objects required for its rituals, and if we practice the Lucumí religion it is to console our suffering on this earth.[15]

Earlier, Guerra had demonstrated an ability to move between religious discourse and the language of science in his efforts to defend his association's beliefs and practices. In 1911, working to buttress his claims to legitimacy through an incorporation of social scientific knowledge, he invited Fernando Ortiz to join the society. As Stephan Palmié has observed, Guerra seems to have used this opportunity to "mobilize discursive authority in [its] fight against the state."[16] From that point on Ortiz muted his calls to eradicate African-derived religious practices.[17] In his public manifestos Guerra displayed his agility with the languages of science, political rights, and the mechanisms of political legitimacy as he carved out a space for his association within the structures of a modern polity.[18]

The Uses of Witchcraft

Despite Guerra's efforts to demystify the impulse behind brujería scares, public thirst for sensationalism in the press continued unabated. In 1917 Ortiz's publisher reissued *Los negros brujos* with a new introduction, leaving the text intact. The following year another brujería scare monopolized the headlines. On September 3, 1918, the editors of *El Día* called upon Cubans of color, as "members of the same race responsible for the spreading virus," to share any insights they might have. Repeating the by-now familiar complaint about *negros brujos* as "an obstacle to our progress and civilization," it asked "upstanding members of the race of color" to use the space offered by the newspaper to consider the problem and propose solutions they thought were available and viable. The appeal requested the participation of an illustrious list of Cubans of color, including Juan Felipe Risquet, Generoso Campos Marquetti, Lino D'Ou,

Manuel Escoto Carrión, Ramírez Ros, Juan Latapier, Miguel Angel Céspedes, and Ramiro Neyra Lanza, as well as "any other black Cubans who loved their country and wanted to assist in its social reform." The editors indicated that the men they had listed embodied the opportunities available to many Cubans of color. Access to higher education and political office, supported by legal equality, had produced exemplary citizens. But progress had not been uniform, and it was against the remaining pockets of "barbarism, ignorance, and of disgusting and cruel fanaticism that adores idols and spills human blood" that the civilized element must fight. The newspaper declared itself at the vanguard of a moralizing, sanitizing campaign against the scourge, promising not to rest until the last brujo had died and anyone invoking a brujista incantation or performing a brujista dance was safely locked away.[19] In this episode the coincidence of what Ada Ferrer has labeled racism and antiracism is striking: El Día recognized the intellectual and moral capacities of certain Cubans of color even as it theorized about the corrosive effects of the "primitive race" at large.[20]

Only one of those named responded to the appeal: Neyra Lanza, editor of the black newspaper La Antorcha, was one of the first to write in. Another ten letters published included three more from journalists, one from an agricultural engineer, and one from a school inspector. One woman and a self-described "espiritista blanco" also replied. Three of the letters published had no information about the authors apart from their names. From this collection three major themes emerged as the respondents tried to situate themselves and "la barbarie" in relation to notions of race and civilization. Within a shared acceptance of the editors' language of "obstacles to progress" lay reactionary, contentious, cynical, and conciliatory moods.

A few letters utilized sophisticated references to Ortiz and his theory of atavism, citing him directly and questioning his inconsistencies and tendency to impute atavism to an entire race rather than a few unfortunate individuals. They were also quick to point out the universal nature of the phenomenon (as one put it, "history, anthropology, and countless pages in literature describe hauntingly similar scenes") and to point to the corruption of Catholicism as the source of the problem.[21] Their proposed solutions included improving education and other reforms, as well as locking up the most egregious criminals: this echoed Ortiz's recommendations. One writer took Ortiz's reformism to a punitive extreme. Muñoz Guinarte, the agricultural engineer, proclaimed that the problem was a "diseased fermentation of superstition rampant in our entire Republic." His harsh recommendations included "severe repression of the charlatans and the repugnant characters who exploit public faith, as well as repression of their victims, those naive and ignorant believers." Revealing both his intolerance for cultural heterogeneity and his faith in the power of the state, he called for the creation of a committee directed by the Ministry of Education "so that spiritual hygiene can be imposed, just as the secretary of sanitation imposes physical hygiene."[22]

Amada Rosa de Cárdenas used the platform to formulate a general critique of Cuban society, shifting the locus of corruption from brujería to the general failure of all Cubans to live up to the nation's liberal, just ideals. She argued that it was Cuba's lack of civilization, its immoral environment, and a persistent colonial heritage that fostered brujería and other social ailments — among them, "prostitution, alcoholism, and gambling." She also espoused an expansive faith in the power of reform, vaguely defined as "encouraging the development of culture and civilized behavior." The burden of change lay within society itself, which lagged behind the ideals set forth in law: "Cuban law and the ideals of justice and humanitarianism forbid the deprivation of a citizen's liberty so long as he does not break the law. It would go against all ideals to institutionalize a repressive system that no just or liberal person would applaud."[23] The danger lay not so much in the effects of brujos and other victims of public neglect, but in the frequently unjust application of repressive measures.

One pervasive theme challenged Ortiz's criminological abstractions with its realpolitik analysis. Respondents argued that brujería had become widespread and irrepressible because it was fostered and supported by local politicians' employment of brujos, who in their turn controlled a large portion of the populace. Marino Barreto, musician, journalist, and contributor to *La Noche*, extended the blame to academics and elite women, contending that both groups somehow depended on the presence of brujos: "In our days of progress, of Cuba Libre and in the full light of day, we hear the sarcastic cackles of the brujo . . . offering his satanic services to the aristocratic and adulterous lady, to the influential gentleman, to the fascinated academic. These are his godsons, they support him and place in his hands large quantities of gold and protect him from persecution." The educated men and women of color who had tried to rid Cuba of the "criminal practices, products of barbarism" were no match for this collection of interests.[24] These views related the problem to whites as well as nonwhites, launching an arrow at the hegemonic edifice of black brujería.

José Rosario Valdes also questioned the extent of the links between brujería and blackness, arguing that Cuban society was deeply corrupt and that the presence of brujería was merely emblematic of moral decay. "From the highest to the lowest spheres of our public and private lives," he wrote, "from the individual sphere to the social sphere, brujería reigns without regard for status, class or color." The practice depended on symbiotic relationships with politicians who had no interest in acting on their promises: "But amongst ourselves everything becomes words, words, words, because the interests that surround the problem produce much talk and very little action." This mutually beneficial system rendered futile any efforts toward reform: "They will continue to enjoy a pleasant and comfortable parasitic existence amongst us, degrading us with their practices."[25]

The debates may have centered on the degree to which brujería was directly linked to black and mulatto Cubans, but never on the assumption that the link existed. At the same time these writers managed to undermine prevailing social scientific theory, insisting, even in the most reactionary versions, that there was no reason to ascribe to the whole race the failings of a few individuals. In apparent allusion to Lombrosian theories of criminal stigmatization, Gerardo Manzano asked what civilized blacks had to do "in order to avoid being unjustly confused with those who support the disgusting cult, for we lack a sign on our forehead that would indicate the contrary."[26] Gabriel Palacios Caussé expressed the same sentiment, adding a dash of political cynicism: "The acts of degeneration of a group of criminals or of a single one do not seem to me reason enough for an entire race—which, like all the others, suffers from the phenomenon of the law of atavism—to have to confess to the entire world, nor to bury itself alive for the acts of a few of its members, used by unscrupulous people during elections against their political adversaries."[27]

To escape the determinist trap these (self-described) black commentators looked, with at times politically divergent agendas, to the power of education, the rule of law, and notions of civility (citizenship). Rather than consenting sycophantically to the "myth of racial equality," they used the trope of brujería and their own status as "blacks above suspicion" to critique society as they variously called for extreme repression, pointed to the inadequacies of the educational system, or denounced political corruption. As their arguments remained within the parameters of the discourse of brujería, they simultaneously called it into question and contributed to its lasting presence.

La Mano del Brujo

March 1919 marked the beginning of a brujería scare that would culminate in the death of eight men of African descent in Matanzas and the lynching of one in Regla, all accused of the kidnapping, ritual murder, and cannibalization of white children.[28] Newspapers reacted to the discovery of nine-year-old Marcelo López's mutilated body by instantly and vituperatively blaming brujería. In the words of *El Día*, "The crime appears to be the work of brujos, of those nefarious brujos who dishonor an era and a nation with their ferocious insanity, with their insatiable thirst for human blood and children's flesh."[29] Despite nonexistent evidence, on April 22 two so-called brujos were arrested and their *objetos* seized in Mariel after the attempted kidnapping of another child. The press advocated lynching. As one editorial declared, "The only thing I regret is not having seen the lynching of one or two of these savage brujos who deserve no compassion whatsoever."[30]

Reports of kidnappings mushroomed. On June 24 *El Día* announced the disappearance of Cecilia, a little girl from Matanzas. On June 28 José Claro, the brujo under suspicion, confessed to murder and cannibalism along with three others, although police investigations had failed to uncover a body. When news of these confessions reached the town's inhabitants, they heeded the newspaper's recommendations. A crowd tried to lynch the prisoners, failing to do so only because military troops protected the prisoners as they were transported to jail.[31]

That same day legislators began discussions about a proposed law against brujería, which was not yet technically illegal. Meanwhile, a newspaper editorial underscored the state's history of neglect or ineffectual responses to the problem, again advocating lynching as the only way to extirpate cannibalism in the face of the government's failure to contain brujería and protect its children. According to this commentary, the specific cause of the present difficulty was the republic's limited vision and inability to control the terrible crimes, in contrast to the colonial government's more effective policing. "During the Spanish regime," the editorial began, "there were no incidents of this nature. What was the motherland's secret for containing cannibalism? We ought to declare that

La justicia del pueblo

CASTIGANDO EL CRIMEN

La Política Cómica, a magazine of political satire, comments on the "law of lynch." (*La Política Cómica*, 1919)

in certain cases, such as this one, we support the terrible *ley de lynch*. When our legislators drafted the penal code they didn't have this terrible crime in mind. A man who extracts a young girl's heart and eats it after stewing it in garlic is beyond any Lombrosian theories, beyond all police accounts."[32]

The next day a crowd in Regla lynched José Williams, a Jamaican immigrant accused of kidnapping and attempted rape of a six-year-old white girl. Police had tried unsuccessfully to protect Williams, who reportedly died gruesomely at the hands of "a furious mob (of all social classes) of over three thousand people." On June 30 in Matanzas a group stormed the Castillo de San Severino, where the defendants in the murder of Cecilia were being held. Prison guards opened fire, killing one man and wounding twelve others. The guards then forced the prisoners to leave their cell and shot them "as they fled," claiming later that the *ley de fugitivos* had dictated their actions.[33] After these two incidents crowds tried to lynch several more prisoners, who survived with police protection. In Matanzas, the military occupied the town and imposed a curfew in an attempt to restore order.

Some Cubans of color protested the repression of brujería. When police raided a Lucumí temple and attempted to arrest members and sequester their objects, a large crowd of black men reportedly tried to attack the police and to free the arrested men. *El Día* linked this protest to the lynching of the previous day: "It seems that blacks have started to mobilize, also, against the lynching in Regla."[34]

Police and law enforcers renewed their attempts to repress anything associated with "African" culture by, as might be expected, arresting suspected brujos and seizing their objects with the slightest provocation. In addition, they began to target healers who relied on other than the most orthodox methods. As if admitting to the paltriness of earlier efforts, legislators once again proposed a law against brujería while expressing admiration for the initiatives taken by the people and the military in defense against the "epidemic." Fernando Ortiz, who was nominated to draft the law, used the current obsession to promote his methodologies: "Let us not lynch the theories of modern criminology."[35]

The themes of civilization and barbarism figured prominently in explanations of the problem and proposals for its solution. Brujería was considered dangerous because it operated beyond "human" understandings of law and justice and occupied a realm of primitive behavior. As such, it posed a constant threat to culture and civilization. According to one commentator, it was essential for Cubans to fight the "barbarous instincts of the degenerates who do not recoil from terrible crimes in order to satiate passions that are understandable only in the depths of Africa, but that cannot be tolerated in the heart of a cultured and civilized society."[36]

Despite the extensive journalistic and scientific expertise that had been devoted to linking brujería with black men and African-derived religious practices, these connections required constant reinforcement. In the case of Marcelo López, for instance, the accused brujos were a white youth and his father. The possibility that white brujería, along with other little understood beliefs and practices, such as *espiritismo* (spiritualism), "oracles, fortunetellers, diviners and seers" formed part of the "pustules of progress that affront our culture" produced ongoing uncertainty about brujería's scope and content.[37]

On the other hand, many observers refused to associate all Cubans of color with the nefarious practices and distinguished, just as in 1912, between those who participated in and those who condemned the maligned behavior: "Those men of the black race who do not share the absurd beliefs behind an execrable and barbarous ritual support the cause of civilization. . . . At the demonstration we saw blacks, many sincere blacks who were the first to criticize the prisoners."[38] A counterdiscourse emerged, condemning brujería but at the same time avoiding an explicitly racialized association of brujería, barbarism, and blackness.

Cubans of color radicalized this discourse. Not only did they divorce barbarism from blackness, following the strategies of politicians in 1912, they also inverted the associations altogether, pointing to the lynchings as proof that the barbarians were white.[39] Juan Felipe Risquet, in other contexts an advocate of more conciliatory racial politics, issued a scathing critique of the practice of lynching: "Lynching is the savage human beast which harms everything in its way . . . it is the symbol of human injustice." But his complex interpretation condemned brujería as well: "Cuban society, for instance, which condemns the brujos, which excoriates those who assassinate children, also condemns those who lynch men who have not yet been judged in the courts." Risquet extended the category of those in need of redemption beyond those accused of kidnapping and devouring children to those who, demonstrating poor judgment, imitated North American lynchers.[40]

Members of the Club Atenas, prominent in Havana's social circles, issued a statement bristling with moral outrage. The club had been founded two years earlier as an attempt to create a new, "modern" society that would guarantee what its largely young, educated constituency regarded as adequate representation before Cuban authorities.[41] Although its founders had aimed to address elite rather than cross-class concerns, in this instance they had broadened their base of support. In addition to many prominent politicians, professionals, intellectuals, and former members or leaders of the Liberation Army, the statement's cosigners included representatives from thirty-eight sociedades from the provinces of Havana, Matanzas, Pinar del Río, Santa Clara, Camagüey, and Oriente.

With impassioned eloquence and careful use of rhetoric, they constructed a new moral hierarchy. They began with a review of the historical contributions of slaves, former slaves, and their descendants to the making of the Cuban nation, insisting that the two could not be separated: "The history of this class is coterminous with that of this nation." The experience of slavery had been a painful but heroic interlude from which arose the concepts of independence and autonomy. The republic ought to be regarded as an achievement of Cubans of color, a majority presence in the Liberation Army. After establishing its version of indispensable black participation in national history, the statement moved on to the recent events in Regla and Matanzas.[42]

Refusing to concede any ground, they insisted that the accusations lacked hard evidence: "Because we still doubt the truth of the kidnapping in Regla as well as of cannibalism in Matanzas. Nothing is clear, in our judgment." Furthermore, regardless of the truth or falsity of the accusations, it was unjust to blame many for the crimes of a few: "And since we want this, which is noble, and that we believe we deserve, we reject, without anger or bitterness, but firmly, any denigrating insinuation, any suspicion, any insulting doubt with respect to our attitude with regard to the savage acts which may have been committed, regardless of the color of those who committed them. We understand that we have the right to be considered civilized men, not barbarians."

Finally, the statement secured the membership's own ethical position within a reconfigured moral code:

> The punishments have scared us because they do not conform, either in form or essence, with the principles of our civilization. Even if the victims of lynching in Regla and gunfire in San Severino had been guilty of the atrocities of which they were accused, they should not have been punished that way. A prominent historian has said: bloody reprisals, just like the crimes that provoke them, pertain to the domain of the barbaric. And Cuba, which so many of us love, should not be home to barbarians, neither cannibals nor lynchers.

The manifesto articulated a complex notion of identity, affirming the link to people of African descent, but at the same time refusing dominant categorizations that criminalized and denigrated them. It emphasized the fractious nature of the "race of color," even as it gestured cautiously toward a sense of collective identity. It shared with the manifesto of 1912 a sense of the need to exercise voice in response to an egregious turn of events, yet the difference between the two documents is striking. The 1912 manifesto had stressed acceptance of state structures and acknowledged the benefits of its egalitarian claims. The tone in 1919 was less accommodating and placed far less faith in the goodwill of white Cubans. It pulled apart more radically than before the association of whiteness with civilization, tying barbarism to whites through lynching while affirming the existence of the "civilized black." Mobilization in response to anti-black violence had impelled the appropriation of "barbarism" and its re-direction toward whites. This was double-edged: the writers of the 1919 manifesto fashioned "black civility" in opposition to "black incivility," as represented by the intractable category of *negro brujo* and thus lent greater credibility to an enduring stereotype. Nonetheless, this episode reveals a growing capacity for political mobilization that would gain relevance in ensuing decades.

Cultures of Mobilization

This mobilization of incipient associational identities and incidents of activism by Cubans of color took place within a context of political crisis and social mobilization in many sectors of Cuban society. During World War I the Cuban economy had been buoyed by high sugar prices as a result of increasing worldwide demand. Immigration, both of Antillean sugar workers and Spanish laborers and of shopkeepers and merchants, increased, as did foreign investment (mostly U.S.), to take advantage of the booming economy. The year 1920 opened amid the prosperous "Dance of the Millions," the culmination of that period. Yet by the end of that year sugar prices had dropped precipitously, from $22^{1}/_{2}$ cents to $3^{5}/_{8}$ cents per pound. A continuing reliance on sugar as the principal source of revenue rendered Cuba what Charles Chapman described as an "economic football: When prosperity gives it a kick it soars high, but when depression boots it, it drives at the enemy's line and is batted back."[43]

With the economic crisis of 1920 came a political crisis. Cubans endured worsening material conditions as wages dropped without a concomitant drop in prices, credit became more difficult to obtain, and unemployment spread in the wake of the reduced demand for sugar. Cubans also endured the very public interventions of U.S. government representatives, including most prominently General Enoch Crowder, sent to Cuba in 1921 in response to Liberal protests of alleged election fraud. He stayed on to oversee the inauguration of Alfredo Zayas's presidency and to initiate a campaign of "moralization." "Moralization" was meant to create discipline and accountability in fiscal and administrative matters: the United States accompanied loan offers with demands that Cuba follow U.S. dictates for spending and eliminate government corruption. Many Cubans reacted to these strictures by expressing discontent over volatile economic conditions and Cuba's inability to remain free of U.S. interference in its domestic affairs.[44]

Many sectors voiced their protest, with labor organizations demonstrating an increasing restiveness. Sugar workers engaged in collective actions regularly, especially in 1917 and 1919. Urban labor, including tobacco workers, dockworkers, and craftsmen, also agitated for the right to organize unions and protect their jobs. By the early 1920s labor activists working toward greater solidarity among different groups of workers created a national labor organization—the Confederación Nacional Obrera de Cuba (CNOC). As part of the island's heterogeneous working class, Cubans of color participated in nationwide labor mobilizations.[45]

The Junta Cubana de Renovación (Cuban Committee of National Renewal), directed by Fernando Ortiz, issued a manifesto condemning government corruption and censuring dependence on the United States; it demanded reform of economic and social policies and of electoral and judicial practices.[46] From the military sector, the Asociación de Veteranos y Patriotas, emerging out of a localized protest against a proposal to cut pensions, expanded and gained support beyond its original constituency with the slogan "For the Regeneration of Cuba."[47] The Grupo Minorista's well-known "Protest of the Thirteen" marked the induction of students, artists, and intellectuals into the ranks of critics of government corruption and fraud, U.S. imperialism, and social inequality in the agrarian and labor sectors.[48] New intellectual streams, including communism and socialism, contributed to the critical voices entering the political stage. In 1925 Julio Antonio Mella, a student at the University of Havana, founded the Cuban Communist Party (Partido Comunista de Cuba—PCC). Together the PCC, the Asociación de Veteranos y Patriotas, the Junta de Renovación, labor groups, and the Grupo Minorista demonstrated the depth of dissatisfaction with corruption and policies that privileged foreign interests. As Robert Whitney has argued, these groups set the stage for the resurgence of oppositional popular politics.[49]

Conclusion

Although these protest movements often faltered, they shifted the political terrain. The Asociación de Veteranos y Patriotas, which threatened armed rebellion, was undermined through repressive measures against its leadership. Even as representatives of the U.S. government grew increasingly skeptical of President Zayas's ability to maintain order, they backed him over oppositional sectors and contributed to their debilitation. Yet even if no single organization was strong enough to pose a serious challenge to the political class, the groups together transformed the nature of politics, forcing leaders to contend with an increasingly mobilized society.

Cubans of color joined the "culture of mobilization" that became part of the political landscape starting in the 1920s. Beginning soon after 1912, black and mulatto associations rebuilt their constituencies and elaborated notions of citizenship. Both secular and religious groups sought to claim space within Cuban social life. Ongoing struggles with the specter of brujería fostered the mutual constitution of "black civility" and "black incivility." In response to violence and threats of violence, tentative notions of community emerged. As these developments laid the foundations for emerging black political identities, Cubans of color found themselves in step with the myriad mobilized collective identities across the island.[50]

And so, with great effort, re-examining everything, attaining the cooperation of all, from the
semicolonial Cuba that we started with, a new
Cuba emerged, very modern and utterly
unknown.

[Y así con tesonero esfuerzo, revisándolo todo,
buscando la cooperación de todos, de la Cuba
semicolonial que recibimos se fue haciendo surgir
una Cuba modernísima, nueva, y desconocida.]

GERARDO MACHADO Y MORALES
Ocho años de lucha (1982)

5

Social Science, State-Making, and the Politics of Time

Gerardo Machado's Liberal Party platform in 1924 obtained substantial support from disenchanted sectors, which were increasingly vocal in their protests against the perceived vulnerability of
Cuban sovereignty. When he claimed to be committed to a "revision of
the Permanent Treaty, eliminating the appendix to the Constitution, and
winning Cuba an independent place in the world," Machado's agenda
resonated with highly mobilized groups, organized around the goal of
"national regeneration," that had ushered him into office.[1]

Machado's program of domestic reform dovetailed with his nationalist, reformist goals. He supported the Customs-Tariff Law, eventually
passed in 1927, which granted protection to national industries. He initiated an extensive public works program intended to remedy economic

Machado's modernizing vision reordered Havana streets and residences. (Secretaría de Obras Públicas, 1929; photo courtesy of Cuban Heritage Collection, University of Miami Libraries, Coral Gables, Florida)

distress by offering jobs to unemployed Cubans. The program's tangible results included a replica of the U.S. capitol in downtown Havana as well as the 700-mile central highway that runs across the entire island.[2] As Jorge Domínguez has observed, the Machado administration initiated a period in which the president, cabinet, and Congress together expanded the powers of government, resulting in a much greater presence of the state in everyday life.[3] But if an expanded state presence meant access to jobs and resources for some Cubans, it meant increased repression for others. Machado swiftly reacted to the creation of the Cuban Communist Party (PCC), the Confederación Nacional Obrera de Cuba (National Confederation of Cuban Workers) (CNOC), and other labor organizations with violence and intimidation. The use of armed forces against strikers and the assassination of labor leaders became standard procedure under Machado. In response to the intensification of mass participatory politics by organized labor, students, veterans, and intellectuals, Machado maneuvered between repression and incorporation.[4]

Reconstructions of the Cuban past accompanied heightened mobilization and dramatic political change. In 1924 Fernando Ortiz published an essay entitled "La fiesta afrocubana del Día de Reyes" (The Afro-Cuban Festival of the Day of Kings). Its descriptions of the colonial practice that allowed slaves and free people of color one day a year (January 6) to engage in ritualistic street dances and celebrations invoked an ordered, well-regulated Cuba. It was a time, he suggested, when slaves and masters existed, if not in complete harmony, then in a negotiated world in which slaves understood and respected the offer of a single day of freedom and reciprocated with obedience. The purpose of the essay was to equate the African origins of these celebrations with European carnival and in so doing to make relativistic claims about the legitimacy of African-derived practices. Drawing almost entirely from nineteenth-century *costumbrista* texts for his description of the festivals, Ortiz reproduced their romantic emphasis on sartorial detail, respect for tradition, and lack of conflict. Like the nineteenth-century painting that served to illustrate it, the article, though it explicitly aspired to "scientific ethnography," offered a still life of a world that was lost.[5]

This version of the romantic turn in ethnography, though increasingly fashionable in anthropological works in Europe and the United States, seems a peculiarly conservative contribution to the demands for reform and national regeneration in which Ortiz himself participated. Yet if "La fiesta afrocubana" rendered colonialism and slavery in a positive light, it also fit African-derived customs into a series of traditions in which the nation was rooted. As many have observed, romanticism's excavation of autochthonous cultural artifacts has often served nationalist enterprises. The extent to which it might aid Cuban state-building as it was constituted in the 1920s, however, was not a foregone conclusion.[6]

Ortiz's work in historical ethnography reflected a broader trend of increased activity in all the social sciences. Machado supported and encouraged scientific activity as part of his program to buttress nationalist sentiment and publicize Cuban contributions to Latin American intellectual endeavors. In a speech delineating his ambitions for Cuba, the production of knowledge was not forgotten: "We must stimulate literary and scientific production . . . since we have received so much knowledge from the rest of the world, we must participate and reciprocate with our own contributions."[7]

What follows is an examination of the heightening of social scientific activity in three arenas: ethnography, which in this period focused on the study of folklore; eugenics, as it underwent a transformation in outlook and purpose; and the growing institutionalization of criminology.

This romanticist painting, by De A. Galindo, 1837, was used to illustrate Fernando Ortiz's 1924 text, "La fiesta afrocubana del Día de Reyes."

I argue that social science was revitalized during Machado's regime, and that, more important, its strategies shifted from reform to depoliticization. Anthropology and criminology in the early years of the republic intended to contribute to a modernist project by demonstrating how their objects of study could be induced to become more like modern political subjects. Though apparently contradictory, one of the primary aims of social scientists had been to find a way to integrate most Cubans of African descent as citizens. By the 1920s, however, the social sciences seemed to lose interest in fostering citizenship and developed new methods for understanding and controlling social order and disorder. At the same time, these methods belied the notion of a race-transcendent Cuba. Instead, social scientists found the concept of race increasingly useful, even if they invested it with distinct and inconsistent meanings.

As ethnography, eugenics, and criminology became institutionally distinct and responded to crises of legitimacy and national identity, their approaches came to be informed by specific deployments of the notion of time. As Johannes Fabian has contended, the use of time is a central strategy operative in any discourse that posits "others" as its object of study. In its inception the discipline of anthropology created distance between the observer and the observed and thus an aura of objectivity, by placing its objects in distant time as well as distant space. Cuban social scientists, with little if any physical distance separating them from their objects of study, arrived at distinctive uses of the concept of time. On the one hand, liberal intellectuals like Ortiz became very interested in folklore and ethnology, evincing a more profound concern with the past than in previous works. Cuban eugenicists, whose fortunes had been in flux in the early days of the republic, distinguished themselves from most other Latin American colleagues as they engaged currents emanating from the United States to create utopian visions of the future. Criminology, however, remained firmly planted in the present, looking to existing criminal bodies for answers to its questions. Although they held disparate ideas about how to proceed, each branch of social science aspired to reign in a highly mobilized society. This chapter explores the utility of these reformulated social scientific endeavors to a state interested in both creating social order and harnessing growing political mobilization.[8]

Rewriting Old Rituals: The Allegory of Salvage

Having authored, during the political crisis of the early 1920s, a critique of contemporary society under the rubric of "renovation," Ortiz sought new national foundations to replace corrupt ones.[9] In 1923 he founded the Sociedad del Folklore Cubano and its journal, *Archivos del Folklore Cubano*, deeming the study of folklore essential to this enterprise. Echoing the recommendations of José María Chacón, one of the earliest promoters of the study of folklore, Ortiz believed that recuperation of forgotten folklore would be crucial in reconstructing a sense of national identity.[10] With a romanticist sensibility he proposed looking at the indigenous, Spanish, and African origins of Cuban culture. The myths, social habits, and linguistic practices of each of these cultures, as he conceived them, would serve as more solid foundations for national identity than the current fascination with all things North American. Suddenly modernity seemed less crucial than the lost riches of the past: "Great treasures remain hidden beneath the layers of modern culture, waiting for studious Cubans to discover, interpret, and classify them for our national civilization."[11]

The works published in *Archivos del Folklore Cubano* rely on the use of the past to describe ethnographic objects, but they shed normative evolutionary explanations and reformist aims. Ortiz and other authors published in *Archivos* ceased to study their objects in order to change them. Instead, they were interested in a more romantic project that James Clifford has called the "allegory of salvage," aiming, with ethnographic descriptions, to capture endangered worlds for their own sake. The concern was no longer to modernize their subjects, or to seek to extinguish the most irredeemable ones, but to study them as part of a search for authenticity and origins.

This turn to a recuperative project was most evident in a long series of texts written by Ortiz on *Los negros curros*. Having already investigated the current-day manifestations of black criminality in *Los negros brujos*, he believed that it was necessary to research the *curro*, an earlier criminal type that had been significant in its day but had subsequently disappeared. The curro was "a perfectly differentiated category of delinquent, which deeply interested our people until the second third of the last century, when he disappeared due to no apparent reason." In contrast to contemporary criminals, curros did not suffer the same prejudices or stigmas attached to brujos.[12] They were all of African descent, but all had been free and *criollo*, or born in Cuba. Although they were assassins and criminals, they never exhibited any signs of remorse. They shared a problematic social status as the "bastards of Don Juan Tenorio with his black slave," the product of illicit sexual relations in the era of slavery.[13] Whereas Ortiz only hinted at the trope of the mestizo as criminal or tainted, eugenicists and criminologists would draw on it frequently. As he had stated the Sociedad's intentions to study the folkloric origins of Spanish, African, and Indian cultures as separate strands, his observations about miscegenation fit uncomfortably within a text more interested in glamorizing its subjects than in identifying sexual exploitation.

Negros curros had been urban, part of their distinction came from their flashy attire, and they had been mostly male (Ortiz promised to describe the female version, but he never did.) Three characteristics formed the essence of the curro: "a highly developed sense of vanity, an exhibition-ist jargon, and professional delinquency." Somewhat nostalgically, Ortiz re-created the scenes in which these figures operated. Meeting in cafés, exhibitionist sparring and feuding with other social groups, loitering, and engaging in petty theft comprised their principal activities. But per-haps because these were intelligible activities, not tainted with a hint of religious mystery or opaque "primitivism," Ortiz rendered them more as peculiar specimens than as threatening aberrations. Indeed, he sug-gested that they were Cuba's version of the picaresque, participants in a well-known tradition of male behavior, which, if not condoned, was certainly tolerated and to some extent canonized in literature: "He is the final and forgotten character in the Spanish picaresque, which the His-panist Mateo Alemán might have immortalized had he painted them in the third section of his *Guzmán de Alfarache*."[14]

With his avowals that curros had disappeared by the end of the nine-teenth century, Ortiz suggested that black criminality in the colonial era was more comprehensible, less menacing, more easily controlled. The transition from criminologist to folklorist was mediated by the use of time. If as criminologist he had relied on newspaper clippings and living informants, as folklorist he worked primarily in the past. His romantic sensibility came at the expense of social utility. In the interest of tackling the problem of an unevenly constituted modernity rife with unaccept-able political subjects, the brujo had been depicted in a harsher light. The curro — exotic, colorful, portrayed almost with an erotic edge — took his place in a gallery of historical tradition, requiring memorialization precisely because he had no connection to the present. Since the curro's political status as a colonial subject rendered citizenship more or less moot, Ortiz depoliticized the issue of black criminality by avoiding it altogether.

Led by Ortiz, the folklore society and its *Archivos* participated in what historians have identified as a shift in the representation of African-derived cultural practices in early-twentieth-century Cuba.[15] The articles included in the journal followed Ortiz's lead in creating a romantic, nostalgic memory of African cultural practices in Cuba to stand alongside the criminalizing but reformist vision of earlier work. But far from being immediately welcomed as a necessary revision, the folklorist approach suffered both neglect and criticism from a number of venues.

The society and the journal existed for seven years (1923–30). The contributors to *Archivos* included the most illustrious members of the Cuban intelligentsia, among them Enrique José Varona; Isis Ortiz, Fernando's daughter; Lydia Cabrera, the daughter of Raimundo Cabrera; Antonio Cosculluela, a respected archaeologist; as well as Juan Marinello, Rubén Martínez Villena, Emilio Roig de Leuschenring, and Carlos de la Torre.

Despite the pedigree of its membership and its stated nationalist intentions, the Sociedad del Folklore Cubano encountered difficulties in obtaining funding for its work. This gradually became apparent, as meetings with government officials and optimistic predictions fizzled into the realization that financial support would have to come from within the group. Initially, the study of folklore had been explicitly approved and supported by the Ministry of Education, which had commissioned José María Chacón to found societies dedicated to researching folklore in cities all over Cuba. He had done so and reported enthusiastic receptions in places such as Pinar del Río, Manzanillo, Bayamo, and Santiago de Cuba. The secretary of education and fine arts, Francisco Zayas y Alfonso, had been so supportive of the project that he had been named honorary president of the society. This was in January 1923, when Alfredo Zayas was president. Optimistically, members of the newly formed society scheduled a visit with Zayas y Alfonso in order to request funding to publish their journal. On February 9, they reported that the meeting had gone well and that the secretary had promised to assist them within the means available to him. Only one week later, however, they stated that the promise had been an empty one: Zayas y Alfonso had sent word in a more definitive manner that the ministry would be unable to offer any assistance at that time.[16]

Government funding was not forthcoming from the Machado administration, either. When the society met to discuss its budget in mid-1927, it was noted that without state support most of the money had come from subscriptions and advertising. The rest came from Ortiz's private funds. But this was to end: as Ortiz stated at the meeting, he could no longer afford to fund the journal. After a lengthy discussion the members reached a solution. The society would cede ownership of the journal to Ortiz himself, who would then contract with a publishing house that had already expressed interest, stipulating that it would publish the journal only if Ortiz was designated sole editor. Evidently, if the appeal of folklore was not wide enough to guarantee a steady readership, Ortiz's name would provide a firmer guarantee. By 1929 the Sociedad was looking to international connections for the affirmation missing at home. The visit of folklorist Aurelio Espinosa from Stanford University seems to have buoyed the members' spirits, as he reminded them of the Sociedad's stature as one of a few formally convened folklore societies in the world and remarked on the extensive demand for their journal abroad. The journal did not last much longer than that, and its pages remained silent regarding the society's internal workings. In 1930 the final volume was released. The study of folklore conceived as a nationalist project did not seem to hold much interest for official circles. Given this lack of government support, the economic crisis of 1929 probably proved fatal to the journal's fortunes.[17]

But the pages of *Archivos* themselves reveal contradictions that may have diminished the Sociedad's appeal. The publication of Nicolás Guillén's poems "Motivos de Son" in the final issue, marking a departure from the usual practice, highlighted growing uncertainty about the nature of recovering folklore. Contradictions appear in Ortiz's introduction to the poems: if the poetry was not strictly folkloric because of its recent composition and because it was produced by a known author rather than an anonymous one, Ortiz argued, the poems fit the category insofar as they "translated perfectly the spirit, the rhythms, the picaresque and the sensuality of anonymous works." Furthermore, imagining a somewhat unimaginable future for one of Cuba's most successful poets, he suggested that "soon these poems will become part of a popular repertory, and their author will be forgotten." He optimistically predicted—indeed, hoped for—their future anonymity so that they might be incorporated into a body of folklore. At the same time, he insisted on the importance of a creative present, expressing disdain for those stuck in a "dead past." Ortiz had placed himself in an untenable position, calling for appreciation of a creative present even as he failed to recognize the awkward fit between a folkloric project based on anonymity and the unique voice before him.[18]

In the same issue *Archivos* also published a series of exchanges about the significance and merit of Guillén's innovative approach, which structured poems around the *son*, the rhythmic song structure of "popular music." These exchanges had taken place in newspapers and in the Club Atenas. At issue was Guillén's use of the vernacular and invocation of lower-class, black lives within the text of the verse. In response to criticism from Ramón Vasconcelos, a black journalist, that his poetry was too easy, vulgar, and not reflective of his considerable talent, Guillén insisted that this, though it had been a difficult and complex task, was precisely his purpose: to create something "truly simple, truly easy, truly popular." Guillén asserted that elite Cubans of color should not denigrate the *son*, but rather recognize it as one of the most elemental aspects of black and mulatto cultural life.[19]

Others had joined this debate, which Ortiz faithfully reproduced in *Archivos*. One of the more prominent voices was that of Gustavo Urrutia, a black journalist who had begun to present himself as a spokesperson for Cubans of color through a weekly column "Ideales de una Raza," published in *Diario de la Marina*. Urrutia used the opportunity to comment on the debates among Cubans of color over the value of the vernacular as it had been invoked by Guillén. Urrutia criticized those who deemed the *son* too uncivilized and unworthy of respect. But he also criticized whites whose appropriation of this music was in most cases a misunderstanding of it: "We have here one of the few cases in which educated blacks do not want to imitate whites and maintain their social taboo against these delicious dances, arguing that whites are the sole consumers of this merchandise which produces and consumes 'blacks.'" He defended Guillén's position, maintaining that those who denied the ubiquity of the vernacular were not deaf but unwilling to discover, "amidst all this sound and fury, the vitality of our collective consciousness."[20]

Urrutia's position revealed much about the politics of "blackness" at this time. It demonstrated that the critique of white consumption of a "black folk" had been made by intellectuals of color. Whether Urrutia's critique was directed specifically at Ortiz is unclear, but Ortiz would certainly fall within the category of those who produced a folkloric image of blackness. More important, this debate took place in other venues, to which Ortiz only enjoyed secondhand access. Urrutia's article, published in *Diario de la Marina*, was a response to a presentation given by Guillén at the Club Atenas, at which Ortiz had not been present. As we shall see in the next chapter, Urrutia was one of several participants in the contentious debates among Cubans of color over representation and political and cultural identity that intensified during the 1930s. But their concerns and goals were increasingly distinct from those of the journal of folklore, which became largely irrelevant before it disappeared altogether. The Sociedad del Folklore Cubano had not proved immediately useful to the state, and it came to follow rather than dictate discussions on the political implications of the excavation and revival of folklore. The relatively new fields of folklore and ethnography entered the 1930s on the margins of political and intellectual Cuban life.

Palaces in the Air

Ethnography and folklore were not the only social scientific endeavors in search of sponsors during this period. Since Machado had explicitly noted the importance of science to his vision of modernity, other disciplines vied for attention and recognition. One of the most active groups of scientists to seek support for their projects worked on eugenics. The theory and practice of eugenics was undergoing a transition just as interest in social scientific inquiry heightened. Eugenicists had been working in Cuba since the inception of the republic, but 1921 marked the waning of "positive" eugenics, oriented toward environmental and reformist projects, and the rise of "negative" eugenics, with its focus on Mendelian genetics, racial purity, and prevention of reproduction for the genetically unfit. Eugenicists now turned their attention away from immediate and possibly remediable issues in contemporary society and began to imagine a racially pure future, to be achieved through exclusion or eradication of undesirables. A brief examination of early eugenics will bring the later emphasis on racial purity into greater relief.

Eusebio Hernández, a physician better known perhaps for his participation in the wars for independence than for his role in Cuban science, initiated the early practice of eugenics on the island. Hernández emerged from the anticolonial struggle with a distinguished military background and one of the more radically egalitarian brands of Cuban liberalism, as well as social and professional connections with the Maceo family. Born in Colón in the province of Matanzas in 1853, he was involved in both the Guerra Chiquita (1879–80) and the final war for independence (1895–98), joining forces with Quintín Bandera, Flor Crombet, José Maceo, and Calixto García. Before the Guerra Chiquita and in the hiatus between the wars he pursued medical studies in Madrid, Paris, and Berlin. During the republic he divided his time between teaching at the University of Havana, where he was professor of gynecology and obstetrics, and participation in party politics, running as vice presidential candidate with Bartolome Masó in 1901 and supporting José Miguel Gómez's presidential candidacy in 1907. In 1923 he supported radical students such as Julio

Antonio Mella, founder of Cuba's Communist Party. His views reflected a belief in the power of social reform: though he often expressed doubts about the current capacity of Cubans for political participation, he also believed in the merits of political inclusion and looked optimistically to the potential of social science and science to craft politically virtuous citizens.[21]

The underlying principles of Hernández's work in eugenics derived from the studies of Adolphe Pinard, a French obstetrician who had popularized the term "puericulture" (based on the Latin word meaning "child-rearing") in the late nineteenth century. Through Pinard's mentoring, Hernández became a proponent of positive eugenics. Pinard held that it was possible to enhance the vigor and robustness of a population by focusing on infant care. Although he gave a nod to hereditarianism regarding the role of parents' fitness in determining the quality of their offspring, his work focused mainly on ensuring that babies were reared in proper environments.[22]

Hernández coined the term "homiculture," which linked human fitness to a nation's capacity for peace, order, and prosperity. He argued that the propensity for corruption and personalism damaged the potential of the Cuban people. It would not be impossible to regenerate Cuban society, but it would require legislative measures to improve the physiological, hygienic, and therefore productive and moral capacity of all Cubans. Homiculture would take its cue from puericulture and work to "cultivate" fit men: "It is crucial to create healthy, useful men, able to work and conscious of their social obligations, strong enough to engage in collective battles and vigorous enough to face all the burdens imposed on individuals today by our complex social structure."[23]

Over the next two decades Hernández dedicated a large portion of his time to attaining this goal. He initiated the process in 1909, when he and his student Domingo Ramos began to present their ideas to public officials in the hope of obtaining funding and support. They had concretized their objectives with plans for a new building in which to shape more vigorous humans. They explained these plans in a series of proposals, first to the secretary of hygiene and welfare, then to the Second National Medical Congress in Cuba, and finally to President José Miguel Gómez.[24] As they conceived it, the enterprise of homiculture was divided into six stages, corresponding to the different stages of the life and maternal cycles: *progonocultura* (care of the gonads), *patrimatricultura* (culture of the parents), *matrifeticultura* (care of the pregnant mother and the fetus together), *matrinaticultura* (care of the mother and baby together), *pueri-cultura* (care of the baby), and *post-genitocultura* (care of the individual after birth).[25] These stages were to be housed, literally, in their proposed Palacio de Homicultura. The Palacio, to be named "Pinard-Hernández" after the Cuban's French mentor (and himself), would embody human life as they conceived it, with separate rooms dedicated to each of the six stages, arranged chronologically so that one could proceed through an entire reproductive cycle by walking through the building.[26] In each of the rooms patients would receive treatment and advice appropriate for the reproductive stage they were in at that moment.

When M. Varona Suárez, the secretary of hygiene and welfare, presented this proposal to President Gómez, he hoped that both the executive and legislative branches would understand the significance of the request. Homiculture was "a subject of such transcendence for the future of our nation, which sees to the physical and mental vigor of present and future generations and the development of citizens who can help themselves and contribute to the nation."[27] The proposals were apparently compelling enough to support the creation of a new department of homiculture within the Ministry of Hygiene and Welfare, decreed in the *Gaceta Oficial* on September 22, 1910.[28]

The idea of homiculture began to take hold in scientific circles, but in a halting, incomplete manner. The government offered occasional gestures of support but withheld consistent institutional backing. In 1913 Hernández and Ramos founded the Liga Nacional de Homicultura, whose members included leading intellectuals like Francisco Carrera y Justiz, Maria Luisa Dolz, Juan Santos Fernández, and Carlos Velasco.[29] *Vida Nueva*, the journal run by prominent Liberal doctor Diego Tamayo, began to publish articles by Hernández, Ramos, and others on various aspects of homiculture and puericulture.[30] Homiculturists tried to ensure that their ideas were disseminated beyond the scientific community. Hernández taught a course in homiculture and preventive sexual care at the Universidad Popular Obrera José Martí. In 1915 the Ministry of Hygiene and Welfare inaugurated its beautiful baby contests. The winners were chosen first at the municipal-level Motherhood Competitions, then competed in the National Motherhood, Homiculture, and Eugenic Reproduction Competitions. Held until 1933, the contests were widely advertised and sponsored by various commercial companies.[31] All of these exhortations and popularizations shared a Lamarckian approach, with an emphasis on enhancing environmental conditions to bring about racial "progress."

Despite the initial surge of enthusiasm for the new science, its most ambitious projects never came to fruition. Four years after the initial proposals, doctors and supporters continued to call for the construction of the Palacio de Homicultura Pinard-Hernández, still, apparently, a utopian dream.[32]

Another variant of eugenic thought arose toward the end of the 1910s. Domingo Ramos, along with Octavio Mañalich and Arístides Mestre, began to devote more attention to Mendelian theories of eugenics. This strand of eugenics held that race was biologically determined and that racial mixing did not result in the amelioration of "inferior traits," but rather in their preservation in "inharmonious" beings. Since miscegenation would therefore only lead to the creation of inferior types, it was important to keep all races separate and prevent interbreeding. As with the emerging interest in folklore, the project of assisting an unprepared citizenry's entry into political life receded. In the case of eugenics, emphasis on stringent control over bodies replaced earlier visions of creating the conditions under which morals, minds, and bodies might flourish.[33]

Ramos quickly took the lead in espousing this new vision, though initially he attempted to integrate it into the environmentalist views held by his mentors Pinard and Hernández. In a presentation to the Second International Congress of Eugenics held in New York City in 1921, his closing words revealed a (vague) synthesis of modes of human engineering: "This is what should be done for the scientific betterment of man, making the human species of the future the outcome of a scientific artificial selection and providing the environment in which it is going to live, artificially modified by the efforts of science which will have overcome existing conditions that would have made its struggle for life extremely hard."[34]

Soon after this conference Ramos turned away more definitively from his mentors and initiated a correspondence with Charles Davenport, director of New York's Cold Spring Harbor Eugenics Office and chief proponent of Mendelian eugenics in the United States. In his letters to Davenport the Cuban demonstrated his increasing adherence to Cold Spring Harbor's emphasis on racial purity. Moreover, he wanted to disseminate the theory and familiarize Cuban physicians with Davenport's views, suggesting that some of them travel to Cold Spring Harbor for training. For his part, Davenport was eager to incorporate Latin America into what Nancy Stepan has described as the "eugenic sphere of influence." He was particularly interested in promoting the racial purification of Cuba, whose mixed population had migrated in significant numbers to Florida.[35]

Ramos was at the center of the institution-building that ensued. He led the founding of the Pan-American Eugenics Committee at the Latin American Medical Congress in Havana in 1922. He must have achieved some influence with other Latin American physicians, for a year later delegates at the Pan-American meetings in Santiago, Chile, elected him head of the new Pan-American Office of Eugenics to be based in Havana. In this capacity he laid the plans for the First Pan-American Conference of Eugenics and Homiculture in Havana.[36]

Ramos's energy, his interest in Mendelian genetics, and Machado's concern with promoting science converged to give Cuban negative eugenics a high national and international profile. The Havana conference took place in December 1927. In it the networking aims of both Latin American and U.S. eugenicists coincided with the nationalist intentions of the Machado administration and produced concrete results. An official decree in 1924 had announced the creation of a Commission of National and International Conferences on Hygiene whose task it would be to control future meetings, all to be held in Havana. These included the First Pan-American Conference on Eugenics and Homiculture, the Sixth Pan-American Conference on Hygiene, and the Fourth International Conference on Eugenics.[37]

Charles Davenport's ideas permeated Ramos's opening speech at the First Pan-American Conference of Eugenics and Homiculture. "For real altrusim," Ramos asserted, those who promoted and directed the development of eugenics in Cuba should "defend, care for and utilize inferior beings, and segregate or sterilize unacceptable or harmful beings, in an act of cooperation that will lead to the engineering of a perfect human."[38] Arguing against the benefits of *mestizaje* (as miscegenation), he advocated instead working toward the improvement of each race as a separate entity. This process of natural selection and evolution, which linked certain characteristics to certain races, had already begun: "In the same manner that we work with the white race, we should also work to improve the black and Indian races . . . whites . . . Indians and blacks, preserving and improving the unique characteristics of each of the three races, for they are all necessary to the task, and each race should take advantage of the opportunities afforded us by peace and liberty."[39]

Also addressing the conference participants, Rafael Martínez Ortiz, secretary of state under Machado, used Ramos's scientific principles as the foundation of a national scheme. The emerging science and its accompanying prescriptions for the creation of a racially healthy population would propel Cuba toward a modernity already enjoyed by other nations, only attainable if inhabited by "collectivities that are more developed, to surpass those that are deficiently constituted."[40] Like Ramos, Martínez Ortiz envisioned a genetically purified future for Cuba, one in which the races were distinctly perceptible. He argued strongly against racial mixing, suggesting that those with faith in the value of mestizaje were sure to see the failure of an unviable illusion, existing, as they did, "in the illusory clouds of a fantastic optimism."[41]

This rejection of mestizaje as the redemptive solution to Latin America's race problem ran counter to the assertions of many delegates at the conference. Nancy Stepan has pointed to the growing appreciation of mestizaje as both a practical and face-saving solution for Latin American scientists and social scientists resentful of European and North American claims to racial superiority. Thus whereas in Mexico José Vasconcelos designed a "Cosmic Race" and in Brazil of the early 1920s the notion of attaining racial health through sanitation prevailed, Cuban eugenicists, especially Ramos, fell under the influence of Davenport's hereditarian antimiscegenationist views.[42]

The discussion that took place at the Havana conference reveals the distance between Ramos as the main proponent of U.S.-influenced eugenics and other Latin American delegates. As Stepan observed, the Code of Eugenics and Homiculture that Ramos had written with Davenport's assistance included some measures that most other delegates considered unacceptable because of their insistence on the importance of racial purity conceived in biological terms. The code called for individuals to be classified as genetically "good," "doubtful," or "bad," and for states to take measures to ensure that "bad" individuals did not reproduce. Another provision allowed for each nation to control immigration and deny entry to undesirable races. Ramos also envisioned the monitoring of marriages: if either spouse was determined unfit to reproduce, a marriage could be annulled or the individuals sterilized.[43]

The code's drafters faced strident criticism from Mexican delegate Rafael Santamarina and Peruvian delegate Carlos Enrique Paz Soldán, both of whom eloquently challenged the code's premises and looked ahead to the potentially dangerous consequences of its adoption. The version agreed upon at the conference's closing session was transformed into a much more tentative document. Provisions that had begun as mandates were changed to nonbinding recommendations. The call for the sterilization of the unfit was eliminated altogether. With regard to immigration, the code allowed each country to determine its own guidelines rather than following a scheme controlled by the Pan-American Office of Eugenics, which is what Ramos had originally envisioned. As Stepan noted, from Ramos and Davenport's point of view, the conference and the attempt to convince all the Latin American delegates to adhere to their Code of Eugenics and Homiculture "must be accounted a failure."[44]

As it turned out, the pinnacle of visibility of Cuba's negative eugenics was also the beginning of its demise. Despite the fanfare that surrounded the conference in 1927, none of the provisions Ramos most desired were ever implemented. He did succeed in convincing the legislature to pass a law requiring marriage certificates, but this proved to be a purely formal measure. Other provisions, such as those for sterilization, suffered a worse fate, receiving debilitating criticism either before they were proposed as law or in Congress. Ramos, originally the most vociferous proponent of negative eugenics, eventually entered the Batista administration and left the field of science.[45]

Ultimately Ramos's vision of a genetically purified future, with its refusal to take into account the heterogeneous and racially mixed present, may have proved too impractical to a state interested in social reform and palpable results. The advocacy of whiteness became part of state policy only when it was politically expedient. The issue of immigration had been tied to the issue of race from the earliest years of the republic, when both the legal establishment and sugar manufacturers had favored admitting Spaniards over the other main sources of labor, Jamaicans and Haitians. Between 1913 and 1920, however, importers of labor had relaxed these preferences in view of the economic prosperity (and greater demand for sugar workers) during the "Danza de Milliones" ("Dance of the Millions") ushered in by World War I. West Indian workers became a major source of labor, especially in the sugar-producing sections of Oriente. Beginning in the early 1920s, however, plummeting sugar prices and ballooning unemployment greatly reduced the tolerance for West Indian immigrants. In a series of conferences and decrees it became increasingly clear that support for the restriction of West Indian immigration was emerging from a variety of sectors. In 1931 Francisco María Fernández, president of the Cuban Academy of Sciences and member of the House of Representatives, proposed to cut off any immigration for the next two years. At the Third International Congress of Eugenics in 1932, Ramos again called for the restriction of "undesirable" immigration and emphasized the dangers of racial mixing. Some labor organizations, perceiving Haitians and Jamaicans as competitors in a tight labor market, also demanded restrictions. By 1933 the eugenicists' anti-immigration stance found resonance with state policy. In 1933 the "50 percent law" to nationalize workers, also called the Ley de Nacionalización del Trabajo, decreed that native Cubans must comprise at least 50 percent of any workforce. Unemployed foreigners without proof of means of subsistence were to be forcibly repatriated.[46] This law greatly affected Haitian and Jamaican sugar workers, the majority of whom had been sent back to their countries of origin by the late 1930s. Repatriation may have achieved a certain measure of "whitening," but it fell far short of the more radical policies including sterilization and marriage certificates that Cuba's Mendelian eugenicists had proposed.

Penitentiary Anthropology and the Science of Race

Of the social sciences, criminology enjoyed the most support from Machado's administration. Certainly part of the reason for this interest was the discipline's utility in controlling and repressing political opponents. But criminology also met Machado's ambitions to propel Cuba into the community of modern nations. Criminology was one of the social sciences most engaged in developing new technologies and updating its theoretical foundations. The restoration of the Model Prison, built on the Isle of Pines and modeled after the Benthamite plan famously interpreted by Michel Foucault, evinced the president's aims in both arenas.[47] If Machado had not seemed overly impressed with Fernando Ortiz's folkloric enterprise, he apparently respected him enough to commission him, in 1926, to draft a proposal to replace the penal code, in use since the colonial era, with one that incorporated the latest scientific theories.

An overlooked moment of coinciding purpose between Machado and Ortiz, the project of the Código Criminal Cubano (Cuban Penal Code) brought together Machado's ambitions and Ortiz's criminological leanings. When Ortiz presented his plan to the Legal Commission, he prefaced his remarks with an acknowledgment of the mutual endeavor, noting that the new code would be a product of "the effort of all, following General Machado's reformist impulse, interested as he is in legislative renewal."[48]

Ortiz's new definition of the delinquent proved the most important innovation in his proposal. In this definition he dispensed with the requirement that a person must commit a crime to be deemed delinquent. All that was necessary, he argued, was a propensity toward criminal behavior. Those who "demonstrate, through their inability to adapt to decent norms or the laws of public security, a state of extraordinary mental, moral or legal inadaptability, which endows them with a propensity for delinquency" ought to be labeled "dangerous persons."[49] In developing his theory, Ortiz disaggregated delinquents into different types. Depending on the nature of their responsibility for the crime committed, they would be classified into the following subcategories: "recidivists, mentally ill, psychopaths, drug addicts, vagrants, political criminals, minors, and members of gangs."[50] A notable array of different "orders of things" constitutes the list. The inclusion of biological, psychological, social, and political factors perhaps reflects early-twentieth-century criminology's confidence in its ability to encompass and address the problem of crime in its multifaceted entirety. It also suggests a broad ambition to demobilize many sectors of society.

This focus on the criminal rather than the crime indicates a shift from classical to positivist criminological theory. Initiated principally by the Italian school of criminology, it rejected the notion of the free will of the criminal and replaced it with the view that the criminal was both constrained and impelled by environmental, biological, and psychological factors. One of the chief proponents of this theory was Enrico Ferri, whose lecture on "The Positivist School of Criminology" in 1885 represented a landmark for historians of criminology.[51] In the succinct analysis of one philosopher: "The person who commits a crime, says Ferri, is a criminal . . . it is no use looking for the motive of his act: the reason for his crime is precisely, his criminality. In a sense these few peremptory words mark the registering of a new object of penal science and practice: *homo criminalis*."[52]

The role of anthropologically derived knowledge was key. Ortiz's new code included methods by which data on inmates were to be gathered: "In each center of detention there will be a Daily Register, managed according to the rules and procedures laid out by the criminal ordinances, which will record the conduct, morality, punishments, rewards, labor, instruction, hygiene, health and rank of each inmate. All inmates will undergo an anthropological examination under the conditions established by the

Criminal Ordinances."[53] It was only by thorough study and analysis of individuals and their criminal tendencies, Ortiz argued, whether they stemmed from biological or environmental factors, that the repression of crime could become a properly rational, scientific endeavor. He recommended the development of university courses, as well as the training of a body of penitentiary personnel and of medical anthropologists.[54] In a formal proposal drafted later he called for the institutionalization of instruction at the University of Havana with the creation of three new professorships in the Law School "for training in Criminology and Penology," "for training in Criminal Anthropology and Policiology" (Ortiz coined the latter term *policiología*), and "for training in Criminal Justice and Penal Law," as well as offering a doctorate in criminology.[55] Once inculcated with knowledge of the most recent technologies and theories, these experts would run the new institutions that Ortiz proposed.

All of this new energy devoted to criminology would be channeled by a National Council of Prevention and Repression of Delinquency. Analogous to the National Council of Hygiene and Welfare, it would serve as "the first line of defense in the war against criminality," assembling government officials and experts in pursuit of greater control over the penological landscape.[56] This council would direct and oversee all operations involved not just in the repression of crime but also in the acquisition of knowledge. Ortiz envisioned that the council would be composed of a member of the judiciary, preferably a high-level judge, and a number of academics, including those named to the professorships of criminology and penology; criminal anthropology and policiology; and criminal justice and penal law. Seats on the council would also be allocated to those involved in more practical matters: the inspector of all penal establishments, the director of the National Bureau of Identification (Gabinete Nacional de Identificación), and the chiefs of corrections personnel. A significant aspect of Ortiz's proposal concerned the collection and systematization of data, including statistics, measurements, and "psychological data."[57]

The proposal generated a wide range of responses that expressed various degrees of enthusiasm. Ortiz's colleague and friend Israel Castellanos, director of the National Bureau of Identification at the time, entered the forum with a proposal of his own to expand the role of state institutions and the experts who would run them. Castellanos wrote from the perspective of a participant within this evolving apparatus, outlining a plan that would fit the needs of the Cuban penal system and nationalists' modernizing ambitions. He praised Ortiz's plan as a step toward the positivist overhaul of the penal system while pointing out that some practices within the penitentiary system had already begun to change in that direction, slightly ahead of the theoretical enterprise. Castellanos and others had already initiated a series of anthropological studies of inmates. Ortiz's plan would support and legitimize his own program for a Laboratory of Penitentiary Anthropology. Through it he would obtain, in as much detail as its techniques allowed, the moral diagnosis and rehabilitative prognosis of each inmate. Once the diagnosis was obtained, criminal anthropologists would formulate a plan by which the inmate would be redeemed socially to the extent possible: "Only on the dual basis of the moral diagnosis and the rehabilitative prognosis will it be possible to establish a rehabilitative plan or moral therapy, a specific scientific treatment of physical and moral reform, for the reintegration of the social life of an inmate."[58] Castellanos accepted the premises of Ortiz's proposal and encouraged their extension beyond the confines of formal law, to the bodies and psychologies of inmates.

The proposed penal code marked a transitional moment in Ortiz's intellectual trajectory. His views (as expressed in earlier works) linking race to crime through atavism were diffused in the text: although a theory of atavism seems to have informed his call for anthropological studies of delinquents, he refrained from making explicit statements about race. By 1928 his actions suggested ambivalence about his criminological roots: he sent copies of *Los negros brujos* to friends even while describing himself as a "former Lombrosian."[59] By 1944 he claimed to be even further removed from his previous endeavors. His letter thanking Rafael Portuondo at the Audiencia de Oriente in Santiago de Cuba for mentioning the new penal code in his own text suggests a disavowal if not an intellectual transformation: "I feel so distant from those studies that when people speak to me of penal issues it feels like they are reminding me of another life."[60]

As Ortiz's career moved on, and fairly bulged with the proliferation of other interests and new points of view, Castellanos took up the thread of positivist criminology and ensured its longevity in the Cuban penal system. In 1930 Ortiz published the "Basis for an Effective Cuban Solution," a manifesto critical of Machado's government. Soon afterward he began a voluntary exile in the United States, during which he joined the Junta Revolucionaria Cubana, an anti-Machado organization in New York.[61] In Cuba Castellanos apparently obtained the support required for the expansion of his nascent project. The plan for a Laboratory of Penitentiary

Anthropology received official backing and was installed in the Model Prison.

For the purposes of the state, ethnography and folklore had seemed too arcane while eugenics proved impractical and too utopian. Castellanos's brand of penitentiary anthropology, however, became a fixture of the Cuban state until at least 1959. His positivist view of race as a measurable phenomenon and insistence on strong ties between race and criminality updated the image of the brujo or ñáñigo. Of Cuban social scientific endeavors, his was the most effective response to heightened mobilization. Rather than excavating distant cultural origins or looking to genes to solve social ills, penitentiary anthropology promised to promote social peace by identifying, analyzing, and incarcerating "delinquents," effectively removing them from contexts in which they might threaten political order.

The Scientific Reality of Mestizaje

Out of Castellanos's interest in criminal anthropology grew a fascination with the use of technology to thoroughly render and represent human bodies. The organizing principle of his long and varied career was an ambition, through statistics, measurements, fingerprints, and blood analyses, to map the Cuban body. For Castellanos, any part of a body could be plumbed for the truths it might reveal.

Both the Laboratory of Penitentiary Anthropology and the Bureau of Identification, which he had directed since 1912, operated efficiently enough to provide the data that would serve a dual purpose: allow assessment of each individual and his or her potential for reform, and provide the raw material from which Castellanos could assemble a series of anthropological guides to Cuba's criminals. Drawing from 100,000 "national files" created between 1909 and 1927, Castellanos's numerous monographs, such as *La delincuencia femenina en Cuba* (1929) and *El pelo en los cubanos* (1933), made public the morphological facts that lay within the walls of the Model Prison and other penal institutions.[62]

Castellanos insisted on the truth and significance of mestizaje in Cuba's racial history. And, like other degeneration theorists at the time, he borrowed freely from and combined seemingly inimical environmental and hereditary notions of change.[63] In contrast to eugenicists, Castellanos was more interested in cataloging racial mixture than in preventing its occurrence. He deplored both the Spanish and U.S. neglect of mestizaje in their censuses, coming down especially hard on the North Americans. Even the benefit of the most recent scholarship engaging "racial factors of delinquency," he chided, had not affected their reluctance to account for mestizaje:

> Disgracefully enough, the North American tables only use the categories "white" and "black," with all data on mulattoes folded into the category of black. In other words, the American ethnic puritanism stubbornly refuses to recognize the anthropological reality of the mestizo. As if obscuring the statistics eliminated the scientific reality of mestizaje, which occurs in North America as in Central and South America. Even in the most recent publication (*Census of Prisoners*, 1923) they maintain their bi-color categorization: black and white.[64]

The problem Castellanos (and, according to him, all conscientious scientists) faced was how to overcome a long history of ambiguous usage, indeterminate criteria, and unscientific principles in order to fix racial categories. Mestizaje, the meaning of which was most elusive, merited special attention. To begin with, the very act of collecting statistical data, so important to his vision of an efficient penal system, had not been practiced systematically. Information was gathered only intermittently: the *Memoria de Estadística Judicial* (1915) (corrections statistics) and the *Informe al Presidente de la República* (*Report to the President of the Republic*) (1921) were the only publications that approached the thorough fact-finding ethos that Castellanos sought to encourage.

But even the initiation of regular anthropological studies under the auspices of his National Bureau of Identification had not produced the consistent categories that Castellanos considered necessary. Castellanos had invented the *ficha-modelo*, a bureaucratic document in which to record the details of each inmate's body. The form included questions on race, complexion, hair, eyes, nose (tip and base), lips, mouth, ears, and tattoos.[65] Despite this regularization and the training of prison staff in the proper meaning of categories, there was a distressing lack of consistency, especially with recidivists. Often, if a woman was classified as white in court documents from an initial incident, she might be labeled "mestiza" the next time around. Similarly, a woman classified as "negra" might return as "mestiza." The root of the problem lay, for Castellanos, in the misguided practice of using class to determine race: "He who, remaining within the cult of chromaticism, puts those men of better families in the 'white' category and those of lower social status in 'black,' dishonors science and is not her disciple." Only "physical, anthropological characteristics," obtained in thorough empirical examinations with complete disregard for social class, could reveal the offender's "real" race.[66]

Castellanos demanded that criminologists recognize the scientific truth of mestizaje because, in his view, miscegenation bred delinquency. The statistics he had processed for female delinquents demonstrated that once foreign blacks were factored out, Cuban mestizas, more than either black or white women, were most prone to criminality. Physical miscegenation, he insisted, was the most important factor in the creation of the contemporary underworld. Cuba's underworld was essentially mestizo, and any study that did not take racial heterogeneity and commingling into account would not, in his opinion, do justice to the phenomenon.

As he noted in *La delincuencia femenina*, Castellanos had tried to impose consistency and scientific criteria on the determination of race, so that whites, mestizas (or *mulatas*—he used these terms interchangeably), and blacks would be clearly differentiated from one another. Yet the challenge of mestizaje had apparently left him with lingering doubts as to the potency of the tools he had developed thus far. A book he published only four years later aimed at further refinement of the technique of reading racial classification from physical signs. Mestizaje posed a theoretical problem for the study of race that could be solved most efficiently, Castellanos contended, through an intensified biological analysis. The uncertainty of mestizos' origins in this case directed criminal anthropologists to biological definitions rather than away from them. If skin color was not to be trusted, the answer was to look more closely at other physical characteristics, assuming that hair or bones would hold truths that trumped potentially misleading skin tones.

Based on an award-winning study he had published in 1928, *El pelo en los cubanos* (1933) looked, as the title suggests, to hair as the key to the racial puzzle Cubans posed. It announced the capacity of new technologies of microscopic observation to discern with a great deal of precision the characteristics of hair: its shape in cross section, tendency to curl, angle of the root, color and thickness. Castellanos believed that in a miscegenated populace, studies of hair would produce a level of certainty not provided by the study of superficial characteristics: "We will obtain a powerful instrument which, in the majority of cases and under normal conditions, will deliver a racial diagnosis."[67] Combined with the observation of other anthropological features, he would be able to pin down those people whose racial vagueness had plagued statisticians. "In the countries of Hispanic America, where mestizaje exhibits a tremendous range, it is necessary to study racial characteristics as specifically as possible, so that together with other details they may orient us and resolve the problems for statistical and anthropological analysis posed by the 'advanced mestizo' and 'backward white.'"[68]

His faith in science and microscopic analysis permeate nearly all 254 pages of *El pelo*. The twenty-five chapters contain numerous illustrations, cross sections, and photographs of different kinds of hair. He claimed to supersede European anthropological authorities with his own contribution centered on racial complexity, or what he called Cuba's "ethnic mosaic." Much like Ortiz, who understood his focus on heterogeneity to be his principal contribution to European social science, Castellanos asserted that knowledge derived from Cuba's particular ethnic makeup would advance criminological studies of hair and race, until then conducted exclusively on homogeneous European races. In the penological arm of the state, mestizaje was a dangerous, precisely identifiable phenomenon.

After completing the study on hair, Castellanos expressed new optimism about progress toward his vision of a completely measured population: "We have measured the height of Cubans according to the laws of anthropology, as well as body weight, both anatomical characteristics which have allowed us to get a more precise idea of the height and weight of all the natives of this country."[69] Fingerprints would also provide vital information. As director of the National Bureau of Identification, Castellanos had been responsible for the implementation of fingerprinting for police and judicial purposes. Spurred by belief in the value of fingerprints as anthropological clues, he had made several attempts to gather larger quantities and engage in further studies. In the early 1930s he had collected the fingerprints of Cubans of color and compared them to those of Haitian and Jamaican immigrants.[70] Later, in an action that satisfied his thirst for data and the requirements of maintaining order, he had ordered that all driver licensees be fingerprinted.

His vision of a thoroughly documented citizenry became the target of popular contention. In 1934, on arriving home from a prolonged research trip in the United States, he learned that his office had been ransacked. Writing to his friend August Vollmer, police captain of Berkeley, California, he expressed his dismay and disbelief:

While I still hold my position, I was surprised and pained to find on my return, that during my absence, my office was broken open and sacked. Everything was taken from the desks, books, observations, scientific material etc. Though I never was a politician, the revolutionists of the former regime stole and destroyed in a moment all the data collected over a period of fifteen years of incessant labor. At the present time, I am enjoying a leave of absence, requested on account of ill health—I have not had sufficient strength to even go see what is left of my office. Perhaps I shall never go there again.[71]

Yet he did return, only to weather another outburst of discontent in 1936. He seemed to understand that his methods had been implicated in protests against an intrusive and unjust regime. "The 'good citizens,'" he wrote, again to Vollmer, "that pretend I am 'violating the Constitutional rights by having honest citizens fingerprinted in our Bureau mixing their fingerprints with those of criminals' started a movement with the purpose of getting rid of me."[72]

Troubles came as well from another quarter: his estranged wife had enlisted the aid of numerous politicians eager to oust him, because "many politicians have been sentenced to prison and they never forget that I am an obstacle."[73] Despite his support from professors of medicine at the University of Havana, the pressure was so intense that he tendered his resignation. Yet by January 1937, after "recent changes operated in our Cabinet," which he hoped would "settle or at least lessen difficulties," he had returned to his post as head of the National Bureau of Identification.

Evidently Castellanos had been swept up in a growing conflict between civil and military government, more specifically between the regime of Miguel Mariano Gómez and the backstage manipulations of Fulgencio Batista. Gómez, who had been elected (fairly by all accounts) in early 1936, had clashed with Batista over the growing power of the military, which had favored a bill reinstating the death penalty and begun to arrest politicians it deemed to be dangerous radicals. Alarmed by the arrest of one of its members, the House of Representatives called for an investigation of police repression. It is likely that Castellanos resigned in the face of attacks on his policing practices. By December 1937, however, Gómez had been impeached and ousted from office, replaced by Laredo Brú, who was more acquiescent to Batista's encroachments. This reshuffling may have been the "recent change in cabinet" that Castellanos credited with enabling his return.[74] In 1954, although quite ill following repeated surgery, he was still acting head of the National Bureau of Identification. Castellanos worked in Batista's regime until it was overthrown. He left his country and his position in 1959 after forty-seven years of service.[75]

The insistent search for the biological manifestations of mestizaje persisted through Castellanos's institutions as a troubling counterpoint to the proliferation of "mulatto poetries." As the state relied increasingly on science and criminology for more efficient means of criminal identification and repression, Castellanos's views about the biological, atavistic nature of race prevailed. Interestingly, in the census, only judicial and penitentiary records used the category of mestizo. In other statistics, such as those accounting for regional population, education, or marital status, census takers used only "blanco" and "de color" (with footnotes explaining that "mixed" and "yellow" were folded into "de color"). Effectively, mestizos did not merit their own separate category except when related to crime—as reflected in judicial and penitentiary statistics.[76]

Castellanos's influence extended beyond the institutions he directly controlled. The secret police, or Policía Secreta Nacional (PSN), sought guidance on issues of identification and analysis of the etiology of crime in Castellanos's work. Through the PSN's Homicide Bureau, which fell under the jurisdiction of Castellanos's Bureau of Identification, members of the secret police were tutored in his criminological theories.[77] The close relationship between Castellanos and the PSN emerges through an examination of articles published in the PSN's journal, *Policía Secreta Nacional*.[78] An article written by Castellanos himself on the technological advances in *policiología* emphasized the use of scientific, physical evidence as opposed to testimonial and therefore fallible evidence.[79] Other articles praised the Lombrosian school of criminology, especially its more subtle version that had evolved in response to criticism. This version stressed the importance of the ongoing study of delinquents and worked from the premise that atavism and degeneration were the sources of criminality. As such, the Lombrosian school was still useful, according to criminologists, for a number of reasons: "For a long time Lombrosian anthropology has determined all the fundamental principles of efficient crime prevention and rehabilitation, from eugenics to moral and mental hygiene, from the struggle against juvenile delinquency to scientific policing, from penal laws to the penitentiary system."[80] Much more evidence of concrete police and penological practices is necessary to draw conclusions about the direct implementation of these ideas. But the tenacious hold of notions of degeneration and the criminal manifestations of Cuba's "ethnic mosaic" within powerful state institutions is undeniable.

Conclusion

Although folklore, eugenics, and criminology enjoyed differential support from the Machado administration, the development of these disciplines reflected a rising interest in theories of racial difference. In their search for cultural authenticity, folklorists and ethnographers drew on racial categories conceived in national terms (African, Spanish, Indian). Eugenicists rejected prevailing "environmentalist" approaches and replaced them with strategies for genetic purification. Criminologists acknowledged racial mixture only as the source of dangerous criminal tendencies. Informed by different uses of time and distinct disciplinary innovations, social scientists worked to depoliticize or demobilize the objects of their studies. From the point of view of folklorists, ethnographers, eugenicists, and criminologists, the transcendence or elimination of racial categories seemed an unfruitful path to pursue. As they designed ways to understand, denigrate, celebrate, mobilize, punish, or purify Cuban bodies, social scientists asserted their continuing interest in race.

The situation was even more dangerous, for
whites and men of color, for both equally, once
certain pseudo-scientific theories, popular in certain European nations, and utilized very astutely
in current times for political ends . . . could reveal
themselves to be a most powerful weapon—
something like a powerful boomerang—in the
hands of men of color in their struggles against
whites.

[Tanto mas peligrosa la situación, para blancos
y hombres de color, para ambos igualmente, ya
que ciertas teorías raciales pseudo-científicas, en
uso en ciertos países europeos y lanzados hoy
en día para fines políticos con gran astucia . . .
podrían revelarse como la mas poderosa arma—
algo como un boomerang muy poderoso—en las
manos del hombre de color en su lucha contra
el blanco.]

ALEJANDRO LIPSCHUTZ
"Sobre el problema del negro" (1938)

The Politics of Blackness
on the Eve of Revolution

In September 1928, 187 sociedades de color from all over
the country staged a spectacular tribute to President Gerardo Machado y
Morales in one of Havana's most prominent theaters. The press accounts
emphasized what one observer called the "sober elegance" of the event.
On display were the best and the brightest of the *raza de color*, including various classical musicians. An aria from *Luchia* sung by Zoila Gál-
vez prompted a deluge of flowers on the stage. The performance and indeed the entire affair demonstrated such a high level of achievement that,
one reporter asserted, it would be criminal to deny these descendants of
slaves their well-deserved place in all institutions of higher learning, since
they enjoyed full access to "the weapons of culture and the benefits of
legitimate triumphs." Organized principally by Américo Portuondo and
Manuel Capestany, both Liberal congressmen and members of the Club

Atenas, the tribute was designed not just to display the uplifted and uplifting talents of the raza de color, but also to explicitly show the participants' gratitude to Gerado Machado for nominating blacks and mulattoes to prominent positions in his administration and for recently supporting the sociedades materially and rhetorically.[1] Portuondo recognized the importance of Machado's actions, as they reflected a qualitative shift in the official view on race: "General Machado has been the first leader to address the problem of the heterogeneity of our society with patriotism and sincerity and to acknowledge the need to treat all of its members equally. The elements of color can be used by General Machado to achieve the loftiest goals, to make Cuba free, cleansed of stains, with pure practices, both public and private." Carefully choreographed, the event exuded a delicately balanced mix of gratitude, reverence, and muted protest.[2]

When Miguel Angel Céspedes took the floor, he began with a tone of civility and references to high culture that fit the tenor of the evening. The raza de color, he declared, understood and appreciated the dignity and privileges of citizenship it had enjoyed in recent years. He noted, for instance, Machado's laudable appointments of men of color to diplomatic positions as representatives of Cuba in foreign countries. When Céspedes brought up Martín Morúa Delgado, he maintained his courteous tone but introduced a counterpoint of dissatisfaction that could not have gone unnoticed on such a civil occasion. In the early years of the republic, the raza de color had grown impatient, he recalled, but Morúa had discretely and prudently prevented the bifurcation of Cuban politics into white and black constituencies. Yet this move, though it had outlawed mobilization along racial lines, had not constituted "the guillotine to our aspirations nor the suicide of our aspirations." These aspirations toward equality in education, in the workplace, and in public life had survived despite Morúa's disapproval of race-based political activity. Now, he asserted, they would use this opportunity to call for equality in practice as well as in the law.

This moment marked the culmination of Machado's strategy to appeal to "blacks" as a political constituency. Early in his presidency, he had very publicly raised the visibility of Cubans of color in his administration. In one of his first acts in office, Machado signed a bill that granted both land and $50,000 to the Club Atenas for the construction of a new building. He had appointed General Manuel Delgado to three secretariats—agriculture, interior, and communications—and named Manuel Capestany subsecretary of justice. In response to frequent complaints about an all-white diplomatic corps, he tapped journalist Ramón Vasconcelos and Dr. Raúl Navarrete for the foreign service. Benjamin Muñoz Guinarte became chief of section in the Secretariat of Agriculture as well as secretary of the Cuban delegation to the Pan-American Conference on Agriculture and Animal Industry.[3] Although elite sociedades had become increasingly visible over the preceding several years, they had shied away from explicit engagement with the state. Machado encouraged this engagement.

The tribute to Machado coincided with a period of crisis in his administration. The previous year he had convened a constitutional assembly in order to extend his term and allow him to seek reelection. Critics, dismayed at what they perceived as a rapid transformation from liberal nationalist to autocratic dictator, raised vociferous protests. With his legitimacy at stake, the spectacle of sociedades de color paying public homage would have served as an exception to intensifying denunciations. With regard to racial ideology, this was a new response to political crisis. In contrast to his predecessors' rhetoric and practices meant to subsume or transcend racial divisions in the interest of national unity, Machado had emphasized racial heterogeneity in his gestures toward Cubans of color.

Rather than insisting that a Cuban national identity rendered racial differences irrelevant, many black and mulatto activists found the vision of heterogeneity valuable as they explored and exploited "blackness" as a political category. In the early years of the republic, as de la Fuente has observed, the professions had come to be characterized by income disparities linked to race. This was more the case in upper-level professions than in manual labor, which was becoming an increasingly multiracial sector and tended to pay poorly regardless of race. As a result, professional and educated sectors were among the most outspoken regarding issues of racial equity.[4] As they confronted limits to their upward mobility, they began to focus on race as an explanation for the dissatisfaction that accompanied rising expectations.

At the same time, by 1928 many Cubans were trying to stave off an economic crisis even as Machado negotiated a political rapprochement. Effects from the steadily falling price of sugar reverberated through all social classes, resulting in an economic downturn that foreshadowed the Great Depression. In addition to eliminating employment for many sugar workers, Cuba's faltering economy produced declining consumption patterns and concomitant unemployment in professional and service sectors.

Even government employees, traditionally buffered against the vagaries of a sugar economy, faced impending salary cuts.[5] Increasingly dire circumstances seem to have forced elite sociedades to confront, however ambivalently, the role of workers and of class disparities in their demands for equality.

With these tensions and contradictions in the foreground, this chapter will shift between the forms of black political organization realized in this period and the ways that intellectuals and activists deliberately posited "blackness" as a political category. I argue that although the specific claims made by social scientists fell under criticism from black activists and were regarded ambivalently by the state, both the state and activists invoked racial categories in their efforts to accrue political power. The converging understandings of Cuba as a heterogeneous society signaled the fading utility of a race-transcendent nationalist ideology. Thus while notions of cultural mestizaje held sway in literary, artistic, and touristic circles, both state officials and black intellectuals came to see races, as well as other constituencies (women, laborers, capitalists), as distinct groups rather than disaggregated collections of individuals or one homogeneous polity. The chapter closes with the explosive encounter between race, revolution, and reaction.[6]

Machado's Constituencies

The racialization of Machado's politics grew out of broader appeals to previously unrepresented sectors of society. Early in his term he had advocated the reform of political representation. In 1926 he proposed the organization of Cuban society into corporations or syndicates to which his government would be accountable. He envisioned "chambers of commerce, blocs of *colonos* and agricultural workers, and associations of all kinds" organized to identify the sources of their economic difficulties. On paper at least he offered the corporations or syndicates a role in shaping policy: "When they came to the Chief of State it would not be to ask for emergency palliatives but rather to propose viable solutions."[7] Thus he envisioned Cubans acting politically not as individuals, but as members of discrete groups.

Although Machado tried to build a broadly based constituency by incorporating many different groups, the demands of industrialists and of those in control of the sugar industry limited his populist strategies. These sectors worried about rising labor unrest and pressured Machado to control labor militancy. For a while he tried to appease both workers and industrialists, an approach that proved difficult to sustain. An early policy to incorporate the labor movement and at the same time control the most radical elements failed. As Marifeli Pérez-Stable notes, "During the 1920s, the Machado administration assassinated militant labor leaders while recognizing the right of maritime workers to unionize in the hope of countering radical labor organizations. . . . A quiescent working class was increasingly elusive."[8] In the late 1920s relations with labor became increasingly strained as Machado responded to unrest with violence and repression.[9]

As a way to maintain the legitimacy that had ushered him into office, Machado sought an alternative to class-based political identities. "Blacks" as a political category, rather than "workers," represented that alternative.[10] Similarly, he directed his energies toward women's groups, promising them the vote if they supported his reelection.[11] In this context his appeal to Cubans of color and women attempted to bypass problematic class-based political identities and invoked an alternative set of issues around which to mobilize citizens.

Social scientific projects increasingly rooted in racial difference that proliferated in this period played a complex role. In his efforts to both instill political order and garner popular support, Machado had included under his wide reformist umbrella groups that were potentially inimical to one another. Even as he sponsored criminological and eugenic theories and practices that continued to privilege whiteness as they linked blackness with delinquency, he fostered, and clearly obtained the gratitude of, sociedades de color. Social scientific projects had proven useful in creating order by demobilizing or depoliticizing potential threats to the state. But as they were largely uninterested in shaping a politically viable citizenry, the social sciences in their ethnographic, eugenic, and criminological incarnations were of limited utility to Machado. Nonetheless, he drew from their assumptions that social categories rested on essential racial differences in his efforts to structure society around his political agenda.

Civil Sociedades

Although the sociedades de color had not waited for Machado's cue to organize, the terms of their engagement with the state remained ambiguous. At this time they faced the challenge of how to assert their rights, critique ubiquitous and problematic (in their eyes) representational practices, and remain within the bounds of "acceptable" behavior, especially when those boundaries were changing.

Even as they navigated these constraints, the sociedades took advantage of the progressivist rhetoric of Machado's regime to extend their activities. Seizing on the allotment of funds and space to the Club Atenas, other sociedades also intensified their public presence, constructing new buildings. They negotiated this greater visibility by relying on accepted idioms and practices to temper the oppositional implications of some of their goals. In January 1928, for instance, the Sociedad Centro Maceo (formerly the Centro de Cocheros) announced that it was opening its own clinic in response to a need "greatly felt within the ethnic group to which we belong." Private clinics run by Spanish immigrant societies were a common institution in Cuba, though they had in fact provoked some protest from the established medical community.[12] The directors of the Sociedad Centro Maceo viewed themselves as extending this privilege to their own, deserving constituency, announcing that the new clinic was intended to serve not just members of that association, but anyone who paid a nominal fee and who qualified as "all those who are moral and lovers of our national institutions, for this is a work of intense patriotism." However attuned to nationalist ideals, the remonstrative impetus behind the organization of this clinic was clear: "We also invite all those people who, due to recent setbacks, find themselves sinking in the deepest pessimism. We ask them to cooperate so that together we may resolve practically our social and economic problems."[13] The society's directors combined sustained suspicion of the state with a sense of urgency for social reform.

The leaders of these societies worked toward citizenship that was defined as egalitarian not just in principle but in everyday life and popular discourse. Chipping away at this issue on a quotidian level, they called for greater visibility in key areas like housing and department store counters, as well as the representation of blacks in cultural events and in historical works. For instance, in a letter to Pedro Hernández Massí, superintendent of schools of the province of Havana, President Machado, and the *Diario de la Marina*, Aquilino Lombard, president of the Club Atenas, registered his concern about a play presented by local schoolchildren to a group of foreign delegates in town for the Pan-American conference. In the drama, little black girls played the parts of slaves in the 1830s. Lombard objected to two things: first, the revival of the memory of slavery, which he argued was still a painful one for many Cubans; and second, the celebratory tone of the play, written in the 1830s, which was not at all critical of the slaveholding regime. The spectacle, he claimed, had retained a ridiculous idiom of luxury and extravagance without any acknowledgment that it had been built "on none other than the tears of our suffering grandmothers and the pain of so many slaves."[14] It was inappropriate, then, to romanticize a slaveholding past using schoolchildren, especially before an audience of distinguished foreigners.

The next day the newspaper printed Superintendent Hernández's response, which began in a defensive mode. Raising the name of Martín Morúa Delgado as cover, he suggested that quibbling over literary matters was not what the renowned politician of color had intended when he had spoken of the regeneration of the raza de color. Lombard's confrontational tactics, in Hernández's view, were far less effective than the focus on education Morúa had envisioned. Yet in the end he conceded that Lombard's argument regarding the significance of representation was valid. The play had been presented, he maintained, to underscore the contrast between the ignominious past and the redeemed present, a transformation wrought by the struggle for independence and the participation of blacks in that struggle.[15] Hernández thus granted the legitimacy of Lombard's claims that historical narrative and its representation of the role of former slaves and their descendants were legitimate terrains for public debate and that the stakes of representation were indeed high.

Members of the sociedades de color seized the moment to achieve a long-standing goal of greater unity, but they also worked to extend their reach and initiated a tentative engagement with the state. The first meeting of all sociedades in the province of Havana took place in 1928. The opening ceremony on May 6 was attended by powerful politicians — among them, Mariano Gómez, son of José Miguel Gómez and mayor of Havana; Antonio Ruiz, governor of the province of Havana; and Matías Duque, president of the Asociación Patriótica. Also present were several representatives from U.S. societies, including George Smith of the Negro Improvement Association, who "spoke frenetically in English,"[16] Leonard Bryan of the Carlington Club, and W. H. Dussel and E. G. Terrelongie of the Grant Brotherhood of Silence, Inc.

The society that arranged the meeting, Santa Eugenia, had been founded in 1925 soon after Machado's election. The organizing committee consisted of prominent men of color, some of whom had been active for years in different venues. In response perhaps to Machado's call for input from corporate groups, their goal was not just to construct a program conducive to the social and economic progress of what they called "the collective," but also to convey their proposals to the leaders of the republic. A preliminary list of reforms issued by this organizing committee cast a wide net over the island's social and economic life:

1. Continuous progress in the life of our societies
2. Socio-moral hygiene
3. Improvement of our civic customs
4. Foundations for our economic future
5. Useful and practical guidance for our youth on choosing careers and professions
6. Protection for our workers, both male and female
7. General social statistics, organized according to profession, wherever one of our institutions resides
8. Construction of a health center
9. Recommendation for a law against juvenile delinquency
10. Recommendation for laws that foster agricultural, scientific, and industrial instruction that will produce adequately trained farmers and industrial engineers.[17]

This platform followed the tendency, exemplified by the Unión Fraternal, of sociedades to forge cross-class alliances and address issues of socioeconomic and, in this case, gender inequity. Some work to achieve these reforms had already occurred and received Machado's approval, who characterized them as "patriotic labor." One proposal involved the archbishop of Santiago, with whom the sociedades were discussing the acquisition of some church-owned land in Cienfuegos to be distributed as small plots to Cubans of color so they might become the Cuban equivalent of yeoman farmers. One observer of this meeting ascribed a regenerative role to its participants, imagining them as productive citizens. Significantly, however, their envisioned productivity would contribute to commerce, industry, and agriculture, while steering clear of "sterile bureaucracy." Their position and goals implied an ambiguous relationship with the state: they called for the inclusion of blacks and mulattoes in any project fashioning Cuba's "improvement" even while evincing nervousness about allying themselves wholly with official structures.[18]

Three days later the meeting closed with a detailed list of goals. Without access to the debates, it is difficult to produce a full account of the negotiations that took place during the session. For the most part, however, the final demands dropped their emphasis on economic and social reform, focusing instead on cultural and artistic activities. These included the publication and circulation of anthologies in prose and verse by authors belonging to "our ethnic Cuban class," as well as of collections of popular music. They sought the establishment of a multiracial acting school that would promote "art informed by the national traditions and customs of all the groups that contribute to Cuba's greatness" and the organization of more congresses. Finally, with a broad and suggestive sweep, they called for "all the activities through which Cuba's personality may be enriched in all aspects of collective life, towards the conservation and development of liberty, the fostering of progress and of Cuba's national conscience."[19] The leaders had danced around the question of what kind of an institution they wanted to create. They called themselves a "social movement," but as is often the case with self-described social movements, it was a self-conception that depended in part on recognition by the state even as it fought for autonomy. In addition, the extent to which they were prepared to expend political capital with proposals aimed at lower-income sectors had evidently been a source of contention. In the end they had retreated from the most risky demands.

These developments had taken place in the months leading up to the lavish tribute to Machado. By that time it seemed neither surprising nor incongruous for sociedades to be thanking him. The process had achieved more than increasing black and mulatto support for Machado's regime. The dynamic of official invocation on the one hand, and mobilization and self-representation on the other, *constituted* "blacks" as a political unit in a way that had never before happened in the republic. Even so, it was a fragile unit, with wary relationships with both the state and nonelite sectors.

Machado had abetted the politicization of blackness by framing his appeals for support in terms of race rather than class as a way of appeasing capitalists worried about increasingly vocal and militant labor movements. The tribute to Machado suggests that associations formed under recreational auspices had the capacity to mobilize for political purposes (it also suggests that the boundaries between the two were blurring). Yet the creation of a political identity required more than official sanction at a time when race-based mobilization could still be imagined as problematic. The Partido Independiente de Color (PIC) had failed for many reasons: because the "myth of racial democracy" left no room for a legitimate "black" voice, because its appeal was too narrow, because its tactics were distasteful to many Cubans regardless of racial identity, and because the violence of repression itself etched a frightening blame on its target. Given this legacy, the journey from a tentative post-1912 sense of collective identity to unapologetic avowals of racial unity was never a foregone conclusion. For many Cubans of color, the leap from "there are no blacks or whites here, only Cubans" to an affirmation of "our ethnic Cuban class" required reflection and deliberation. Intellectuals of color took advantage of newly opened political space to think explicitly about the politics of blackness.

He May Complain, but Urbanely

In 1928 an eloquent voice gave sustained public life to the question of the political and social identity of Cuban blacks. Gustavo Urrutia launched his career in Havana's prominent newspaper *Diario de la Marina* as the creator of the column "Ideales de una raza" with a utopian vision: "An ideal, based on my understanding, is the abstract limit of moral, civic or aesthetic perfection towards which we ought to strive, even if we can never reach, because by coming closer every day we contribute to the general progress and happiness of all."[20] From then until 1959, Urrutia used his space in the *Diario de la Marina* to shape an emerging sense of the raza de color as a social entity. The column fueled, from the perspective of an intellectual claiming to speak for blacks, a shift from a race-blind society to one composed of distinct races. From the beginning, Urrutia eschewed the language of a single "Cuban race," preferring instead to speak of Cuba as composed of two races. At the same time, his notion of citizenship extended beyond formal political rights to a concept that stressed greater participation in social and economic spheres as well as demanding a crucial if difficult-to-define sense of respect from fellow citizens.

Urrutia had in the course of his life crossed invisible and unofficial color lines in Cuba. The only student of color in Havana's Institute of Commerce, he had graduated at the top of his class and found employment in Jorge Fortún's accounting firm, where he was quickly promoted to head accountant. Soon after that he became the first Cuban of color to serve as the representative of a large department store, a position that included making sales calls to the homes of wealthy Cubans. In his next job he occupied a prominent position as a government employee in the office of the Lottery, where he was the only trained accountant.[21]

At the age of thirty-two, Urrutia decided to change careers and enrolled in the University of Havana's School of Architecture. As a practicing architect he drew praise for his design of a church, the Banco de Libertad, and the Frontón Jai-Alai—all in downtown Havana. How or why Urrutia shifted from accounting to architecture and eventually to journalism and activism remains unclear. A biographical sketch written by Mercer Cook in 1943 for W. E. B. Du Bois's journal *Phylon*, one of the few published works on Urrutia, explains the move to activism as the result of a conversation between Urrutia and three friends: Miguel Angel Céspedes, Ramiro Cuesta, and Agapito Rodríguez. The conversation must have galvanized his sense of purpose, for, according to Cook, the next day Urrutia wrote to the *Diario de la Marina* requesting space for a new column that would address issues of race explicitly. He posed it as a project not of confrontation but of communication and exposition: "I come to ask hospitality for two or three articles per week. Our whites know but the two extremes in the Negro race: their domestics and their bootblacks, people who interest me as others do—and Juan Gualberto Gómez at the top. Between these two extremes, there is a class of Negroes, the real negro race, of whom the white Cuban is ignorant. I want to reveal to the white Cuban the soul and mentality of these folk. To tell him how the negro thinks and what he wants. To negroes also I have something to say."[22]

Given its reputation as one of Havana's more conservative publications, the *Diario de la Marina* was not an obvious home for such a column. However, the newspaper's extensive cultural section was directed by Marxist intellectual José Antonio Fernández de Castro, who in the 1920s had created a forum for many leftist poets and essayists. Most likely Fernández de Castro supported Urrutia's proposal and made space in his pages for the column.[23]

Urrutia's column, renamed "Armonías" in 1931, eventually expanded to a full-page feature that was published every Sunday. Urrutia used it to forge connections with other prominent Cubans of color, including Juan Gualberto Gómez and Nicolás Guillén, whose contributions he published as part of his feature. He also drew attention to black activists and organizations in the United States, writing about individuals like Booker T. Washington, W. E. B. Du Bois, Marian Anderson, William Pickens, and Paul Williams (another architect), as well as reporting on the campaigns in defense of the Scottsboro Boys and the activities of the NAACP and the Urban League. Evidence suggests that he claimed a wide readership. Many of his columns contained letters from his readers and his responses. "Armonías" was reproduced in *Adelante*, a black newspaper that made many efforts to reach a socioeconomically diverse population.[24]

The column and its politicizing intentions were recognized by Havana's white political and intellectual elite. During a visit to New York in 1930, Fernando Ortiz referred to Urrutia as a "race champion among Havana's Afro-Cubans."[25] This reputation survived the fall of Machado and propelled Urrutia to government posts in subsequent regimes. In 1934 he was appointed to the Council of State, where he advocated socialized medicine, the creation of a workers' party, and the elimination of racial discrimination in private hospitals. He also criticized election practices. Apparently discontented or frustrated, he resigned by the end of the year. In 1936 he was appointed director of culture for the city of Havana. Yet his place in politics remained somewhat ambiguous. Although he ran twice for office, he was never elected. Nor did he ever affiliate with a political party.[26]

His aims included serving as commentator and interpreter of the processes unfolding at that moment. The day after the tribute to Machado, Urrutia affirmed the emergence of a determined political unit that had finally overcome its reluctance to mobilize. "The raza de color, in accordance with its ethical and democratic principles, resists the need to act as a unified class, but in response to historical realities it has begun to organize and better itself, in order to contribute to the well-being of the republic in this new era." Indebted as he was to Machado, however, he insisted that much of the impetus must continue to come from the membership: "We applaud General Machado and praise his actions as a revolutionary leader, but we do not believe that our social revindication ought to depend solely on official actions." The raza de color would make itself even more visible, he predicted, with the organization of another conference, the establishment of a federation of all sociedades de color, the publication of a newspaper, and the organization of agricultural and industrial cooperatives.[27]

The question of visibility could not be separated from the problem of respect in everyday life. Thus he worried not just about numbers and representation in employee rosters, but also about how blacks were treated when they entered commercial establishments: "Blacks are denied the same treatment as whites . . . I refer to barbershops, most hotels, some movie theaters, rooming houses, etc."[28] But it was more than a matter of numbers. He directed his efforts at a certain kind of freedom: "Certainly the aim of the black race is not to dispense ribbons, stationery, or sundries from behind a counter, nor to conduct trams . . . but to be able to choose to do so."[29]

The problem of everyday life was at the heart of the matter because, Urrutia argued, racial discrimination did exist in Cuba. Furthermore, contrary to popular belief, it was evident not in official discourse and practices, where the effort to appear egalitarian prevailed, but rather in private interactions: "The majority believes that hypocrisy resides in the grand patriotic gestures and invocations of nationalist sentiment, and that deeply rooted feelings of fraternity lie in everyday relations, with their banalities and their intimacies. This is the great error that embitters the lives of many Cubans."[30] The problem grew not out of hatred but rather ignorance, especially with regard to the progress and achievements of "civilized blacks." His column was hence part of his proposed solution, in which he would expose the true beliefs and aspirations of blacks to white readers, revealing common ground rather than incommensurable values. "Our ideals, after all, are identical to those of all civilized peoples, therefore it is not the purpose of this column to discover them, since everyone knows what they are."[31]

Urrutia's cordial articulation of dissatisfaction reflected an underlying vision, expressed in many columns, of the most efficacious strategy to achieve his ends. The newspaper had granted him space on his terms in order for "a modest, average black man to sing out the pain of his race."[32] Yet he would do so with a modicum of courtesy: "He may complain, but urbanely."[33] His white readers had nothing to fear: "I will demonstrate through words and through deeds, that if whites lay aside their fears, blacks will not swarm in like savage hordes."[34] He bore no grudges, he insisted, even as he brought injustices to light. The voice he adopted must have been appealing to readers and acceptable to editors, who ran the column for thirty years. Its tone, at once oppositional and conciliatory, suggests the elaboration of an approach difficult to classify as either "resistance" or "integration."[35]

Inquietud Negrista: Mestizaje and the Politics of Race

Urrutia was one of a group of black intellectuals whose public discussions honed the notion of a black political identity. They engaged proliferating racial discourses. In the early republic, Cubans of color experienced arbitrary criminalization upheld increasingly by state and scientific institutions, confronted widespread discrimination in public spaces, and continued to suffer from economic disadvantages justified by claims of their racial inferiority. Not all racial discourses, however, presumed negative notions of blackness. Alongside Castellanos's and eugenicists' definition of mestizaje as the perpetuation of black degeneracy, some nationalist intellectuals had come to celebrate mestizaje as a paean to authentic Cuban identity.[36] In step with Ortiz's search for authentic cultural roots, musicians and writers had initiated Afrocubanismo, which sought to valorize the contributions of African cultural forms. Yet some black intellectuals approached the celebration of racial mixing and acknowledgment of "African roots" in national culture with caution. Maneuvering between excavations of an exoticized "folk" and a variety of views on mestizaje, they struggled to create a language of race they could abide by and use to promulgate social, economic, and political reform.

Through interrogations of the language of mestizaje these writers arrived at qualified validations of cultural and biological miscegenation. Entering the debate they tried to pry apart the aspects they deemed justly affirming of "blackness" and those they deemed inimical to the interests of racial equity, even as they formulated and argued about what precisely they meant by racial equity.

In the interest of addressing what they referred to as "the black problem" (el problema negro), they oscillated between ideals of race transcendence, binary views of racial divisions, and tempered recognition of cultural and biological mixture. Such navigations may imply inconsistent thinking, but it is important to consider other interpretations. At times these writers advocated a strategic deployment of the languages of race. They often deliberately chose the degree of emphasis to place on the issue of race according to circumstance. Just as often, however, because they could not control every situation or predict every outcome, they groped, without a clear plan, toward a usable language from within their parameters of political and intellectual possibility.

Both Nicolás Guillén and Urrutia (who was by the 1930s an established voice in discussions of race and politics) attacked the notion of mestizaje. Urrutia understood the advocacy of mestizaje to be just as dangerous as American Jim Crowism, even if it led to a different outcome:

> In the United States the white race strives to isolate the Negroes and segregate them in every possible way. The Anglo-American considers his Negrophobia as a natural and legitimate sentiment,

and he gives expression to it frankly. For the Spanish Cubans it is a shameful sentiment which they will not on any account confess to the Negroes. They try to dissolve the black race in a torrent of Aryan blood, and aim at their extinction in every possible indirect way. The ultimate aim in both cases is to exterminate the Negroes.[37]

For Guillén the answer was not to reject mestizaje but to rewrite it by bringing to light its tragic origins. Most literary critics and historians regard Nicolás Guillén as the most renowned and eloquent proponent of mestizaje as the source of *cubanidad*. They look both to his explicit statements about Cuba's African heritage and its profound strengthening of history and culture, as well as to those that take into account both Spanishness and Africanness in the formation of a syncretic national culture.[38] For Antonio Benítez-Rojo, for instance, Guillén articulated and envisioned "a mestizo reality understood as unity."[39]

But Guillén's life and work extended beyond the poetic invention and rendition of racial harmonies. He was born into a politicized milieu and cultivated and maintained his connections to national and international radicalisms in different ways throughout his life. His father (also named Nicolás Guillén) had been a senator under José Miguel Gómez and participated in the uprising of 1917, during which he was killed. Through his father's friendship with Lino D'Ou, Guillén had formed a relationship with the outspoken black politician and come to admire him a great deal. As a young law student at the University of Havana, Guillén had fallen in with a group of student radicals led by Julio Antonio Mella. The admiring Mella published Guillén's first poem in his literary and political journal, *Alma Mater*. During the early stage of Machado's regime, Guillén's Liberal Party connections (again, through his father) had led to an appointment in the Secretaría de Gobernación (Ministry of Interior). By 1937 he had traveled to Spain to join the fight against fascism.[40]

His career as a poet at times intersected with and at other times veered away from his political life as a journalist. During the struggles against Machado he remained somewhat distant from the active opposition, but it was at this time that he published his most overtly "black" poetry. In 1935 he became the editor of Cuba's first communist newspaper. In 1936, during a period when evading censorship was difficult, he began another journal, *Mediodía*. Self-described as a literary magazine, *Mediodía* also published essays on domestic and international politics. His words in 1937 suggest bifurcated but not opposing intentions: "A poet may make revolution, but at the same time he *must* make poetry, that is, create art."[41]

In many essays and some poems, Guillén articulated a more complex acknowledgment of the limitations as well as the strengths of the "mestizo reality." The notion of mestizaje as racial harmony needed qualification. In 1929, for instance, he declared that "the race of color in Cuba still has problems and still needs to struggle a great deal in order to resolve them."[42] He injected into racial mixture the violence at its source. Riddled with pain and humiliation, mestizaje had not been born of harmonious coexistence but of the power struggles that permeated social relations. Thus Cuban men had repeated their fathers' habits, seeking ambivalent lovers and populating the island with a mixed race, initially outcast: "And often, following the example of their fathers, once they became men they sought amongst the black women a lover both ardent and resigned, out of whose womb would emerge, in time, the seeds of the island's future—and present—mestizaje."[43] The final stanza of the poem entitled "Mulata" from *Motivos de Son* (1930) rejects mestizaje in favor of a more authentic blackness:

Si tú supiera, mulata
la verdá;
que yo con mi negra tengo
Y no te quiero pa na!

If you knew, mulatta
The reality
That with my black woman I have so much
And you are nothing to me

Black intellectuals also engaged ethnographic Afrocubanismo and argued for distinctions between trivializing and meaningful versions. Writing for his regular Cuban audiences in 1932, Urrutia had denounced anthropological theory and pointed to the potentially damaging consequences of Afrocubanismo: "The anthropological pronouncements of whites regularly devalue the black race. . . . From that we derive the current subordination of all activities to the racial imperative: black literature, black history, black religiosity, black heroism, in all of which there is just as much reactionary sentiment as an authentic desire for integration. If whites are moved by racialism, blacks have responded accordingly."[44] Guillén also looked askance at the legacy of anthropology: "Possibly, the method came with the fashion . . . the scientific fascination awakened by the work of Frobenius and other ethnographers in the African jungle immediately generated a literary fad. Opportunistic tourism that paid no attention to human tragedy. Excursions to photograph palm trees, monkeys, drums, naked blacks."[45]

Both Guillén and Urrutia found ways to salvage what they thought indispensable about the current fashion of "blackness." Urrutia apparently felt more at ease with "black religiosity" if he enjoyed some control over others' access to it. With visitors present he became a proud presenter of African-derived traditions, including himself as part of that world. In *The Crime of Cuba*, Carleton Beals remembers Urrutia's role in introducing him to the rituals and legends of the Gangá, whose "picturesque acquaintance he made only as a result of Urrutia's intervention."[46] For Guillén the answer was to derive struggle from banality: "For some, the answer is *fashion*, because they don't understand the profound meaning of the appearance of dark-skinned men on the universal scene; for others, it is the means, the means of the struggle between oppressors and oppressed."[47]

Drawing from but also criticizing these concepts, they crafted black political identities based on notions of equality and honor, and in dialogue with the mixed blessings of tradition and cultural survival. But those were fragile constructs, their tensions apparent. Guillén's oscillation between the poetry of African rhythms and the harshness of racial realities and Urrutia's apprehensions about the dangers of "racialism" even as he became an outspoken voice of la raza de color reflect ongoing struggles over the meanings of blackness.

Yet their responses to different situations suggest an ability to deploy meanings of race strategically. Guillén's faith that "language is very important in the struggle between classes" may have informed the deliberate deployment of particular discourses in particular circumstances.[48] If categories were ambiguous and unsettled, language might prove a powerful instrument. Thus, at times they advocated a deliberate and politicized sharpening of categories. Federico Ibarzábal, the poet, novelist, and journalist, acknowledged that miscegenation's production of so many different kinds of people in Cuba posed "a real problem for even the most experienced ethnographer." But if for some whites mestizaje was a "fantasy of absorption," then it ought to be challenged, because "being present at their own extermination has never been an ambition of the races." He maintained that, despite demographic truths, Cuban blacks ought to resist claims of "absorption" and insist on essential distinctions.[49]

Urrutia concretized this aim. When school officials tried to register his granddaughter as white, he objected. The contingency of categories, he argued, meant that in certain situations Cubans of color could and ought to choose the race to which they belonged. It was important, given the betrayal of Martí's vision, that blacks not abandon their race if given the option. They had spent far too much time internalizing the stigma of color. "The black man saw himself as ugly and humiliated; he sought to advance his people by mixing his blood with that of whites. He began to hate the dark color that had subordinated him and to escape his race as if he were escaping an inferno."[50] Echoing eugenicists' rejection of mestizaje but with very different reasons, he asserted that if blacks accepted the notion that mestizaje implied "progress" or "betterment" they would be ceding to white claims of racial superiority. This would be desertion: "Each desertion, each humiliation of the black man, deviates whites from the doctrine of the *mambís*; from the salutary goal of uniting humanity with dignity and justice."[51]

The languages and strategies of blackness developed in response to transnational as well as domestic concerns. In the 1920s and 1930s the intersection of labor activism, anti-imperialism, and domestic politics had given rise to various forms of black radicalism in the United States and the Caribbean. Marcus Garvey's United Negro Improvement Association, which linked Christianity, Pan-Africanism, and labor activism, had established a wide network of organizations throughout the region, including in Cuba, Trinidad, the United States, and Jamaica. Although his particular brand of radicalism enjoyed differential success in each of these places, his newspaper *Negro World* and peripatetic self-promotion promulgated the use of blackness and African ancestry as political tools. In Haiti, the U.S. occupation (1915–34) and its promotion of a mulatto elite fed *indigénisme*, articulated by Jean Price-Mars's *Ainsi Parla L'Oncle* (*So Spoke the Uncle*) (1928), which looked to the black peasantry as a source of authentic, autochthonous national values. In the complex terrain of Haitian racial politics, *noirisme*, the political myth of anticolonial revolution, overlapped with the cultural premises of *indigénisme*, drawing new attention to blackness and its cultural parameters. This period in Haitian cultural history has been cited as the precursor to *négritude*, the Francophone Caribbean literary movement that emerged in the 1940s.[52]

Marxism and communism became intertwined with black radicalism in a variety of political and cultural movements. Internationally, this period witnessed a surge in mutual interest between people of African descent and Marxists, ranging from the Parisian publication of the anticolo-nial *Légitime Défense* by Martinican students in 1932, to C. L. R. James's brilliant excursion into the Haitian Revolution, to African Americans' and Afro-Caribbeans' close monitoring of wars in Ethiopia and Spain.[53] The 1935 Italian invasion of Ethiopia became a rallying cry for the com-bined battle against fascism and defense of Africa. As Robin Kelley has shown, this struggle extended to the Spanish Civil War.[54] In Cuba as well, men who had allied themselves with communism and the struggle for racial equity also became involved in the war in Spain. Among them were Nicolás Guillén and Juan Marinello.

Cuban intellectuals drew from these currents of knowledge and activ-ism. They also looked to expressions of black identity emanating from the United States, drawing inspiration from the writings of Langston Hughes, the collecting and recording ambitions of Arturo Schomburg, and the NAACP's organizing capacities. Guillén and Hughes, both mem-bers of Communist Parties, initiated a noted friendship.[55] Often the thrust of the activism centered on intellectual exchanges and publica-tion of those exchanges. While Urrutia wrote often about the visits and projects of North American activists, radical journalist Carleton Beals praised Urrutia, Guillén, and their circle for their work.[56] After a trip to Cuba in 1932, Schomburg published an article describing his "quest for negro books."[57] Often they aspired to publicizing a comparative view of race relations. In 1938 Schomburg wrote to Hughes about the importance of translating Guillén's work. Different versions of politicized blackness thus nourished Cuban efforts to conjure up a collective consciousness.

The Cuban Communist Party (PCC) drew from both local and inter-national issues in an effort to increase its membership. The party's cam-paigns in defense of the Scottsboro Boys extended to Cuba, where it orga-nized rallies and protests at the U.S. embassy. The PCC was at the forefront of protests against the Ku Klux Klan, which had organized a Cuban chap-ter in 1928 and then again in 1932.[58] It drew the attention of its members to events in Latin America, denouncing the role of "yanqui imperialism" in Bolivia, Paraguay, Peru, and Colombia and calling for solidarity with "workers, peasants, Indians, and students."[59] Further research is neces-sary to understand the extent and nature of these appeals. But it is clear that the PCC attempted to incorporate Cubans into a transnational net-work in solidarity with "oppressed nationalities" that included not only the United States, but also Latin America, Europe, and Africa.

By the late 1920s labor organizers had begun to appeal to workers in racialized terms. The Confederación Nacional Obrera de Cuba (CNOC) and the PCC, both founded in 1925, had initially denied racial and national divisions in the interest of "proletarian internationalism." They shifted their strategy, however, after the Comintern's Sixth Congress in 1928, which both expressed its support for the Stalinist theory of oppressed nationalities and called on Communist Parties to strengthen interethnic solidarities. As in the United States, the PCC could make racialized appeals based on the notion that people of African descent were oppressed nationalities within a system of U.S. imperialism.[60] As early as 1929 the CNOC called for the inclusion of all black workers in the professions. In 1932 the PCC's electoral platform demanded the elimination of racial discrimination in economic, political, and social spheres, as well as the creation of a multiracial alliance against discrimination, the rescinding of the Morúa law, and "total equality." That year the PCC also initiated the short-lived proposal for a "Franja Negra" or zone of black self-determination in Oriente, which was dropped by the end of 1934.[61]

Recent research has documented increasing numbers of Cubans of color in the ranks and leadership of the PCC and CNOC. During the sugar mill occupations of 1933, field workers—often multiracial groups that included Cubans of color and West Indian immigrants—initiated the mobilization. The Communist leadership came to include men like Blas Roca Calderío, a shoemaker from Manzanillo, who was general secretary of the party after 1934, and Antolín Dickinson Abreu, a sugar worker who was editor of the National Sugar Workers' Union newspaper, *El obrero azucarero*. In the mid-1930s Sandalio Junco became the PCC's first Negro affairs specialist and Lazaro Peña led the CNOC.

Significantly, however, the PCC was not universally successful in organizing workers of African descent, nor did it unquestioningly support racial mobilization. The party's protests against the nationalist 50 percent law, which proposed to eliminate scores of foreign workers from the ranks of Cuba's employed, diminished support among Cubans of color, who perceived foreign workers as threats to their jobs. By December 1933, for instance, participants at the Fourth National Workers Congress of Labor Unity lamented the lack of black mobilization and called for renewed efforts to appeal to black workers. The PCC expelled leaders, such as Sandalio Junco, for Trotskyist tendencies and denounced the Club Atenas and Unión Fraternal as reformist and some of their members as "traitors." Among those were many who had benefited during Machado's regime, like Miguel Angel Céspedes, Américo Portuondo, and Aquilino

Lombard.[62] In the complex politics of the early 1930s, the PCC and CNOC competed with Machado and nationalists for the loyalty of Cubans of color. In doing so they both mobilized and exacerbated the divisions among them.

In such a charged climate, their use of language was important. All of the PCC documentation referred explicitly to "blacks" and "black masses," emphasizing a biracial system. Perhaps relying on North American categories, perhaps also drawing from emerging emphases on "blackness" in Cuba itself, this language fortified black political identities and challenged race-transcendent ideals. Although it may have proved jarring to some Cubans who held to those ideals, this use of "blackness" also served as a source of racialized political identities, adding to those that had emerged during the previous decade.

Revolution, Violence, Regeneration

Having revitalized a tradition of associational life and a faith in autonomous institutions, Cubans of color met Machado's efforts to mobilize a racialized political identity with agendas of their own making. If somewhat ambivalent about their relationship to the state, they nonetheless took advantage of the opening to advance their goals. As part of the process, and in dialogue with intensified black activism throughout the Atlantic region, the notion of blackness and an implied notion of citizenship came to be defined against mestizaje, imbued with the idea of dignity and respect and, to a certain extent, imagined across class boundaries. However, this proceeded in a halting, fragmented manner, as articulations of political identity and citizenship were rife with tensions, as well as the source of disagreement among Cubans of color. A more serious problem was rising antiblack hostility. If politics had been crucial to the formation of these identities, then subsequent events would test their resilience.

Many historians have written of Machado's ouster in the "revolution of 1933." By 1930 the expectations raised by Machado for regeneration and reform in material and political life were crushed, both by dire economic circumstances and the president's own machinations to remain in office. In 1928 Machado had requested and obtained a constitutional reform ensuring his reelection. Once a group of prominent lawyers declared this move illegal, the perception that Machado had betrayed the republic grew, and opposition to his regime became increasingly strident and violent. The depression left its mark on Cuba—its effects on manufacturers and industrialists as well as agricultural workers and producers were devastating. As government revenues fell, scores of public servants found themselves out of work. By 1933 many and varied opposition groups, including students, labor, the military, and intellectuals, converged on whatever scraps of legitimacy were left of Machado's rule and decimated them.[63]

In the years leading up to and immediately following the Machadato, violence became the mode of conducting politics. All sides relied on it: both Machadistas and anti-Machadistas engaged in bombing, kidnapping, and assassination to terrorize opponents and wrest concessions. Mass protests often turned deadly when government forces intervened, and those deaths in turn spurred retaliatory measures. As both supporters and opponents of Machado's regime, Cubans of color became enmeshed, like all other Cubans, in these practices. In one of many examples, Havana police chief Estanislao Mansip, a Machado supporter who was said to "control the Negro Liberal vote in Marianao" and "had been energetic in running down terrorists" was targeted and wounded by a bomb in the fall of 1932.[64]

Alongside evidence of multiracial violent acts, some evidence suggests that violence itself became racialized. Part of the anti-Machadista strategy was to "blacken" and therefore discredit Machadista forces. By the same token, observers commented on the "negro masses" threatening order in unstable times. In the eyes of one U.S. observer, the "race question" had terrified white women, who worried about "insults and attacks by Negroes," especially in Camagüey and Oriente, where "agitation is growing steadily and it is feared may bring on a repetition of the Negro rising of 1912."[65] Participants on all sides of the unfolding struggle were able to draw on the gendered, racialized stereotype of the dangerous black man as they vied for power.

In many cases it was difficult to prove who had perpetrated the disturbances. In December 1933, for instance, bombs exploded in a number of buildings that housed sociedades de color, including the Club Atenas, Unión Fraternal, Jovenes del Vals, Minerva in Cienfuegos, and Bella Unión in Santa Clara. Although they may have been targeted by ABC, an anti-Machado organization that allegedly initiated a number of racist campaigns across the island, these sociedades had also been criticized by the Communist Party for their "traitorous bourgeois" tendencies the previous year.[66] To be sure, many who had benefited during Machado's regime, such as Aquilino Lombard, Américo Portuondo, and Generoso Campos Marquetti, were arrested by the army or fled the country. But other Cubans of color profited from the revolutionary upheaval, including those who joined Batista's army, which came to include a higher percentage of men of African descent.[67]

In the wake of violence and rapid political change, activists used opportunities to reform faltering sociedades de color and continue their pursuit of equality. One of the galvanizing incidents was the so-called race riot of January 1934 in Trinidad, actually a series of incidents in which homes and businesses of blacks and mulattoes were sacked and Rafael Soler y Santana, a white youth, and Félix Justo Proveyer, a cousin of José Maria Proveyer, editor of the Afro-Cuban publication *Alma Joven*, were killed.[68] Many Cubans responded quickly and angrily to the violence in Trinidad, generating a debate about the nature of the problem. Writers like Urrutia, Juan Marinello, and Jesús Plasencia countered hollow claims about racial harmony with descriptions of the recent increase in antiblack violence. They blamed several factors: the socioeconomic inequality suffered by most blacks, the influence of fascist racial violence, and persistent "white chauvinism" ("the theory that discriminates against blacks, reducing them to a position of inferiority under the pretext that they constitute a backward race guided by savage instincts"). One explanation relied on Max Nordau's theory that the bourgeoisie "is no more than a series of lies, of conformity, of pathetic proportions, which shrinks infinitely in contrast to the civilization of other eras."[69] In any event, these incidents revealed the disturbing, unintended consequence of a decade of black social and political mobilization, provoking a new round of debates among Cubans of color about how best to proceed.

The Comité por los Derechos del Negro (Committee for Black Rights) was formed in an effort to clarify conflicting accounts and rumors that had been circulating in the aftermath of the events in Trinidad. Among the participants were writer Juan Marinello; Federico de la Cuesta, a lawyer and veteran of the wars for Independence representing the Unión Fraternal; Manuel Alonso, a tobacco worker; and Juan Martínez, a representative of the Club Atenas. More than an investigative committee, it resolved to draw attention to this and similar incidents. In addition, its membership reflected recent shifts in the character of the Club Atenas and Unión Fraternal. In the face of criticism by their younger members, these associations had shed some of their elitism and aloofness and regained a prominent voice in reconfigured racial politics. This cross-racial committee, which comprised activists with a range of political affiliations, would provide the impetus for renewed black mobilization in the populist context of the late 1930s.[70]

As Ambrosio Fornet has observed, the need to explain what was essential about the vast, changing, and contradictory visage of society during the Machadato and its aftermath animated intense public discussion.[71] As the revolution of 1933 gave way to the consolidation of Fulgencio Batista's leadership, contentious voices found themselves fully engaged, if not fully impressed, with Batista's own vision of the role of the state in social, political, and economic life. In this, black intellectuals and activists did not stand apart from other Cubans.

> Representation, taken generally, means the
> making present *in some sense* of something which
> is nevertheless *not* present literally or in fact.
> HANNAH PITKIN
> *The Concept of Representation* (1967)

7

From Comparsas
to Constitutions

On January 30, 1937, Mayor Antonio Beruff Mendieta of Havana asked the Sociedad de Estudios Afrocubanos whether it was advisable, as part of the upcoming Fiestas de Carnaval, to allow the performance of comparsas. Hoping to overturn the prohibition since 1913, the Commission of Tourism had recommended the inclusion of comparsas in the fiestas with the expectation that tourists would flock to the display of traditional culture. The mayor agreed that the reauthorization of the public processions would attract tourists. He also hoped that they might reacquaint the city's own residents with their rich history and folklore. But critics of this plan had warned him that comparsas would incite "racial conflicts and public disturbances." Was there any truth to this, and could the Sociedad please provide some expert advice? Fernando Ortiz,

A comparsa in Havana, 1930s. (Courtesy of Cuban Heritage Collection, University of Miami Libraries, Coral Gables, Florida)

then president of the society, sent Beruff Mendieta an extensive reply in which he urged that comparsas be allowed.[1]

This seems to have allayed the mayor's fears, for the comparsas took place as scheduled. Soon afterward historian and Sociedad member Emilio Roig de Leuchsenring contributed a description of the brilliant, surreal scene. Nine different comparsa companies had paraded through the streets, each with a different theme: Los Mambises, Los Compone-dores, Los Colombianos modernos, Los Marqueses, Los Guaracheros, Las Bolleras, Los Modernistas, El Barracón, and Los Guajiros. The groups had between fifty and one hundred performers each, many of them carrying musical instruments or banners, the others executing the choreography in all of its syncopated complexity. Whereas some of the groups had retained traditional themes, others followed a more ironic path. In what represented to Leuchsenring a wry commentary on the entire proceedings, the men in Los Modernistas paraded as Indians, carrying bows and arrows, while the women wore Parisian haute-couture fashions. An observer or participant might well have agreed with Ortiz's assessment of the pageant's unifying potential: "It is precisely these collective amusements that integrate the people, through the most emotional and intimate aspects of culture."[2]

But a look just beyond the street-level proscenium reveals that the comparsas provoked a heated controversy. The performance set off an extensive debate in *Adelante*, Havana's new black monthly newspaper dedicated to promoting racial equality. If the Sociedad de Estudios Afrocubanos and the mayor believed that the comparsas had afforded Havana's visitors and residents lively and even instructive entertainment, *Adelante*'s commentators viewed them with varying degrees of hostility, bickering over the quality and degree of exploitation in evidence. For many, these performances only signaled blacks' and mulattoes' continued marginalization as less-than-equal citizens. This dispute over the politics of representation raised familiar questions, still unresolved: How should traditional cultural practices fit into a nationalist vision premised on modernity? To what extent did paternalistic state-sponsored displays of those practices detract from the realities of persistent social and economic inequality? Who—among social scientists, politicians, or political activists, white or of color—ought to control the representation of cultures? (None of the participants in the debate devoted much attention to the perspectives of artists or musicians.)

At issue was the actual experience of the law as opposed to the ideal of equality as it had been granted in article 11 of the 1901 constitution. A notion of citizenship defined as "a set of mutual contested claims between agents of states and members of socially constructed categories" is useful here.[3] Combined with T. H. Marshall's concept of "social worth" as crucial, beyond the recognition of formal equality, to the experience of equality, the idea of citizenship as a set of mutually contested claims provides a framework for understanding the link between comparsas and citizenship. Critics of the comparsas argued that this particular use of African traditions demonstrated that though formal equality was recognized, social worth was experienced tenuously. Social inequality, these critics argued, was persistently underscored and in some ways reproduced by these renditions of African traditions as stereotyped spectacles. As such, they were an obstacle to the meaningful social equality that ought to accompany citizenship.[4] Citizenship, in the minds of those in pursuit of racial equality, became linked to representation in its dual sense: that which referred to portrayals or depictions of a particular group as well as the meaningful presence of that group in the structures of the state. This late 1930s struggle over the meaning of citizenship is the subject of this chapter.

A new constitution, written and adopted in 1940, included an article declaring illegal and punishable all discrimination based on race, color, sex, and religion. My contention is that black political activists and intellectuals took advantage of an unusually consensual episode to bring, more explicitly than ever before, the issue of discrimination to the law-making agenda. The combined outcome of years of mobilization, both through autonomous institutions and through intensified, if uneven, engagement with the state, had changed the terms of the struggle. No longer on the defensive about claiming "blackness," intellectual critiques of the politics of culture—in this case, tourist versions of folklore—did not need to rest on "high culture" as a common referent. With regard to constitutional debates, activists came to demand more of the state than mere recognition of equality. The pursuit of "civil citizenship" with its emphasis on autonomy had slowly fallen away as autonomy became less and less tenable, and incursions into public arenas had all too often animated hostility. They thus engaged a rapidly changing political context with ambivalent memories of failed strategies and a sharpened sense of the contingency of their status. Although mobilized Cubans of color were not a uniform or homogeneous entity, they issued a clear demand with regard to the constitution. Further research will undoubtedly expose more fault lines and tensions within the raza de color. For the moment, however, I will focus on the conditions that allowed their powerful and significant presence in the constitutional convention of 1940. The debates over the article in the constitutional assembly demonstrate that there was broad agreement (at least in public) about the desired ends. But there was also profound uncertainty about the means required to achieve those ends. The ultimate adoption of the constitutional ban on discrimination amounted to an uneasy victory that created rich grounds for subsequent contention.

Batista: Slippery Populist

The reconsideration of citizenship by Cubans of color took place in a national context of reconfigured roles for state and society. In the aftermath of the Machadato in 1933, Fulgencio Batista had accumulated power as the head of the politically dominant military forces. With military backing he had contrived an uneasy peace after years of depression-induced hardship and violent terrorism perpetrated by both the government and its opposition. In 1934 the Mendieta government, under Batista's vigilance, had negotiated the Jones-Costigan law to placate sugar interests as it raised sugar prices and guaranteed U.S. markets for Cuban sugar. When a wave of strikes demanding agrarian reform and the end of military rule swept the island in 1935, Batista suspended civil rights, jailing hundreds of opposition leaders and dissolving all labor unions. The momentary stability gave Batista some room to maneuver, which he used to shore up his legitimacy beyond the military and sugar interests.[5] A growing consensus in support of increased state intervention in economic and social arenas consolidated Batista's authority. Both conservatives and progressives began to look toward an expanded state: for the left it seemed to promise economic well-being, and for the right it would serve to anchor "stability" with regard to labor unrest and access to foreign markets.[6] After 1936 this allowed Batista to create initiatives that, as Robert Whitney has observed, were cast as appeals to "*el pueblo.*" Batista would then fashion himself as a populist with gestures and spectacles appealing to the people. But ultimately he ought to be considered, as Alan Knight has suggested, a "slippery populist" due to his ability to smoothly maneuver among bitterly opposed interests.[7]

The sweeping social and economic measures set out in his Three-Year Plan, or Plan Trienal (1937), show the extent to which Batista aimed to create a more interventionist state. Large estates would be abolished and a new national banking system, health insurance, and literacy programs would be introduced. Moreover, the sugar industry would be reorganized into a profit-sharing enterprise for producers and laborers, with the state acting as mediator between the two. Although the level of intervention and the direction of redistribution gave rise to dissatisfaction within the Cuban Association of Sugar Manufacturers, it did not dissuade the membership from subscribing to the general principle that an expanded state would serve it in the long run, providing stability and efficient economic structures.[8]

Efforts to generate a dependable source of revenue included the revival of tourism after a lull induced by the depression and fears of political violence. To placate critics of the industry's corrupting and immoral influence, government officials promoted cultural tourism. They began to emphasize historical sites, museums, folkloric practices, and natural beauty over the casinos, cabarets, and horse races that had dominated tourism in Machado's era. Comparsas formed part of this scheme to exhibit national cultures as wholesomely as possible.[9]

Batista's proposal to draft a new version of the constitution provided another way to garner support. Machado's 1928 unilateral constitutional reform and subsequent dictatorship had stripped the existing constitution of any legitimacy as the blueprint of Cuban democracy. In the transitional years after the fall of Machado, many sectors had pressured for a new constitution. Batista, realizing that heeding this call would nurture the legitimacy he sought, had by 1938 given top priority to producing that document. In the interest of giving life to the unfinished business of the revolution of 1933, he swept aside his own Plan Trienal and ceded to the calls for a new Cuban "Magna Carta."[10] In a flash of self-abnegating rhetoric he cast himself as both in control of and responsive to the people. As a contemporary observer described it, "in a dramatic and unexpected statement, the strongman of the island told the people that he was sacrificing his plans for social and economic reconstruction of the Republic because of the clamor for a constitutional assembly."[11]

This growing faith in the role of government as mediator of social conflict mirrored developments abroad. In Latin America, postdepression states expanded in an effort to rescue shattered economies and to harness discontent. Governments across the political spectrum partook of this strategy. One of the legacies of Mexico's left-leaning revolution was an expanded state, as was Getúlio Vargas's Estado Novo, the ideological content of which is still debated by historians. In the Dominican Republic, Rafael Trujillo had found ways to consolidate his dictatorship by ensuring that the state was far more present in everyday life than ever before. Likewise, in the United States the New Deal ushered in an era of unprecedented state growth.[12]

Whether or not Franklin Roosevelt's New Deal served as a model for Cubans looking to ease economic and political tensions that had intensified during the depression, U.S. foreign policy directly affected the landscape of Cuban politics. The United States's retreat from intervention gave Batista more freedom and greater leverage in domestic politics. After an initial period of violence and repression, he began to cultivate much-weakened labor and leftist movements, allowing him to expand his popular base after 1937. Batista's negotiations with leftist groups, especially the Cuban Communist Party (PCC), would become unimaginable in later years.[13] As the concerns (and the membership) of black associations and the PCC overlapped during this period, it proved a particularly auspicious time to mobilize around issues of socioeconomic and racial equality.

Dead Letters, Live Letters

After 1935 the state's failed egalitarian promise became the focal point of activists' calls to action. Offering his grim assessment of current affairs, black activist Salvador García Agüero asserted that "there exists, undeniably, a widespread neglect of blacks in all arenas of national life, perpetuated at given intervals by those who keep prejudice alive. This has rendered equality before the law and in the Constitution a dead letter."[14] The notion of "dead letters," a ubiquitous trope in the writings of black intellectuals, indicated a faltering faith in the constitution's ability to implement the republic's egalitarian ideals. Recent history, they argued, had proven that if the republic's founding words — *con todos y para todos* (with all and for all) — had exuded moral power in earlier years, the thorns of prejudice had punctured their core and drained the life out of them.

Working as they were in a period of considerable strides toward inclusion and mobilization as well as recurrent episodes of discrimination and antiblack violence, activists took advantage of the public voice they had acquired to press for new measures in pursuit of equality. If Cubans had not done enough to integrate the commitment to equality with the practices of everyday life and with the agendas of institutions, it would be up to leaders such as García Agüero to marshal available resources and accrue the moral and political force to revive, or reincarnate, those letters.

Adelante, founded in 1935 with national and often radical aspirations, grew out of this conviction. In its monthly publication, chroniclers of the Havana-based association looked back to the antiblack violence that followed Machado's fall as a turning point that had animated their oppositional stance. Ernesto Pinto Interián, one of *Adelante*'s contributors, blamed the intensified overt racism on an uncharacteristically inappropriate remark made by one of Cuba's eminent intellectuals. When a dying Enrique José Varona had said that "the race of blacks has been indifferent to the sufferings of our Republic during the bloody struggle to topple Machado's tyranny," he had unleashed, according to Pinto Interián, "a systematic and unjust persecution against the black race."[15] As a result, he argued, the few blacks with civil appointments had been ousted in the chaos that ensued after Machado's fall. Pinto Interián saw in the betrayals of blacks by white political patrons who reneged on promises of protection the stuff of which the "tragedy of blacks in their political phase" was made.[16] Already mobilized groups would have to demonstrate greater singularity of purpose: "As black societies began to mobilize, it became necessary to leave behind uncooperative individuals, so that we could create a more unified collective and work to determine our own future." Later, with growing institutional aspirations, he asserted, "We agreed, in concord with the Sociedad Santo Domingo . . . to the proposition of initiating the preparations to organize a convention of black societies, in order to articulate and record the feelings, hopes, and ambitions of our ethnic conglomerate."[17]

The association's aims signaled the convergence of a number of approaches to the mobilization of black political identities. Pursuing multiple strategies, it advocated the invigoration of autonomous institutions even as it sought to reform state structures. *Adelante*'s contributors argued that eliminating or attenuating economic disparities ought to be a principal focus of those concerned with racial inequality. Indeed, many contributors, such as Salvador García Agüero, Juan Marinello, and Romulo Lachatañeré, were also active in socialist and communist organizations. But the leadership also drew attention to discrimination in public sectors such as education and private employment, sustaining strategies that had been the purview of Juan Gualberto Gómez, Rafael Serra y Montalvo, Gustavo Urrutia, and others who had suffered less from economic disadvantage than from social humiliation. Although they articulated an array of positions as to the precise origins of the problem, they were more certain of what was immediately required: "We must work intensely, until we achieve the kind of understanding and cohesion necessary to achieve the status we deserve and the rights that have been eternally denied us . . . GREATER UNITY FOR ALL."[18]

The directors of Adelante strove not only to galvanize a broadly based black political identity but also to encourage higher degrees of contention and dissent. They supported and reported on large gatherings such as the Convención de Sociedades Negras (Convention of Black Societies) in Santiago in 1936. They also tried to influence the everyday practices and beliefs of blacks throughout Cuba, advocating the formation of local groups called "friends of Adelante." These clubs were intended to promote education and exercise vigilance over local discriminatory practices by bringing them to the attention of local authorities. Adelante kept track of the many clubs that sprang up, creating a network of information about like-minded activists all over the country.[19] Blacks were also asked to exercise their strength as consumers by choosing establishments that advertised in *Adelante*.

Through commemorations of struggles for equality in various regions of the country, the editors created a sense of shared purpose. Blacks in Havana, they showed, were just as prone to rebuff or humiliation as those in Santiago.[20] Articles transported the minds of readers not only across Cuba but from Cuba to the United States as well. A regular column featured articles on North American activists, such as W. E. B. Du Bois and Paul Robeson, as well as contributions by noted writers like Langston Hughes. Essays on Antonio Maceo, Quintín Bandera, Martín Morúa Delgado, Juan Gualberto Gómez, and the poet of color Gabriel de la Concepción Valdés, known as Plácido, constructed a genealogy of military, political, and literary efforts on behalf of equality over time. Notably, this genealogy tended to overlook past conflicts among Cubans of color over the nature of their objectives. Women, engaged in their own struggles for greater equity, also received attention, especially through the astute writing of one outspoken feminist, Cloris Tejo. The goal of greater unity led the editors of *Adelante* to tackle a prickly issue: the existence of tense divisions between blacks and mulattoes, which until that time had been a public secret. Santiago in particular was infamous for this, as many mulatto sociedades excluded blacks and vice versa. The editors encouraged exchange regarding this troubling practice with a survey that invited readers to send in their ideas on why this occurred and how to end it.[21]

Despite such efforts, progress, inevitably, was uneven. After the first eight months production had tripled in volume and the newspaper attained nationwide circulation. Another group of black intellectuals, aspiring to start a publication of their own entitled *Igualdad*, bowed out after a few months, acknowledging their redundancy and *Adelante*'s fine work. But *Adelante* did not always manage to persuade by example. Although a great deal of enthusiasm heralded the Convención de Sociedades Negras, in the end *Adelante* expressed, with pointed allusions to frivolity and wasted time, its disapproval of the societies' priorities and comportment. For its three-year anniversary in 1938, the editors issued an ambivalent retrospective: if on the one hand they had survived and garnered considerable support, they were nonetheless disappointed with lukewarm responses from some key (unnamed) constituencies. In addition, "dishonorable activities," to which they had euphemistically alluded earlier, forced them to exclude some sociedades from their rosters.

Lively debates and stubborn disagreements filled the pages of *Adelante*. The convocation of a collective consciousness did not seem to stifle ideological heterogeneity. Prominent intellectuals, both white and of color, contributed regularly. They included Gustavo Urrutia, Alberto Arredondo, Emilio Roig de Leuchsenring, José Luciano Franco, and Angel Pinto along with Marinello, García Agüero, and Lachatañeré. Debates arose over the relationships of blacks to political parties, over the question of separatism versus integration, and over the extent to which racial characteristics were shaped by biological or cultural factors.

The Past in the Present:
Comparsas and the Politics of Culture

When the issue of the comparsas arose in 1937, interlocutors presented it as a debate over the question of representation: What was the merit in parading African-derived musical practices as symbols of a valued tradition in a context of economic distress and widespread social animosity? Although the coexistence of comparsas and contempt did not necessarily indicate a relationship between them, many—and disagreement ran along precisely this fault line—felt that the presentation of Afro-Cuban spectacles would deflect attention from the reality of racial animosity. Whose vision of the place of blacks in the imagined national community would dictate policies and practices? As Urrutia told an audience at a new institute for social reform, the Instituto Nacional de Previsión y Reformas Sociales, a "new negro" was one who "does not limit himself to the diverse definitions, both friendly and hostile, that whites have produced to describe blacks."[22] One of the major sources of these "diverse definitions" was the Sociedad de Estudios Afrocubanos.

Ortiz's tireless efforts at institutionalization had resulted in the founding of the Sociedad in 1937. Reflecting the ascendance of public discourse firmly embedded in racialist categories, it promised to produce and disseminate the most recent and sophisticated information concerning "the race called black, of African origins, and that called white, or caucasian." In so doing it hoped to promote egalitarian, cross-racial interactions and make progress toward "the happy realization of our common destinies." Its membership reflected these goals. On its initial roster, for example, were Miguel Angel Céspedes and Nicolás Guillén, vice presidents; Salvador García Agüero, treasurer; and Gustavo Urrutia, member. Election to an office of the association did not imply total agreement with the positions or strategies of the Sociedad. It meant instead that critiques of representation, whether they were, in Urrutia's words, "friendly or hostile," could be formulated in closer dialogue with the creators of those representations.[23]

Romulo Lachatañeré expressed perhaps the most direct critiques of Ortiz, current representations of African-derived religions, and the stubbornly persistent trope of brujería. A black anthropologist trained by Ortiz himself, Lachatañeré challenged Ortiz's early writings on brujería in the pages of the *Estudios Afrocubanos*. Pointing out that the categorization, and therefore criminalization, of all religious practices as brujería did a grave injustice to legitimate beliefs, he offered a complex narrative tracing their origins and noting distinctions between various African religions that had been transposed to Cuba.[24]

As they became more and more familiar with anthropological theory, intellectuals of color thus contended with the representation of Afro-Cuban culture on its terms. In their valorization of African-derived traditions they vied for greater control over those terms, rather than, as had earlier generations, distancing themselves from such practices. The issue of the comparsas produced a heated discussion in which black intellectuals engaged, and dissented from, the opinion of the Sociedad de Estudios Afrocubanos.

A consistent "allegory of salvage" informed the Sociedad's support of the comparsas. These musical performances, it claimed in response to the mayor's inquiry of January 1937, had originated in Africa but traveled to the New World with the slaves who had originally performed them. As such, they ought to be valued as "contemporary survivals" from that lost world. The comparsas would afford the residents of Havana an opportunity to engage in what Ortiz called "internal tourism." Through them one could perceive glimpses of the "remote religious ideas" that had given sustenance to Afro-Cuban rituals. Although they were relics from a remote past, they might still retain the power to harmonize a dissonant society.

Thirty-five years earlier the arrested celebrants, in similar costumes (though engaged in different practices), had posed a threat to the tentative boundary between freedom and civility. In the transition from U.S.-occupied territory to republic, those costumes had served religious, criminological, and anthropological understandings of race. By 1937 the costumes had taken on additional roles as emanations of an essential "Cubanidad" and as sources of income for the Commission on Tourism.[25] But the threat of incivility lingered. In its advocacy of the performances, the Sociedad de Estudios Afrocubanos included a warning against *congas*: comparsas too often and too easily degenerated into lascivious free-for-alls when enthusiastic observers joined in the dancing. This development might also be a traditional practice, but it ought to be discouraged.

Neither the cautious supporters nor the vehement critics in *Adelante*'s pages seemed to care much about resurrecting (or re-creating) the past. In fact, this justification drew the bitterest complaints. For María Luisa Sánchez, the comparsas represented an idealized past and obfuscated exploitation. They had originally been performed, she pointed out, during the *zafra* (sugar harvest) by slaves to keep their spirits up. Their rebirth as frivolous entertainment, in her view, served as a drug, an opiate that spread docility and erased the memory of suffering.[26] Likewise, Alberto Arredondo challenged the notion that the comparsas would be salubrious revivals of cultural traditions. He rejected any claims of their artistic value with counterclaims that constantly evolving musical forms had long since superseded them: they were "without a doubt, an artistic stage long ago surpassed." Rather than a valuable memory of the past, they were manifestations of the injustice of the present. "Since blacks are in a situation so dire that they barely have enough with which to feed and clothe themselves, the town council had to finance the *comparsas* and supervise them so that they might take on 'artistic value.'" Arredondo also criticized alleged supporters of the performances for their hypocrisy. No member of the Club Atenas (who had supported the comparsas, apparently) nor from *Adelante* had attended, much less participated. This was irresponsible, especially "in this historic moment, when it is necessary to lead through example." Worse still, the performances had fed reactionary racism. Arredondo, who had attended the processions, noted in a later article that most of the spectators had been intolerant whites, sneering among themselves about the backwardness and barbarism of the pageant. The *Diario de la Marina*'s opinions reinforced his belief that the spectacle provided far too much grist for reactionary mills: "The *comparsas* must have proffered few benefits to the masses, and they must have been presented with an absurd intention to enclose the past within the present, otherwise the *Diario de la Marina* would not have sung their praises on the front page."[27]

Yet these critics did not speak with a unified voice. Even those who defended the comparsas (and even, cautiously, the *congas*) resisted characterizing them in terms of an inert past, choosing instead to see them as reflections of the present. Black activist Angel Pinto charged critics like Arredondo with holding overly negative views. To denigrate the art form was to blame the victim, he argued, since blacks remained tied to these cultural forms because of economic disadvantage and lack of education. Reproaches by insensitive intellectuals would not help matters: "Blacks will continue to play their music and dance the conga, despite Mendieta's wishes or those of the *Sociedad de Estudios Afrocubanos*, and despite 'our intelligentsia,' which continues vomiting, with unsurpassed insensitivity, their bitter and virulent reproaches of our brothers, who as victims of the oppression that weighs on them and that causes their ignorance, have remained in their primitive state."[28]

Despite these disagreements, *Adelante*'s contributors shared certain premises. They clearly believed that black intellectuals ought to shoulder the responsibility for improving the political and social status of what they called "the masses." Battles over representation were directly connected, in their view, to battles over rights and citizenship. While nationalists had integrated Afrocubanismo into a more heterogeneous cubanidad, the growing acknowledgment of the profound influence of African culture had proved double-edged. Time and experience had demonstrated that some versions of Afrocubanismo were all too easily yoked to a conservative agenda.

Disappointment with social scientific endeavors and legal structures that had failed to yield social equality or greater economic parity impelled black activists to refine their strategies. As the constitutional convention of 1940 approached, they transplanted concerns over the meaning of citizenship and equality to new ground, reframing issues of marginalization and cultural representation raised by the comparsas to issues of legal and political representation. They began to formulate demands that took into account the consensus supporting expanded state power, asserting that the state's protection against discrimination rather than mere recognition of equality seemed an apt use of constitutional reform.[29]

From Rites to Rights

As the constitutional convention opened on February 9, 1940, it evinced a remarkable degree of consensus, having quickly overcome initial disputes between heterogeneous factions. The factions that con-stituted the opposition included the reformist socialist Partido Revolu-cionario Cubano, led by Ramón Grau San Martín; the ideologically slip-pery ABC, led by Jorge Mañach; the Partido Acción República, consisting mostly of supporters of Miguel Mariano Gómez, the impeached former president; and the Demócrata República, led by Mario Menocal and rep-resented by "moneyed sectors and those aligned with the old guard." Those standing up for the interests of the government included the "con-servative and discredited" Partido Liberal and Unión Nacionalista Parties as well as the Unión Revolucionaria Comunista (URC).[30] In addition to the aforementioned agreement on the need for a more interventionist state, international developments had pushed the Cuban political spectrum to the left. Both an intensified relationship with Lázaro Cárdenas's Mexico (which had nationalized its oil companies in 1938) and a growing reaction against fascism in Europe fed labor and Communist support and isolated the contingent of disgruntled conservatives.[31]

The constitutional convention commenced with speeches reflecting a sense of renewal and optimism. Yet beneath lofty invocations of democ-racy, cooperation, and justice ran a somber undercurrent that commemo-rated the conflict and violence that had permeated recent political events. Marinello, speaking on behalf of the URC, acknowledged the profound injustices that continued to corrode the social fabric. Many complicated issues would have to be addressed, he suggested, for the convention to deliver its promise.[32]

Participants seemed prepared to fight for their proposals with a good deal of energy. Black activists, mobilizing on a number of fronts, con-tinued to work in the Comité por los Derechos del Negro and Adelante and began to develop strategies to end discrimination in private spaces and the workplace, as well as objectionable representations of blacks in media and public discourses.[33] They had founded the National Federa-tion of Cuban Societies of the Race of Color (Federación Nacional de Sociedades Cubanas de la Raza de Color) in 1938, hoping that increased numbers would give them a more viable voice.[34] Marinello and Salva-dor García Agüero had led other activists for racial and socioeconomic equality in founding the Unión Revolucionaria, which linked racial issues to party politics in the most explicit manner (except for the Communist Party's "Franja Negra" experiments) since 1912.

As the convention opened, representatives of the National Federation, calling themselves a "new social presence," presented a long written statement to the delegates. Its membership had grown, they claimed, to include over 90 percent of Cuban sociedades, from Oriente to Pinar del Río. Furthermore, they claimed to represent all Cuban blacks: "Given the national scope and the truly popular following of our constituent societies, the principles, demands and activities of this national federation not only represent the beliefs, needs, and mandates of all the affiliated societies, they also act on behalf of those groups of blacks which are not specifically represented."[35] They cast their net even more widely, careful not to make overly specific demands. The reforms they advocated would in theory alleviate the hardships of the "rural and urban proletariat, women, peasants, and even the middle class" in addition to Cubans of African descent. Nonetheless, they insisted on addressing the problem of race directly: "In order for this gathering of forces to be effective it is necessary to propose specific solutions to the specific black problem." Their demands included a series of interconnected political, social, and economic reforms. Fragmentary approval of some reforms and not others, they argued, was unacceptable. Nor were empty resolutions — "lyrical declarations which live only on paper." The National Federation insisted on the need for the threat of force, lest the adopted measures become a "juridical fiction," like article 11 of the 1901 constitution.[36]

Their boldest demands called for guarantees of protection in addition to basic rights. They asked for the penalization of discrimination and the prohibition of public manifestations of racism, as well as of secret organizations. Other requirements were just as far-reaching: among them, a 50 percent law (50 percent of employees must be native-born); proportional representation in the workplace; a labor code with special protections for women, children, and domestic servants; extensive social security measures; and attention to education, family, and agricultural policy. Their demands for "political rights" included a requirement that the racial composition of rosters of candidates supported by all political parties correspond proportionally to the racial composition of those parties. They also advocated immigration restrictions to mitigate competition in the labor market.[37]

As leaders of the URC, Juan Marinello and Salvador García Agüero (who was also a member of the National Federation) responded to this manifesto by proposing that an amendment banning racial discrimination be presented as part of the official deliberations. This amendment had been adopted by the PCC in its platform of 1938, soon after it was granted legitimacy and merged with the Unión Revolucionaria to form the URC, which sent delegates to the convention.[38] This move suggests that in this instance the PCC had not subsumed race to class interests, but rather that this merger depended on the continued viability of both forms of political categorization and had occurred because of shared ideology and political contingencies. Although struggles for racial equity and labor rights have been considered separately more often than not, historians have begun to uncover an early history of civil rights that centered on labor rights as its primary focus in the United States. At this time U.S. activists envisioned battles for civil and labor rights as intertwined, rather than incompatible. This seems to have been true in Cuba as well.[39]

Yet integrating concerns about discrimination and racial equality in the URC platform did involve some ideological gerrymandering. In a speech to the Club Atenas, party president Marinello conflated Cuban workers with Cuban blacks as he spoke of the benefits to both of state control of latifundia and redistributive measures. In the end (or perhaps because he was addressing the Club Atenas), he produced an impassioned if frangible synthesis: "It is not enough to declare equality for all citizens . . . the black question is so transcendent, and its existence wounds our democracy so deeply, that we call for firm state intervention in private activities, especially in the spheres of labor and the economy."[40] Blas Roca, the URC's vice president, utilized a slightly different strategy. Although he acknowledged the role of economic disadvantage in racial discrimination, he distinguished more clearly between the two issues. Joining concern for the working class with demands that elite black associations had been making for years, he called for unimpeded access to public spaces, educational institutions, and high-level jobs.[41]

The URC's proposal to amend article 23 attempted to define discrimination as broadly as possible in order to include the array of expressed goals. The proposed article 23 had already superseded article 11 with protections against discrimination. Article 23 read as follows:

All Cubans are equal before the law. The Republic does not recognize any special rights or privileges.

All discrimination due to sex, race, class or any other motive harmful to human dignity is declared illegal.

The law will establish sanctions for those who violate these norms.

The amendment eschewed the term "discrimination" and substituted a specific list of rights:

All Cubans are equal before the law. The Republic does not recognize any special rights or privileges. All behavior or action that prevents any citizen from full access to public services or public places, the right to work and culture in all its aspects, or the full enjoyment of all his civil and political activities, due to his race, color, sex, class or any other discriminatory reason, shall be declared illegal and punishable. Within six months following the promulgation of this constitution, the law will establish the sanctions incurred by those who violate these norms.[42]

The shared premises and subtle differences between the article and the amendment set the stage for a debate not just over the nature of discrimination, but over the extent of the state's responsibility and capacity to remedy the problem. In these debates, García Agüero, a schoolteacher, eloquently but insistently compelled the assembly to linger over the question of race. As a member of both the National Federation and the URC, he was well qualified to address the issues from slightly different perspectives. Born in Havana, he had participated in the political upheaval of the late twenties and the thirties. In his youth, he had volunteered to teach night classes sponsored by the Unión Fraternal. His politicization continued when he became a founding member of the National Teachers' Union just after the fall of Machado, and he was asked to publicize his views in a contribution to *Adelante*. The conflict in Trinidad in 1934 thrust him in the public eye, beginning with an invitation, as a member of the Comité por los Derechos del Negro, to speak to the cabinet at the Presidential Palace. More important, through the Comité he met Juan Marinello, who was also a member. Once Marinello became editor of the first legal communist newspaper, *La Palabra*, he invited García Agüero to contribute. García Agüero then embarked on an increasingly public life of speaking tours, radio shows, and participation in a cycle of conferences organized by the PCC. The National Federation of Cuban Societies of the Race of Color elected him a member of its national executive committee and vice president of the delegation from Havana. When the Unión Revolucionaria joined forces with the PCC, García Agüero became second vice president under Juan Marinello and Blas Roca.[43]

It was not until April that the assembly began to discuss individual rights. García Agüero quickly turned the debate into a lesson on the history and meaning of discrimination. Although they had been granted formal equality and participated in the political process, blacks had nonetheless suffered ill-treatment and exclusion "in the crucial aspects of culture, work, and in the enjoyment of all rights that accompany citizenship." He refused to lay full blame on slavery, which was often targeted (and served to shift blame onto Spanish colonialism) as the source of Cuba's troubling racial dynamic. Discrimination, he argued, was a historical phenomenon that emerged from the political and economic circumstances of the republic as much as from the institution of slavery: "From then until now, due to a series of reasons—which I really ought to elaborate on—this process has been growing; and if in the first moments it [discrimination] emerged out of the slaveholding regime, at present, a series of economic, political and social developments has resulted in the continuation of prejudices which create harmful oppressions, difficulties, obstacles and limitations for the human potential of this sector of the national population."[44]

He tried to point out the grave implications for all Cubans, not just those of color, by appealing to their sense of honor, their aspirations to stability, material welfare, and modernity. "These constitute not only a stain for any democratic organization or country, but also a danger to its internal stability and an obstacle to its progress and economic, political and social development. One can see manifestations of this reality particularly in the three aspects mentioned in the amendment I just proposed."

While García Agüero drew attention to these issues from within the ranks of the convention, ordinary citizens demonstrated their concern with a flood of postcards addressed to the assembly. Approximately one hundred postcards filed along with the documents produced by the constituent assembly attest to the investment ordinary Cubans had in the lawmaking at hand. Dozens wrote in support of the article and amendment banning discrimination. It is possible that the National Federation of Cuban Societies of the Race of Color organized the effort, for many of the cards expressed their support with exactly the same wording. These made their request succinctly:

> We ask this assembly to approve the following demands:
>   1. Absolute equality of all Cubans before the law.
>   2. A law against discrimination and specific sanctions.
>   3. Proportional representation in the labor force for blacks.

Others sent in more elaborate statements. Pedro Pablo Toledo, Nicolás J. Terry, Lázaro Bravo, Perfecto Quiñones, José Antonio Aponte, José I. Angera, and Juan Mederos invoked citizenship and nationalism with their wide-ranging demands:

> As a conscientious and responsible citizen who prays for equality, justice, fraternity and above all for peace in the Republic of Cuba, I ask and implore that for the good of the nation, the following demands be supported and approved in the Constitution that is now being elaborated:
> 1. Equality for whites and blacks.
> 2. Punishment for discriminators.
> 3. Proportional representation in the labor force for blacks.
> 4. Secular education.

Still others distilled their appeal into one basic point. Gustavo Martínez was very direct: "The author of this card would like to notify those delegates representing the Cuban people that the principal desire of those who want to live in this nation with true fraternity, is the cessation of discrimination due to color, sex, etc., because after all we are all Cuban, or human."[45] These postcards formed part of a mobilization campaign in which many sectors, including peasants, students, and women as well as Cubans of color, voiced their demands through postcards, letters to delegates, and rallies outside the convention's meeting halls, creating an unprecedented atmosphere of vigilance and accountability just as the constitution was being drafted. Blas Roca attributed the progressive nature of the constitution in part to this mobilization, arguing that reactionary and conservative delegates who would have fought against progressive measures buckled under the pressure to appeal to *el pueblo*.[46]

In the end García Agüero lost the battle for his amendment on a vote of 23 to 20 but won the war to penalize discrimination. Those siding against the amendment argued that it was unnecessary, since it addressed issues already covered by the article's broad language. Their reasoning reveals widespread recognition (in public debate, at least) of the problem of discrimination and of the need to penalize it. Even Nuñez Mesa, the only delegate who broke the consensus, beat a hasty retreat when he was caught in a contradiction. Nuñez Mesa first asserted that there was no discrimination in Cuba, then said that the problem of discrimination could be redressed by the laws already in place. García Agüero pointed out the inconsistency of his claims and forced him to concede. No other delegates used their allotted time to argue that race relations were acceptable as they stood.

With debate on the amendment terminated, García Agüero extended the discussion by requesting that the article be modified to differentiate "color" from "race." The notion of distinct or pure races, he argued, drawing from recent anthropological thought, had proved false. If distinct races had ever existed, miscegenation had blurred the boundaries to the extent that one could only describe Cuba (and, indeed, many other parts of the world) as a nation of mestizos. Yet this had not prevented discrimination. To the contrary, it had heightened the importance of color and created new divisions, introducing an insidious array of exclusionary practices based on slight differences in skin tone. This twist on prevalent claims about Cuba's racial intermixture further demonstrated that accepting the notion of a mestizo nation did not necessarily imply agreement that racial harmony had been achieved. Echoing the ambivalence about mestizaje expressed by Urrutia, Guillén, and others, García Agüero insisted that instead of eliminating problems, mestizaje reconfigured them. The assembly honored his request and modified the article, adding color to sex, race, and class in the list of illegal bases for discrimination.[47]

Examined thus far, the debates relating to the proposed article indicate that there was little room for public dissent from the claim that racial discrimination existed in Cuba. The fact of this consensus in 1940 reveals the distance from the days when the very mention of inequality or exclusion prompted accusations of disloyalty to the Cuban republic. Instead, the assembly agreed that the expectations raised by the declaration of equality in the 1901 constitution had not been met. The "myth of racial democracy" was no longer the powerful silencer it had once been.

As the state came to "see" races as a political category, its duty came to be understood (ideally) as protecting and enforcing individual and group rights. Thus the social scientific reinvention and perpetuation of race as a viable category had shaped political outcomes. Although politicians and black activists had found social scientific versions of this category either objectionable or ineffectual, they had ultimately rendered it an indispensable political category. Transcendence of racial categories, an admirable ideal perhaps, had been found lacking by too many sectors seeking equality, or order, or modernity as they remade, reentrenched, and politicized blackness and whiteness.[48]

Conclusion

Most historians agree that the final document produced by the 1940 convention was Cuba's most liberal and progressive constitution. In a matter of months the delegates had crafted a utopian document that contained 286 articles confirming universal suffrage, free elections, freedom to organize political parties, and a large variety of protected civil and political rights, including rights to speech, association, religion, and publication. It created extensive provisions for social rights, such as care for the elderly, accident and other forms of insurance, and protections for women and children. It regulated working conditions, specifying maximum hours, minimum wages, and annual one-month paid vacations for every worker. Finally, it guaranteed the right to strike.[49] If implemented, the 1940 constitution would create a state that was present in many more aspects of daily life than before, not only granting freedoms but also alleviating material hardships for many of the worst-off citizens.

In addition to the article criminalizing racial and other kinds of discrimination, the constitution dictated social and civil rights for Cubans of color in other arenas. Article 74 prohibited discriminatory practices in the workplace, and article 44 conceded rights to the children of unmarried parents, which would affect many blacks and mulattoes (as well as whites). Although it was still illegal to form political parties based on race, class, or gender (article 102), minorities were guaranteed representation in elected bodies at the federal, provincial, and municipal levels (article 103).[50]

As the convention drew to a close, Blas Roca expressed a great deal of optimism and enthusiasm about the constitution's merits. It was "progressive, democratic, contained principles of revindication for the popular classes, and capable of serving as a tool for economic improvement." Yet as Samuel Farber and others have pointed out, if the progressive vision was its strength, it would be its weakness as well, as it became mired in the vagaries of political life and legal structures. Many of the measures included a provision dictating that enabling laws must be drafted by future legislative assemblies, which opened up the process to political contingency. Many provisions never received the legislative backing they required. Campaigns for laws to enforce the criminalization of discrimination, initiated in 1941 and again in 1944, died on the Senate floor. After 1948, the Communist Party, which had been the principal advocate of these laws, lost much of its power as it fell victim to the exigencies of the Cold War.[51]

Nicolas Graizeau describes the problem as one of "parliamentary apathy," arguing that the gap between the "real structures" of the state and its "formal constitution" were too wide to allow for the codification of the most idealistic measures. "Real structures"—public opinion, political culture, corruption and the use of political violence—and the economy failed to provide enough support for the codification of the kind of regime envisioned by the constitution. An alternative explanation is that a conservative contingent had cynically allowed for the passage of articles without having any intention of seeing them through the legislature. Additionally, as Robert Cottrol has pointed out in the case of Brazil, criminalizing discrimination may in fact have made enforcement more cumbersome. Comparing Brazil's case to that of the United States, he observes that the most effective measures against discrimination have come as a result of civil litigation rather than criminal prosecution. If Cuban activists focused on criminalization rather than civil suits, in part because that was the most accessible route, they may have comparably hindered the pursuit of racial equality. In any case, full access to the rights of citizenship, which includes, in Guillermo O'Donnell's formulation, recourse to the law and legal apparatus, were denied.[52]

It was a fundamentally ambiguous moment. In addition to enumerating these failures of codification, it is also important to underscore the exceptionally idealistic, progressive nature of the constitution in relation to most of the Americas at that time, when disregard for rights prevailed. In much of the United States, segregation laws made a travesty of political equality. In the Dominican Republic and Argentina, authoritarian governments would not have considered allowing the expression of popular voice (however mediated) in the form of a new constitution, and in 1940 Mexico witnessed a shift, under the regime of Manuel Avila Camacho, to conservative government policies. Moreover, during this period visibility and effectiveness of black political mobilization were rare, if not unprecedented, in Latin America. Black activists in Brazil, for example, enjoyed a brief opening with the formation of the Frente Negra in 1930, but this was shut down along with other opportunities for expanded political participation with the initiation of Getúlio Vargas's Estado Novo.[53]

Still viable in some contexts, the aspiration toward race-transcendence had been challenged from all sides, by social science, the state, and activists of color who increasingly invoked collective political identities. But if that myth unraveled, perhaps a new unstated myth arose—that of popular participation and the merits of social and political rights for a society conceived as a set of distinct groups, including blacks, women, youths, workers, and industrialists, rather than an agglomeration of individuals. Struggles over the terrain and content of citizenship had created new venues for political participation and set high stakes that would be the source of further conflict in the years to come.

:: Epilogue

How does this examination of the processes by which social scientists, state officials, and activists of color made, legitimated, and disseminated meanings of race fit into broader national narratives? Any response must take into account two historiographic understandings of the Cuban past. The first is a teleological narrative that culminates with the revolution of 1959. This account stresses the frustration of nationalist goals due to corruption and mediated sovereignty in the republic. As precursor and counterpoint to the revolution, the republic is cast as a weak state with self-serving leadership and ineffectual social movements. The year 1940 only underscores the disregard for the rule of law that characterized the entire period. A second historiographic assumption dovetails with the first through assertions of cultural and social unity. Linking nationalist visions from Martí to Ortiz, the vision of unity acknowledges heterogeneity only to note that it was subsumed within a national identity.[1] This cubanidad might have failed to find the right channels through which to assert itself in the republic, but its continued presence and consistently homogeneous content provided the link between the end of the wars for independence and the beginning of the revolution. Thus early versions of race-transcendence flow smoothly into later conceptions of cultural unity, such as Ortiz's well-known *ajiaco*, which imagined Cubanness as a harmoniously blended stew of different flavors.

It was not the purpose of this project to overturn those narratives, but rather to understand the republic and the conditions of its making, taking into account contingencies, contradictions, and tensions that might not fit so well in teleological interpretive schemes. Looking at the postemancipation adoption of formal equality exposed an array of voices that challenged assumptions about the unity of national identity. These voices made it difficult to characterize the republic as either the incubator of democratic ideals or the seat of the utter disregard of those ideals. Instead, their visions, dissent, and negotiations bring into relief the highly contradictory and contentious tenor of politics and culture in the republic, as democratic aspirations both flourished and dissolved.

Rafael Rojas has suggested that the constitution of 1940 provoked Cubans' "obsession with the imperceptibility of their destiny."[2] As a reconfiguration of state in the service of nation, what did its promise yield? By most accounts the 1940 constitution proposed such profound changes in the domain and role of the state that it could not but prove disappointing. The governments that followed found ways to circumvent or ignore what they viewed as the most troublesome provisions, such as those intending to reform labor relations and working conditions. Laws that might implement the changes sought by reformers seldom materialized, and when they did enforcement was inconsistent at best. At the same time, however, this context of continual disregard of the constitution's progressive aims served to legitimize protest against corruption and social injustice.[3]

This was also true of efforts to ban discrimination. A number of proposed laws were deliberated within legislative bodies but were ultimately rejected. Black activists invoked the constitution's codified commitment to social equality as they continued to mobilize against discrimination. The complex interplay between civil society and political parties through which these struggles transpired is beyond the scope of this project. Further inquiry into this problem would also have to address the impact on Cuban social science of World War II and the horrifying fascist implementation of racialist schemes.[4]

Seen through my original problem regarding the tensions between democratizing tendencies and the reinforcement of racial hierarchies, 1940 was perhaps as rife with contradictions as 1902. But they were different contradictions. In 1902 a liberal polity had imagined citizens as equal. In response, social science had concentrated its efforts to reform within a paradigm that emphasized racial difference in order to contain it, as a prerequisite to the acquisition of modernity. Between these realities Cubans of color had both attained new levels of equality and suffered various modes of racial antagonism. While holding to various degrees of racial and nationalist self-identification, most desisted from mobilizing politically around race-based claims.

Four decades later the state's perceived duty to foster social justice had grown, despite frequent observations of its weakness and corruption. Social science had by this time splintered in different directions, some currents persistent in their convictions of the inherent inferiorities of Cubans of African descent, while other strands shed explicitly hierarchical views and turned to "African culture" with an eye to its redemptive possibilities. Activists of color engaged a context of increasing mobilization to politicize blackness in new ways. Thus Cubans in 1940 deemed politicized blackness both necessary as a way to redress ongoing inequality and acceptable at the level of official discourse previously premised on race-transcendence. This placed a new paradox at the center of Cuban politics, society, and culture.

:: Notes

ABBREVIATIONS

Anales	*Anales de la Academia de Ciencias Médicas, Físicas y Naturales*
ANC	Archivo Nacional de Cuba, Havana
AUH	Archivo de la Universidad de la Habana, Havana
BLCAV	Bancroft Library, University of California at Berkeley, August Vollmer Collection
BNJM	Biblioteca Nacional José Martí, Havana
CCC	Fernando Ortiz, *Proyecto de Código Criminal Cubano* (Havana: Comisión Nacional Codificadora, 1926)
CMFO	Colleción Manuscrita Fernando Ortiz, Biblioteca Nacional José Martí, Havana
CMUF	Cinco monografías Unión Fraternal
exp.	expediente (file)
ILL	Instituto de Literatura y Lingüística, Havana
leg.	legajo (bundle)
Los negros brujos	Fernando Ortiz, *La hampa afro-cubana: Los negros brujos (apuntes para un estudio de etnología criminal)* (Madrid, 1906)
NYT	*New York Times*
RG	Record Group
USNA	National Archives, Washington, D.C.

INTRODUCTION

1. Montalvo, de la Torre, and Montané, *El craneo de Maceo.*

2. For the complex process of the emergence of antiracism and its continuing co-existence with racism in the context of the wars for independence, see Ferrer, *Insurgent Cuba.*

3. For a rich discussion of this issue, see Jeremy Adelman, Introduction to *Colonial Legacies.*

4. Martí, "Mi Raza," *Obras completas,* 2:299–300. Martí's race-transcendent ideology was nonetheless fraught with unresolved tensions between the need to overcome race and the admission of the impossibility of that goal: his strategy amounted to an attempt to overcome by forgetting.

5. For debates leading to the adoption of universal manhood suffrage, see de la Fuente, *A Nation for All*.

6. L. A. Pérez Jr., *Cuba and the United States*.

7. Barreras, *Textos de las constituciones*, 142.

8. Ibid., 144.

9. Cooper, Holt, and Scott, *Beyond Slavery*.

10. Adams, *Wellborn Science*; Chamberlin and Gilman, *Degeneration*; Nye, *Crime, Madness*; Galera, *Ciencia y delincuencia*; Pick, *Faces of Degeneration*; Rodgers, *Atlantic Crossings*; Peard, *Race, Place, and Medicine*.

11. Stepan, *"Hour of Eugenics"*; Schwarcz, *Spectacle of the Races*; Hale, *Transformation of Liberalism*.

12. Tocqueville, *Democracy in America*, vol. 1, chap. 18.

13. R. J. Scott, *Slave Emancipation*; Ferrer, *Insurgent Cuba*.

14. Helg, *Our Rightful Share*.

15. de la Fuente, "Myths of Racial Democracy."

16. For a very limited sample of this extensive literature, see, e.g., Whitten and Torres, *Blackness in Latin America*; Andrews, *Blacks and Whites*; Marx, *Making Race and Nation*; Skidmore, *Black into White*; Wade, *Blackness and Race Mixture*; Arocha, "Inclusion of Afro-Colombians"; Grandin, *Blood of Guatemala*; J. Gould, *To Die in This Way*; and Appelbaum, Macpherson, and Rosemblatt, *Race and Nation*. For twentieth-century Cuba, see, e.g., B. Carr, "Identity, Class"; Chomsky, "Aftermath of Repression"; Guridy, "Racial Knowledge; Cooper, Holt, and Scott, *Beyond Slavery*; Sarduy and Stubbs, *Afro-Cuban Voices*; Fernández Robaina, *El negro en Cuba*; and García Martínez, Martínez Heredia, and Scott, *Espacios, silencios*.

17. Fields, "Ideology and Race"; Holt, "Marking"; Wade, *Race and Ethnicity*. For a compelling study of the making of racial difference as a departure from a literature noted for its studies of "racial democracy," see Weinstein, "Racializing Regional Difference."

18. Geertz, *Interpretation of Cultures*, 314.

19. Military Order 250, December 28, 1899, AUH, Fondo Secretaría General, exp. 365, 1900. Named as professors were Carlos de la Torre y Huerta, Raimundo Castro y Allo, Antonio Govín y Torres, José González Lanuza, Eusebio Hernández, and Diego Tamayo. Tamayo and González also received political appointments at the time.

20. T. D. Stewart, *Hrdlicka's Practical Anthropometry*, 5–12.

21. *Anales* 37 (1900–1901): 42.

22. Ibid., 44.

23. *Anales* 38 (1901–2): 7.

24. Danielson, *Cuban Medicine*.

25. Academia de Ciencias Médicas, *Homenaje al Dr. Diego Tamayo y Figueredo* (session held on December 10, 1921), and *Diego Tamayo* (paper delivered at the Ateneo de la Habana by Dr. Evelio Tabío, supreme court judge of Cuba, vice president of the National Institute of Criminology, and president of the National Association of Members of the Judiciary).

26. Barnet, "Concepto actual de la medicina," *Anales*, May 15, 1902.

27. For a thoughtful analysis of race and politics in this period, see de la Fuente, *A Nation for All*. See also Fernández Robaina, *El negro en Cuba*; Portuondo Linares, *Los independientes de color*; and Ibarra, *Cuba*. For an insightful analysis of nationalist discourse, see Martínez Heredia, "El problemático nacionalismo."

28. For the process of emancipation, see R. J. Scott, *Slave Emancipation*. For the formation of voluntary associations, see Howard, *Changing History*, and Hevia Lanier, *El directorio central*.

29. *La Fraternidad*, November 10, 1888, cited in Fernández Robaina, *El negro en Cuba*, 25–26.

30. Fernández Robaina, *El negro en Cuba*; Deschamps Chapeaux, *El negro en el periodismo cubano en el Siglo XIX*; Helg, *Our Rightful Share*.

31. Ferrer, *Insurgent Cuba*, chap. 7.

32. R. J. Scott, "Reclaiming Gregoria's Mule"; Zeuske, "'Los negros hicimos la independencia.'"

33. Horrego Estuch, *Juan Gualberto Gómez*, 177; de la Fuente, *A Nation for All*, 66–67.

CHAPTER ONE

1. For the linked nineteenth-century struggles for independence and emancipation, see R. J. Scott, *Slave Emancipation*, and Ferrer, *Insurgent Cuba*. On politics and society in the republic, see L. A. Pérez Jr., *Cuba under the Platt Amendment*; Ibarra, *Cuba*; Yglesia Martínez, *Cuba*; H. Thomas, *Cuba*; Anuario de Estudios Cubanos, *La república neocolonial*; and LeRiverend, *La República*.

2. Iglesias, "José Martí"; L. A. Pérez Jr., *On Becoming Cuban*; Ferrer, *Insurgent Cuba*, chap. 7.

3. "Proceso de asociación ilícita," 1902, ANC, Audiencia de la Habana, leg. 214-5, 223-4. For a different analysis of the same incident, see L. Guerra, "From Revolution to Involution."

4. Clifford, "Objects and Selves," 244.

5. Holt, "Marking," 7. Holt also stresses that "everyday" does not necessarily refer to "non-elite," a point that cannot be overemphasized.

6. I have borrowed the term "large processes" from Tilly, *Big Structures*. My analysis of the meaning of objects, especially in the context of cultural exchanges, is informed by a provocative set of texts that includes Pietz, "The Problem of the Fetish, I," "II," and "IIIa"; N. Thomas, *Entangled Objects*; Appadurai, *Social Life of Things*; Kopytoff, "Cultural Biography of Things"; and Spyer, *Border Fetishisms*. My thanks to Stephan Palmié for bringing my attention to many of these texts.

7. Palmié, *Wizards and Scientists*, 168.

8. Pietz, "The Problem of the Fetish, I." For religion and the meanings and uses of ritual objects, see, e.g., MacGaffey, "Eyes of Understanding"; Brown, "Toward an Ethnoaesthetics of Santería Ritual Arts"; Legêne, "From Brooms to Obeah and Back"; and Palmié, *Wizards and Scientists*.

9. It is difficult to provide an accurate portrait of ñañiguismo, as secrecy was a

primary characteristic. What I am trying to do here is interpret the official documentation and to underscore that its categories and assumptions often differed radically from those of the religious practitioners they sought to describe.

10. R. J. Scott, *Slave Emancipation*; Hevia Lanier, *El directorio central*.

11. January 4, 1901, USNA, RG 140, entry 3, 6725 1/2.

12. Moore, *Nationalizing Blackness*, chap. 3.

13. Ibid., 229.

14. "Declaración de Carlos Masso Hechavarría, Capitán de Policía," ANC, Audiencia de la Habana, leg. 214-5.

15. Sánchez Martínez, *Guía del policía cubano*, 269.

16. Ibid., 208.

17. Carreras, *Historia del estado*; Spain, Ministerio de Ultramar, *Spanish Rule in Cuba*, 35.

18. Cuba, *Penal Code*, art. 180, no. 1.

19. R. Carr, *Modern Spain*, 8.

20. Sánchez Martínez, *Guía*, 226. For more on the 1901 constitution, see the Introduction above.

21. Brooke, *Civil Report*, 15.

22. Cuba, *Penal Code*, 76–77.

23. Sánchez Martínez, *Guía*, 208–9.

24. "Proceso de asociación ilícita," ANC, Audiencia de la Habana, leg. 214-5, 223-4.

25. S. Stewart, *On Longing*.

26. L. A. Pérez Jr., *Cuba under the Platt Amendment*, 90, and chaps. 3, 4.

27. Brooke, *Civil Report*, 256.

28. Anonymous letter to the chief of the Havana Detective Bureau, December 21, 1900, USNA, RG 140, entry 3, box 105 (letters received), file 4163.

29. Ibid.

30. Letter from President of the Court of Havana to Dean of the University, August 2, 1902, 12, AUH, Fondo Secretaría General, exp. "Laboratorio y Museo Antropológico" 334, 1901.

31. Some of these objects may have been household items taken by accident in the sweeps conducted by police. (Suggested by Reinaldo Román in a personal communication.) The objects in translation were identified with the help of Stephan Palmié (personal communication). *Abakuá* is a male secret society thought to be derived from similar groups in Africa.

32. AUH, Fondo Secretaría General, exp. "Laboratorio y Museo Antropológico" 334, 1901, 14–15.

33. Mestre, *La política moderna*, 8.

34. Stocking, "Paradigmatic Traditions," 351. On the construction of distinctions between "biological" and "cultural" understandings of race, see also Wade, *Race, Nature, and Culture*.

35. Stocking, *Race, Culture, and Evolution*, 48.

36. *Anales*, vols. 38, 37, 40.

37. S. J. Gould, *Mismeasure of Man*, 25.

38. This was a society not of anthropologists, but of doctors, lawyers, and literary scholars interested in anthropological questions. Lafuente, Elena, and Ortega, *Mundialización de la ciencia*; Rivero de la Calle, *Actas*.

39. Mestre, *Montané en la Antropología Cubana*; Montané, "Rapport sur l'état des sciences anthropologiques."

40. AUH, Fondo Secretaría General, exp. "Luis Montané 301; University of Havana, *Memorias anuarios*.

41. S. J. Gould, *Mismeasure of Man*, 86. See also the assumptions revealing the close relationship between polygenist thought and Broca's brand of physical anthropology in Stocking *Race, Culture, and Evolution*, 56.

42. S. J. Gould, *Mismeasure of Man*, 124.

43. Responding to criticism, Lombroso ultimately settled on a rather uneasy combination of degeneration and atavism to explain innate criminality. See Pick, *Faces of Degeneration*.

44. S. J. Gould, *Mismeasure of Man*, 125; C. Lombroso, *L'Homme Criminel*; Pick, *Faces of Degeneration*.

45. S. J. Gould, *Mismeasure of Man*, 74.

46. Stocking, *Race, Culture, and Evolution*.

47. E. Williams, "Art and Artifact at the Trocadero"; Clifford, "Objects and Selves."

48. Stocking, *Race, Culture, and Evolution*, 121. See also Wade, Afterword, in Appelbaum, Macpherson, and Rosemblatt's *Race and Nation*.

49. On the distinctions between biological and hereditarian concepts of race, see Wade, *Race, Nature, and Culture*.

50. Fabian, *Time and the Other*.

51. F. Guerra to Secretary of Provincial Governor of Havana, President of the Republic, and Luis Montané ("Con esta fecha presento ud. el diseño de las Panderetas correspondiente al género de musica que en sus fiestas cívicas y religiosas usa el culto de Santa Bárbara."), ILL, Fondo Fernando Ortiz, carpeta 34C. See Barkan and Bush, *Prehistories of the Future*, for the ways the appropriation of objects destabilizes distinctions between savage and civilized, as the act of appropriation inevitably mixes violence with aestheticism, inadvertently valorizing what it sets out to excoriate.

52. "Contra Pascual García Almirante y Juan Llanes Basallo por asociación ilícita," May 24, 1902, ANC, Audiencia de la Habana, leg. 223-4.

53. Stocking, "Paradigmatic Traditions," 346. For this interpretation of the function of museums, see Bennett, *Birth of the Museum*.

54. Anderson, *Imagined Communities*, esp. chap. 10.

CHAPTER TWO

1. My account summarizes the Zoila case as reported in *El Mundo* between November 1904 and January 1906. For other accounts, see Román, "An Indignant Public Opinion: The Cuban Press and the Negros Brujos Scares, 1904–1943," "Conjuring Progress and Divinity"; Palmié, *Wizards and Scientists*; and Helg, *Our Rightful Share*, 109–14.

2. *El Día*, September 6, 1918, 1, 12.

3. Brazil shared many of these features, with the exception of universal manhood suffrage.

4. de la Fuente, "Race and Inequality" and *A Nation for All*.

5. Although the period just after the war saw a reconfiguration in the language of civility and race, "civilization" became a new yardstick with which to measure blacks' capacity for leadership. See Ferrer, "Rustic Men, Civilized Nation."

6. Palmié, *Wizards and Scientists*, chap. 3.

7. Helg, "Race in Argentina and Cuba," 48–49.

8. Figueras's notion of "pacific penetration" is not clearly spelled out.

9. Carrera y Justiz, *El municipio y la cuestión de razas*.

10. Céspedes Casado, "La cuestión social cubana," 7.

11. Román, "Conjuring Progress and Divinity."

12. *El Mundo*, December 18, 1904; Román, "An Indignant Public Opinion."

13. Palmié, *Wizards and Scientists*, chap. 3; Helg, "Black Men, Racial Stereotyping." For the prevalence of male witches in Brazilian social scientific and literary discourses, see Borges, "Healing and Mischief."

14. Ferrara, *Anuario estadístico*, 165.

15. On the press and print culture in Cuba, see Fornet, *El libro en Cuba*, and Ricardo, *La imprenta en Cuba*. For the importance of newspapers in making crime a public phenomenon, see Nye, *Crime, Madness*.

16. For Zequeira's extensive role in this case, including his participation in the investigation itself, see Román, "An Indignant Public Opinion."

17. *El Mundo*, December 13, 1904, 1, 8.

18. Ibid., 2.

19. *El Mundo*, January 5, 1906, 5, 8.

20. Ibid.

21. Ibid.

22. Ibid.

23. C. Lombroso, *L'Homme Criminel*; Pick, *Faces of Degeneration*.

24. *El Mundo*, January 5, 1906, 5, 8.

25. "De la reorganización del servicio de vigilancia como una necesidad de la administración de la justicia en lo criminal," AUH, Fondo Secretaría General, exp. "Fernando Ortiz" 9975. The literature on Ortiz is extensive—see, e.g., Bremer, "Constitution of Alterity"; Coronil, Introduction to Fernando Ortiz's *Cuban Counterpoint*; Iznaga, *Transculturación en Fernando Ortiz*; Ibarra, "La herencia científica de Fernando Ortiz"; Palmié, "Fernando Ortiz and the Cooking of History"; and Quiza Moreno, "Fernando Ortiz y su hampa afrocubana."

26. Ortiz, "Tarjetas postales y la criminología," and "Niños y Salvajes," in *Azul y Rojo* 2, no. 1 (January 1903).

27. *Hampa* is defined as "a group of miscreants, villains and ruffians who live on the margins of the law and dedicate their lives to committing crimes."

28. Ortiz, *Los negros brujos*.

29. For this problem in anthropological thought, see Fabian, *Time and the Other*.

30. Ortiz, *Los negros brujos*, 102.

31. Ibid., 103.

32. Ibid., chap. 3.

33. Ibid., 242. The question of Ortiz's view of the nature of Cuba's relationship to Spain is a difficult one. Though he was educated there and clearly owed a considerable intellectual debt to its criminologists, he also sought to differentiate himself and Cuba's intellectual circles from Spanish ones. This is most clearly expressed in his *La Reconquista de America* (1911). See Halperín Donghi, "España e Hispanoamerica," *El espejo de la historia*, for an insightful discussion of the processes of differentiation and self-definition engaged in by Latin American intellectuals in the initial years of independence from Spain.

34. For these letters, see "Brujos," ILL, Fondo Fernando Ortiz, carpeta 36, #542–550.

35. Anonymous letter to the chief of the Havana Detective Bureau, December 21, 1900, USNA, RG 140, entry 3, box 105 (letters received), file 4163.

36. Discussed at the end of this chapter.

37. *El Mundo*, July 16, 1906, 2.

38. *El Comercio*, July 10, 1906, 3.

39. *Diario de la Familia*, July 10, 1906, 3.

40. *La Discusión*, August 12, 1906, 11.

41. *La Unión Española*, November 5, 1906, 3.

42. *El Mundo*, October 8, 1906, 4, November 25, 1906, 10.

43. Chávez Alvarez, *El crimen de la niña Cecilia*, 26–28.

44. For a history of the laws against brujería (or lack thereof) in Cuba, see Palmié, *Wizards and Scientists*, chap. 3. For Brazil's contrasting outcome, see Borges, "Healing and Mischief."

45. For the cases between 1904 and 1923, see Chávez Alvarez, *El crimen de la niña Cecilia*. Court cases, ANC, Audiencia de la Habana, leg. 459-5, 781–6, 781–9.

46. "Que informan sobre el destino que los objetos ocupados tienen en la *brujería*," ANC, Audiencia de la Habana, leg. 555-10.

47. "Causa criminal contra Diego Ozeguera y otros por asociación ilícita," January 10, 1913, ANC, Audiencia de la Habana, Juzgado de Instrucción de la seccion segunda, 43, leg. 223-2.

48. ANC, Audiencia de la Habana, leg. 223-2, pp. 16–18.

49. Ibid., p. 29.

50. "Declaración del Vigilante 1247 Amador Prío Rivas," ANC, Audiencia de la Habana, leg. 223-2, pp. 31–32.

51. "Declaración del Vigilante 534 Juan González," ANC, Audiencia de la Habana, leg. 223-2, p. 33.

52. Ibid., 34.

53. "Causa criminal contra Diego Ozeguera y otros por asociación ilícita," January 10, 1913, 43. Herrera Sotolongo was probably referring to the original formulation of the law against illicit association, which in colonial times targeted conspiracies against the government. It is notable that none of the cases I examined in the republican era involved political rebellion.

54. "Declaración del Vigilante 1247 Amador Prío Rivas," 94–111. This text is very similar to parts of Roche y Monteagudo, *La policía y sus misterios*, a striking and extensive example of police production of ethnographic texts.

55. "Declaración de Luis Sánchez, ANC, Audiencia de la Habana, leg. 223-2, p. 118.

56. "Causa criminal contra Diego Ozeguera y otros por asociación ilícita," January 10, 1913, 49–50.

57. On the civil law system, see Merryman, *Civil Law Tradition*.

58. S. J. Gould, *Mismeasure of Man*.

59. University of Havana, *Memorias anuarios*, 97–98. Darwin was not on the initial syllabi. For a discussion of Darwinism in Cuba, see Pruna, *Darwinismo y sociedad*.

60. University of Havana, *Memorias anuarios*, 1906–7, published in 1908. The 1906 university reform also created a new course on "Derecho Municipal e Historia de las Instituciones locales cubanas," in the Escuela de Derecho Público (Municipal Law and History of Local Cuban Institutions in Law School), taught by Carrera y Justiz.

61. Ibid.

62. Ibid. For the disagreements between French and Italian anthropologists, see Nye, *Crime, Madness*, esp. chap. 4.

63. Mestre, "Brujería y criminalidad," 318.

64. Ricardo, *La imprenta en Cuba*, 152.

65. Ferrara, *Anuario estadístico*.

66. On the United States, see Rodgers, "In Search of Progressivism," and Gerstle, "Protean Character of American Liberalism." On Europe, see Nye, *Crime, Madness*; Stocking, *After Tylor*; and Pick, "Faces of Anarchy" and *Faces of Degeneration*. Rodgers, in *Atlantic Crossings*, has also recently demonstrated the intimate relationships between European and U.S. progressives.

67. For Latin America, see Graham, *Idea of Race*, and Hale, "Political and Social Ideas." See also Zimmermann, *Los liberales reformistas*; Stepan, *"Hour of Eugenics"*; and Schwarcz, *Spectacle of the Races*. Zimmermann assumes that racialist theories were transposed from Europe to Argentina with minimal change. I would suggest that particular circumstances in Cuba led Cuban commentators to reshape European ideas.

68. Editorial, *Vida Nueva* 1 (January 1921).

69. For autobiographical information on Castellanos, see his "Confidencias." For biographical information, see Galera, *Ciencia y delincuencia*, 141–72.

70. Castellanos, *Brujería y el ñañiguismo*, 9. For another comparison of Ortiz and Castellanos, see Naranjo Orovio and Puig-Samper, "Delincuencia y racismo."

71. His claims here reflect an inconsistent view of race: sometimes the two forms of delinquency are exclusively black, and at other times they are mixed, including whites as well. But they are never wholly white. Thus even if the biological paradigm for criminal identification was extended to whites, it never was detached from its association with blacks.

72. For a brilliant exegesis of Castellanos, including a comparison of his and Ortiz's attitudes toward their subject matter, see Palmié, *Wizards and Scientists*, chap. 3.

CHAPTER THREE

1. Domínguez, *Cuba*, 11. See also L. A. Pérez Jr., *Cuba under the Platt Amendment*.

2. I mean to invoke multiple meanings of "civil," including (1) nonmilitary, (2) the practice of citizenship, and (3) polite.

3. de la Fuente, *A Nation for All*, 69.

4. See L. A. Pérez Jr., *Cuba under the Platt Amendment*, chap. 6, for the ways access to state power was linked with access to economic resources in the early republic.

5. For the organization and history of the PIC and of the uprising in 1912, see, e.g., Portuondo Linares, *Los independientes de color*; Fernández Robaina, *El negro en Cuba*; Orum, "Politics of Color"; de la Fuente, *A Nation for All*; Fermoselle, *Política y color*; Helg, *Our Rightful Share*; L. A. Pérez Jr., "Politics, Peasants"; and Roig de Leuchsenring, *Males y vicios*. For an eloquent analysis of racial politics in republican Cuba and of the memory of the repression, see Fernando Martínez Heredia, Prologue to Portuondo Linares's *Los independientes de color*.

6. Deschamps Chapeaux, *Rafael Serra y Montalvo*, 23–28.

7. On this period, see, e.g., Ferrer, *Insurgent Cuba*, chaps. 4, 5.

8. Serra cited in Deschamps Chapeaux, *Rafael Serra y Montalvo*, 28.

9. Ibid., 27–28.

10. Serra, *Para blancos y negros*, 54.

11. Deschamps Chapeaux, *Rafael Serra y Montalvo*, 162–81.

12. Ferrer, *Insurgent Cuba*, chap. 5.

13. Serra, *Para blancos y negros*, 98–99.

14. Ibid., 22, 39.

15. Ibid., 94.

16. Ibid., 100.

17. Ferrer, *Insurgent Cuba*, chap. 7.

18. Serra cited in Deschamps Chapeaux, *Rafael Serra y Montalvo*, 157.

19. Serra, *Redención* (1903), cited in Deschamps Chapeaux, *Rafael Serra y Montalvo*, 161.

20. Deschamps Chapeaux, *Rafael Serra y Montalvo*.

21. Serra, *Para blancos y negros*, 204.

22. Portuondo Linares, *Los independientes de color*, 236.

23. Scott and Zeuske, "Property in Writing"; R. J. Scott, "Provincial Archive"; Ferrer, *Insurgent Cuba*.

24. L. A. Pérez Jr., *Cuba under the Platt Amendment*, 90.

25. Portuondo Linares, *Los independientes de color*, 66–68.

26. Ibid., 56.

27. Horrego Estuch, *Juan Gualberto Gómez*, 217; R. J. Scott, "'Lower Class of Whites'"; Portuondo Linares, *Los independientes de color*, 131.

28. *El Mundo*, May 21, 1912.

29. *La Discusión*, May 21, 1912.

30. *El Popular*, vol. 2, no. 70, May 30, 1912.

31. *El Mundo*, May 22, 1912.

32. L. A. Pérez Jr., *Cuba under the Platt Amendment*.

33. de la Fuente, *A Nation for All*, 73–75.

34. *Política Cómica*, May 26, 1912.

35. For an alternative interpretation, see Helg, *Our Rightful Share*.

36. For a local study of this dynamic, see Bronfman, "Más allá del color."

37. Interview with journalist Sixto López, *La Discusión*, May 31, 1912.

38. "La camara y los sublevados," *El Mundo*, May 23, 1912.

39. *El Mundo*, May 23, 1912.

40. *El Mundo*, May 26, 1912.

41. Editorial, *El Mundo*, June 6, 1912.

42. *El Mundo*, June 7, 1912.

43. *El Mundo*, June 9, 10, 1912.

44. "A nuestro pueblo," *El Mundo*, June 4, 1912.

45. Ibid.

46. Helg, *Our Rightful Share*, 206–7.

47. "A nuestro pueblo," *El Mundo*, June 4, 1912.

48. L. A. Pérez Jr., "Politics, Peasants."

49. Portuondo Linares, *Los independientes de color*, 251.

50. For descriptions of the massacre, see, e.g., L. A. Pérez Jr., "Politics, Peasants"; Helg, *Our Rightful Share*; Fermoselle, *Política y color*; and Portuondo Linares, *Los independientes de color*. Underexamined in all accounts (including my own) are the perpetrators and the victims of the "butchery." Without that analysis, we can only speculate on how or why this happened.

51. Holt, "Marking," 3.

CHAPTER FOUR

1. Gómez cited in Horrego Estuch, *Juan Gualberto Gómez*, 220.

2. On the role of memory in the formation of collective identities, see LeGoff, *History and Memory*; Fentress and Wickham, *Social Memory*; and Fabre and O'Meally, *History and Memory*. On the "culture of mobilization" and practices of citizenship beyond formal elections, see Sabato, "Citizenship, Political Participation."

3. Horrego Estuch, *Juan Gualberto Gómez*, 221–22.

4. de la Fuente, *A Nation for All*, 168–70.

5. "Documentos relativos a la asociación Unión Fraternal de la Habana 9 mayo, 1917," ANC, Fondo Adquisiciones, box 75, no. 4317, CMUF essay 2.

6. Ibid. For a comparative discussion of the integration of African American memory into master historical narratives, see Fabre and O'Meally, *History and Memory*, esp. David W. Blight, "W. E. B. Du Bois and the Struggle for American Historical Memory" (chap. 4), and Brundage, *Where These Memories Grow*.

7. On sociedades in the nineteenth century, see Hevia Lanier, *El directorio central*; Howard, *Changing History*; and R. J. Scott, *Slave Emancipation*.

8. CMUF essay 5. On the treatment of recruits in the wars for independence, see Ferrer, *Insurgent Cuba*.

9. CMUF essays 1, 5. On memories of 1912, see also Fernando Martínez Heredia, Prologue to Portuondo Linares's *Los independientes de color*.

10. de la Fuente, *A Nation for All*, 83–85.

11. CMUF essays 1, 2, 4. On the relationship between urban life and citizenship, see Appadurai and Holston, "Cities and Citizenship."

12. CMUF essays 2, 3.

13. "Manifiesto," Culto religioso Africano Lucumí, Santa Bárbara, Sociedad Santa Rita de Casia y San Lázaro. "Al honorable Presidente, Secretario de Gobernación, Secretario de Justicia, al Sr. Alcalde Municipal de la ciudad de la Habana y al pueblo en general": LA VERDAD, CON CARA AL SOL!," July 19, 1913, ILL, Fondo Fernando Ortiz, carpeta 34C.

14. Fernando Guerra, July 5, 1913, ILL, Fondo Fernando Ortiz, carpeta 34A.

15. "Manifiesto," Culto religioso Africano Lucumí.

16. Palmié, *Wizards and Scientists*, 252.

17. ILL, Fondo Fernando Ortiz, carpeta 34C.

18. For more on Guerra and his contributions to the mutual constitution of modernity and tradition, see Palmié, *Wizards and Scientists*, chap. 3.

19. *El Día*, September 3, 1918, 1, 14.

20. Ferrer, *Insurgent Cuba*.

21. *El Día*, September 8, 1918, 1, 12.

22. *El Día*, September 15, 1918, 1, 11.

23. *El Día*, September 25, 1918, 1, 10.

24. *El Día*, September 20, 1918, 1, 12.

25. *El Día*, October 7, 1918, 1, 8.

26. *El Día*, September 10, 1918, 1, 10.

27. *El Día*, September 17, 1918, 1, 12.

28. On persecution of and violence against minorities, see Nirenberg, *Communities of Violence*. On the fear of cannibalism, see Morris, "Anthropology in the Body Shop."

29. *El Día*, March 23, 1919.

30. *El Día*, April 22, 25, 1919.

31. *El Día*, June 24, 28, 1919.

32. *El Día*, June 28, 1919.

33. It is not entirely clear who these men were. In *Our Rightful Share*, Helg writes that eight men died, but the newspaper reports one dead and twelve injured. *El Día*, June 29, 30, 1919.

34. *El Día*, July 1, 1919.

35. *El Día*, July 3, 1919.

36. *El Día*, June 29, 1919.

37. *El Día*, March 23–30, 1919. In the original, the term *pitonisas* refers to the priestesses or oracles at Apollo's temple in Delphi; it was used by extension to signify clairvoyants and women who foretold the future. The *cartománticas* were fortune-tellers who relied on cards, a practice that seems to have been associated with "Gypsies" and Canarios who advertised heavily in the press. *Adivinas* and *videntes* are fairly generic and nearly synonymous terms. I am indebted to Reinaldo Román for this information. For the contingent relationship between "blackness" and "Africanness," see Palmié, "Color of the Gods."

38. *El Día*, July 3, 1919.

39. For a similar strategy deployed by Ida Wells in critiques of U.S. lynchings, see Bederman, *Manliness and Civilization*, chap. 2.

40. On Risquet, see Helg, *Our Rightful Share*, 186, 283 (n. 36), and *El Día*, July 2, 1919.

41. de la Fuente, *A Nation for All*, 168–71.

42. "Manifiesto relativo a los sucesos ocurridos en Regla y Matanzas a consecuencia de las prácticas de brujería y canibalismo," ANC, Fondo Adquisiciones, box 65, no. 4201 (source of quotations in this and the next two paragraphs). Also published in *El Día*, August 2, 1919.

43. Chapman, *History of the Cuban Republic*, 609–13.

44. LeRiverend, *La República*, 181–97.

45. Dumoulin, *Azúcar y lucha de clases*; Grobart, "Cuban Working Class Movement"; B. Carr, "Mill Occupations"; Whitney, *State and Revolution*, chap. 1; de la Fuente, *A Nation for All*, chap. 3; Stubbs, *Tobacco on the Periphery*.

46. L. A. Pérez Jr., *Cuba under the Platt Amendment*, 235; Chapman, *History of the Cuban Republic*; Ortiz, *La decadencia cubana*.

47. L. A. Pérez Jr., *Cuba under the Platt Amendment*, 241–44; Cairo Ballester, *El Movimiento de Veteranos y Patriotas*; Buttari Gaunaurd, *Boceto crítico histórico*.

48. L. A. Pérez Jr., *Cuba under the Platt Amendment*, 236; Cairo Ballester, *El grupo minorista*; Ripoll, *La generación del 23*; Kapcia, "The Intellectual in Cuba." In the *protesta del trece* thirteen intellectuals led by Rubén Martínez Villena disrupted an official ceremony in 1923.

49. Whitney, *State and Revolution*.

50. L. A. Pérez Jr., *Cuba under the Platt Amendment*, 214–48.

CHAPTER FIVE

1. L. A. Pérez Jr., *Cuba under the Platt Amendment*, 252; de la Fuente, *A Nation for All*; Pérez-Stable, *Cuban Revolution*; Domínguez, "Seeking Permission to Build a Nation."

2. L. A. Pérez Jr., *Cuba under the Platt Amendment*; de la Fuente, *A Nation for All*; Pérez-Stable, *Cuban Revolution*; Domínguez, "Seeking Permission to Build a Nation"; Machado, *Ocho años de lucha*; Foreign Policy Association, *Problems of the New Cuba*.

3. Domínguez, *Cuba*, chap. 2.

4. L. A. Pérez Jr., *Cuba under the Platt Amendment*, 263–64.

5. Ortiz, "La fiesta afrocubana del 'Día de Reyes,'" *Archivos del Folklore Cubano* 1, no. (April 1924), 1, no. 3 (1925), 1, no. 4 (June 1925).

6. Stocking, *Romantic Motives*; Linke, "Folklore, Anthropology."

7. Machado, *Declaraciones*, 19–20.

8. Fabian, *Time and the Other*.

9. Ortiz, *La decadencia cubana*.

10. *Archivos del Folklore Cubano* 1, no. 1 (January 1924): 77.

11. Ibid., 7.

12. *Archivos del Folklore Cubano* 2, no. 3 (October 1926): 211.

13. Ibid., 222.

14. Ibid., 221–22 (source of quotations in this and the next paragraph).

15. Morejón, *Nación y mestizaje*; Benítez-Rojo, *Repeating Island*; R. Moore, *Nationalizing Blackness*; Kutzinski, *Sugar's Secrets*; J. Martínez, *Cuban Art and National Identity*; de la Fuente, *A Nation for All*; Martínez Furé, *Dialogos imaginarios*.

16. *Archivos del Folklore Cubano* 1, no. 1 (January 1924): 83–93.

17. "Noticias y comentarios: Reorganización de la sociedad del folklore cubano," *Archivos del Folklore Cubano* 3, no. 1 (January–March 1928): 93–95; "Sociedad del Folklore Cubano: Acta de una sesión extraordinaria," *Archivos del Folklore Cubano* 4, no. 2 (April–June 1929): 191–92.

18. "Motivos de son, por Nicolás Guillén, con glosas por Fernando Ortiz," *Archivos del Folklore Cubano* 5, no. 3 (1930): 222.

19. Ibid., 232.

20. Ibid., 236–37.

21. Biographical details are drawn from Cepeda, *Eusebio Hernández*.

22. On Pinard, see Schneider, *Quantity and Quality*, esp. chap. 3, and Stepan, *"Hour of Eugenics,"* chap. 3.

23. Hernández cited in Cepeda, *Eusebio Hernández*, 123.

24. Hernández and Ramos presented their proposals to the secretary of hygiene and welfare once in 1909 and on October 2, 1910; to the medical congress on February 24–28, 1911; and to Gómez on March 25, 1911.

25. The terms are from Hernández, *Homicultura*, and the translations are from Stepan, *"Hour of Eugenics,"* 79, except for *matrinaticultura*, which is my own.

26. Hernández, *Homicultura*; M. Varona Suárez, "Informe del Secretario de Sanidad y Beneficencia al Honorable Presidente de la República," March 25, 1911; "Informe de los Dres Hernández y Ramos al Secretario de Sanidad y Beneficencia," October 2, 1910. See also Stepan, *"Hour of Eugenics,"* and García González and Alvarez Peláez, *En busca de la raza perfecta*.

27. M. Varona Suárez, "Informe," 57–58.

28. Ibid.

29. García González and Alvarez Peláez, *En busca de la raza perfecta*, 130–31.

30. A few of these articles in *Vida Nueva* include Steinhardt, "La Madre debe ser criandera"; Amador, "Eugenica"; Arteaga, "Los Ancianos"; and D. F. Ramos, "Algo sobre la homicultura."

31. García González and Alvarez Peláez, *En busca de la raza perfecta*, 282–83.

32. Mañalich, *La homicultura*; Primera Conferencia Panamericana de Eugenesia, *Actas de la primera conferencia Panamericana de Eugenesia*.

33. Stepan, *"Hour of Eugenics,"* chap. 6.

34. D. F. Ramos, "Homiculture in Its Relation to Eugenics," 432–34.

35. Stepan, *"Hour of Eugenics,"* chap. 6; García González and Alvarez Peláez, *En busca de la raza perfecta*, chap. 5.

36. On Ramos and Davenport, see Stepan, *"Hour of Eugenics,"* 174–78.

37. García González and Alvarez Peláez, *En busca de la raza perfecta*, 174.

38. Conferencia de Eugenesia.

39. Ibid., 54–55.

40. Ibid., 36.

41. Ibid., 34.

42. Stepan, *"Hour of Eugenics,"* esp. chap. 5; Skidmore, *Black into White*; Kevles, *In the Name of Eugenics*; Adams, *Wellborn Science*; Peard, *Race, Place, and Medicine.*

43. Conferencia de Eugenesia; Stepan, *"Hour of Eugenics"*; García González y Alvarez Peláez, *En busca de la raza perfecta.*

44. Stepan, *"Hour of Eugenics,"* 178.

45. García González and Alvarez Peláez, *En busca de la raza perfecta*, chap. 6.

46. For a detailed discussion of immigration law, see Naranjo Orovio and García González, *Medicina y racismo en Cuba*, 34–54. On Antillean immigration, see McLeod, "Undesirable Aliens: Haitian and British West Indies Immigrant Workers" and "Undesirable Aliens: Race, Ethnicity, and Nationalism." For economic and political conditions during this period, see, e.g., L. A. Pérez Jr., *Cuba under the Platt Amendment.*

47. Domínguez, "Seeking Permission to Build a Nation"; Machado, *Ocho años de lucha*; Foreign Policy Association, *Problems of the New Cuba.*

48. Ortiz, "Ponencia a la Comisión Certificadora," BNJM, CMFO, carpeta 356.

49. Ortiz, *CCC*, 14.

50. Ibid., 13–14.

51. See Beirne, "Adolphe Quetelet," and Pasquino, "Criminology," 7.

52. Pasquino, "Criminology," 18. The line of influence between Ortiz and Ferri may be drawn through their connections to Césare Lombroso, whose impact on Ortiz's early work has been well documented. Ferri studied with Lombroso in the 1880s, during which time they became friends and colleagues, working together on key positivist concepts such as the born criminal and the use of anthropological data. Ferri's proposed reform of penal law in 1921 was in many ways a model for Ortiz's *Código Criminal Cubano.*

53. Ortiz, *CCC*, 50–51.

54. Ortiz, "Ponencia a la Comisión Certificadora," BNJM, CMFO, carpeta 356.

55. Ibid.

56. Ibid.

57. Ibid.

58. Quintiliano Saldaña, cited in Castellanos, *Un plan para reformar*, 15.

59. Ortiz to Sr. Dr. Mariano Ruíz-Funes, March 16, 1928, BNJM, CMFO, carpeta 403: Correspondencia variada.

60. Ortiz to Rafael M. Portuondo, November 2, 1944, BNJM, CMFO, carpeta 325: Correspondencia: P. I am grateful to Consuelo Naranjo Orovio for bringing this letter to my attention.

61. Apart from García-Carranza, Suárez Suárez, and Quesada Morales's *Cronología Fernando Ortiz*, this period of Ortiz's life has not received much scholarly attention.

62. Castellanos notes the number of files (*expedientes*) at his disposal in the preface to *La delincuencia femenina*, 1:7. For comparable practices in Brazil, see Gomes da Cunha, *Intençâo e Gesto.*

63. Nye, "Sociology and Degeneration."

64. Castellanos, *La delincuencia femenina*, 2:101.

65. For a reproduction of the *ficha-modelo*, see ibid., 2:61.

66. Ibid., 2:66.

67. Castellanos, *El pelo*, 101.

68. Ibid., 98. Castellanos used the terms *mestizo adelantado* and *blanco atrasado* in apparent allusion to racial categories formulated with the notion of whitening in mind. The best discussion of the complex dynamics of color and class identification is Martínez-Alier, *Marriage, Class, and Colour*, although it is important to exercise caution when asking how nineteenth-century terms transferred to the twentieth century.

69. Castellanos, *El pelo*, 11.

70. Castellanos, "Program for the Biological Study of Fingerprints," copy of grant application to the John Simon Guggenheim Memorial Foundation, enclosed in Castellanos to August Vollmer, December 21, 1933, BLCAV, box 7.

71. Castellanos to Vollmer, February 13, 1934, BLCAV, box 7.

72. Castellanos to Vollmer, July 28, 1936, ibid.

73. Ibid.

74. Phillips, *Cuba*, chap. 2; LeRiverend, *La República*; L. A. Pérez Jr., *Army Politics in Cuba*, chap. 9.

75. Castellanos to Vollmer, May 27, 1954, BLCAV, box 7. For biographical information on Castellanos, see Galera, *Ciencia y delincuencia*, and Castellanos, "Confidencias." After leaving Cuba Castellanos spent eleven years in Puerto Rico working with the police force; he later traveled to Miami, where he taught courses in criminology at the University of Miami. He died in 1977.

76. Cuba, *Census of the Republic of Cuba, 1919*.

77. *Policía Secreta Nacional* 1, no. 1 (November 1937): 3–5.

78. It seems odd that the secret police would publish a journal, thus publicizing their supposedly secret practices. But it did.

79. Castellanos, "La Policía Técnica."

80. Benigno Tulio, "La antigua y la nueva antropología criminal," *Policía Secreta Nacional* 1, no. 3 (February 1938): 49.

CHAPTER SIX

1. de la Fuente, *A Nation for All*, 91–92.

2. *Diario de la Marina*, January 23, 1928, 14 (source of quotations in this and the next paragraph).

3. de la Fuente, *A Nation for All*, chap. 5.

4. Ibid., 137.

5. L. A. Pérez Jr., *Cuba under the Platt Amendment*, 265–69.

6. J. Scott, *Seeing Like a State*.

7. "Discurso leido el 31 de Mayo de 1926, por el General Gerardo Machado y Morales en contestación al del Dr. José A. Del Cueto, en el Acto de la investidura del grado de Doctor en Derecho Público Honoris Causa que le fue conferido" (Speech given on May 31, 1926, by General Gerardo Machado y Morales, in response to Dr. José A. del Cueto, on the occasion of the awarding of an honorary degree in public law), in Machado, *Ocho años de lucha*, 186.

8. Pérez-Stable, *Cuban Revolution*, 38–39.

9. L. A. Pérez Jr., *Cuba under the Platt Amendment*, chap. 10; Whitney, *State and Revolution*, chap. 3.

10. This is not to say that class and race were interchangeable, but to suggest that at this moment they both fell under the rubric of *clases populares*.

11. Stoner, *From the House to the Streets*, 65–72.

12. Danielson, *Cuban Medicine*.

13. *Diario de la Marina*, January 1928.

14. "Del Presidente del Club Atenas al Honorable Señor Presidente de la República," *Diario de la Marina*, February 5, 1928, 5.

15. "El Dr. Hernández Massí contesta al Presidente del Club Atenas," *Diario de la Marina*, February 6, 1928, 25.

16. *Diario de la Marina*, April 2, 1928, 3.

17. "Las sociedades de color de esta provincia celebrarán pronto su primer congreso en la Habana," *Diario de la Marina*, April 2, 1928, 3. The members of the organizing committee included Alfredo Colás, Coronel Lino D'Ou, Juan Canales, Ciriaco Villaurrutia, Manuel Cartes, Hipólito Martínez, Policarpo Madrigal, Pío Sandoval, Alfredo D. Azauza, Juan M. de García, Alberto Céspedes, Ventura Ruíz, Sabas Hernández, Moisés Sariol, Alfonso Estaurias Guerra, Alfredo Frades Veranes, Prudencio González, Facundo Ación, Miguel Gómez, Eduardo Gree de Mc Carthy, Justo de Lara, and its president, Dámaso T. Randich.

18. *Diario de la Marina*, April 10, 1928, 4, April 2, 1928, 3.

19. *Diario de la Marina*, May 9, 1928, 21.

20. Gustavo Urrutia, "Ideales de una Raza," *Diario de la Marina*, April 19, 1928, 8.

21. On Urrutia, see Cook, "Urrutia"; Schwartz, "Cuba's Roaring Twenties"; and Fernández Robaina, "Marcus Garvey in Cuba."

22. Urrutia, *Diario de la Marina*, May 6, 1938, cited in Cook, "Urrutia," 225. The translation is Cook's, which may account for its Du Boisian language.

23. Fernando Martínez Heredia, personal communication.

24. Alejandro de la Fuente, personal communication. For an extended discussion of *Adelante*, see chap. 7.

25. Schwartz, "Cuba's Roaring Twenties," 112.

26. Cook, "Urrutia." The literature on Urrutia is sparse. I am grateful to Tomás Fernández Robaina for sharing his unpublished material on Urrutia.

27. Urrutia, *Diario de la Marina*, September 10, 1928, 10.

28. Ibid., May 31, 1928, 9.

29. Ibid., April 19, 1928, 8.

30. Ibid., July 11, 1928, 10.

31. Ibid., April 19, 1928, 8.

32. Ibid., May 5, 1928, 9.

33. Ibid., July 29, 1928, 9.

34. Ibid., May 15, 1928, 8.

35. For a theoretical account of the limits of this dualism and of the possibility of conceiving of political mobilizations in other terms, see D. James, *Resistance and Integration*.

36. de la Fuente, *A Nation for All*, chap. 5.

37. Urrutia, "Racial Prejudice," 473–74.

38. See, e.g., Morejón, *Nación y mestizaje*, and Martínez Furé, *Diálogos imaginarios*.

39. Benítez-Rojo, *Repeating Island*, 126.

40. Augier, *Guillén: Notas*; Guillén, "Estampa de Lino D'Ou," in Augier, *Guillén: Prosa de prisa*, 269–77.

41. Guillén, cited in Augier, *Guillén: Notas*, 2:51.

42. Guillén, "El Camino de Harlem," *Diario de la Marina*, April 21, 1929, reprinted in Augier, *Guillén: Prosa de prisa*, 3–6.

43. Guillén, "Racismo y cubanidad," *Mediodía*, January 15, 1937, reprinted in Augier, *Guillén: Prosa de prisa*, 65–67.

44. Urrutia, "Armonías: Teamwork," *Diario de la Marina*, November 9, 1932, 10.

45. Guillén, "Cuba, negros, poesía: Esquema para un ensayo," *Hora de España* (Valencia) 11 (1937), in Augier, *Guillén: Prosa de prisa*, 94–100.

46. Beals, *Crime of Cuba*, 51.

47. Guillén, "Cuba, negros, poesía."

48. Jacques Roumain, cited in Guillén, "Charla en el Lyceum," in Augier, *Guillén: Prosa de prisa*, 304. Guillén cites Roumain, then says, "I would like to have written those magnificent words."

49. Ibarzábal, *El problema negro*.

50. Urrutia, "Armonías: Complejos de inferioridad," *Diario de la Marina*, November 26, 1932, 14.

51. Urrutia, "Armonías: La misión magistral del negro," *Diario de la Marina*, November 10, 1932, 16.

52. Hill and Bair, *Marcus Garvey*; Yelvington, "War in Ethiopia and Trinidad"; Trouillot, *Haiti*, chap. 4; Shannon, *Jean Price-Mars*; Richardson, Introduction to *Refusal of the Shadow*.

53. Richardson, Introduction to *Refusal of the Shadow*; C. L. R. James, *Black Jacobins*; Kelley, *Race Rebels*, chaps. 5, 6; Yelvington, "War in Ethiopia and Trinidad."

54. Kelley, *Race Rebels*, chap. 6.

55. Ellis, "Nicolás Guillén and Langston Hughes."

56. Beals, *Crime of Cuba*, 65.

57. Arturo S. Schomburg, "My Quest for Negro Books," *Opportunity*, February 1933, 48–50.

58. de la Fuente, *A Nation for All*, chap. 5; Guridy, "Racial Knowledge," chap. 4.

59. Instituto de Historia, *El movimiento obrero cubano*, 320.

60. B. Carr, "Identity, Class" and "Mill Occupations"; Kelley, *Race Rebels*, chap. 5.

61. Instituto de Historia, *El movimiento obrero cubano*, 122, 288, 560.

62. B. Carr, "Identity, Class"; Instituto de Historia, *El movimiento obrero cubano*, 488; Rosell, *Luchas obreras contra Machado*, 205.

63. Among the many accounts of this period, see, e.g., Aguilar, *Cuba, 1933*; L. A. Pérez Jr., *Cuba under the Platt Amendment*; Pérez-Stable, *Cuban Revolution*; Tabares del Real, *La revolución del 30*; Farber, *Revolution and Reaction*.

64. "Bomb Blast in Cuba Kills Two Officials," *NYT*, September 7, 1933. See also, e.g., "Revolt by Terror Going on in Cuba: Fear of Riot Grows," *NYT*, April 2, 1933; "Wild Disorder in Havana," *NYT*, August 13, 1933; "Six Dead in Cuba in Communist

Riot," *NYT*, September 30, 1933; "Many Hurt in Riot of Students in Cuba," *NYT*, February 24, 1934; "Four Are Wounded in a Riot in Cuba," *NYT*, May 8, 1934; Tabares del Real, *La revolución del 30*; de la Fuente, *A Nation for All*; L. A. Pérez Jr., *Cuba under the Platt Amendment*; and Guridy, "Racial Knowledge," chap. 5.

65. "Six Dead in Cuba in Communist Riot," *NYT*, September 30, 1933.

66. de la Fuente, *A Nation for All*, chap. 5; Guridy, "Racial Knowledge," chap. 5; Rosell, *Luchas obreras contra Machado*, 205.

67. Guridy, "Racial Knowledge," chap. 5; de la Fuente, *A Nation for All*, chap. 5.

68. For an extended description of this incident, see Guridy, "Racial Knowledge," chap. 5.

69. Jesús Plasencia, "Hitler en Trinidad?," *Aurora*, March 1934; Marinello, "Linch en Trinidad" and "Carta a un Trinitario airado"; Gustavo Urrutia, "Armonías," *Diario de la Marina*, January 13, 1934, 2.

70. Serviat, *El problema negro*; Foreign Policy Association, *Problems of the New Cuba*; de la Fuente, *A Nation for All*, chap. 5.

71. Fornet, *En blanco y negro*, 79.

CHAPTER SEVEN

1. The letters of Beruff Mendieta and Ortiz are reproduced in Ortiz, Vasconcelos, et al., "Las comparsas populares." On the history and content of comparsas, see Moore, *Nationalizing Blackness*, chap. 3.

2. Roig de Leuchsenring, "Las comparsas carnavalescas"; Ortiz, cited in Ortiz, Vasconcelos, et al., "Las comparsas populares," 131.

3. Barreras, *Textos de las constituciones*, 142. Charles Tilly offers this definition ("A notion of citizenship") as a synthesis of the work of various scholars. Tilly, "Citizenship, Identity," 6.

4. Marshall, *Citizenship and Social Class*, 40.

5. Thompson, "Cuban Revolution."

6. Whitney, "Architect of the Cuban State"; Knight, "Populism and Neo-Populism"; Farber, *Revolution and Reaction*; Phillips, *Cuba*.

7. Whitney, "Architect of the Cuban State"; Knight, "Populism and Neo-Populism."

8. Batista, *Revolución social o política reformista*; Whitney, "Architect of the Cuban State," 438.

9. Schwarz, *Pleasure Island*, chap. 6.

10. Whitney, "Architect of the Cuban State"; Pérez-Stable, *Cuban Revolution*, chap. 2; Phillips, *Cuba*, 188.

11. Phillips, *Cuba*, 187.

12. Hamilton, *Limits of State Autonomy*; Knight, "Cardenismo"; Gilly, *El Cardenismo*; Turits, "Foundations of Despotism"; Derby, "Magic of Modernity"; D. Williams, *Culture Wars in Brazil*; Weinstein, *For Social Peace in Brazil*.

13. Domínguez, *Cuba*, chap. 3; Whitney, *State and Revolution*, chaps. 6, 7.

14. García Agüero, "Una promesa estimable," *Adelante*, November 1935, 12. See also Betancourt García, "Igualdad de derechos," *Adelante*, January 1936.

15. Pinto Interián, "En torno a la convención de sociedades negras," *Adelante*, May 1935, 11.

16. Pinto Interián, "En Marcha," *Adelante*, July 1935, 3.

17. Pinto Interián, "En torno a la convención de sociedades negras."

18. Pinto Interián, "En Marcha."
Adelante, July 1935, 3.

19. The records of these clubs, if they have survived, might provide fascinating glimpses into local racial dynamics in distinct regions.

20. "Discriminación," *Adelante*, July 1936, 11.

21. See esp. *Adelante*, January, February, March, May, July 1936, August 1937. Responses to the survey appear in issues from January to December 1937.

22. Urrutia, "El Nuevo Negro" (lecture given at the Instituto Nacional de Previsión y Reformas Sociales), *Adelante*, October 1937.

23. "La Sociedad de Estudios Afrocubanos contra los racismos: Advertencia, comprensión y designio"; "Estatutos de la Sociedad de Estudios Afrocubanos"; and "Miembros de la Sociedad de Estudios Afrocubanos"—all in *Estudios Afrocubanos* 1, no. 1 (1937): 3–10.

24. Lachatañeré, "El sistema religioso," Parts 1 and 2. For Ortiz's response in which he rather ambivalently accepts Lachatañeré's critique, see Ortiz, "Brujos o santeros," *Estudios Afrocubanos* 3 (1939): 85–90. On Lachatañeré, see Palmié, *Wizards and Scientists*, chap. 3.

25. Ortiz, Vasconcelos, et al., "Las Comparsas Populares," esp. 132–37.

26. María Luisa Sánchez, "Zafra y comparsas," *Adelante*, April 1937.

27. Alberto Arredondo, "El Arte Negro a Contrapelo," *Adelante*, July 1937.

28. Angel Pinto, "Una aclaración," *Adelante*, June 1937.

29. On race and the constitution of 1940, see also de la Fuente, *A Nation for All*, and Cohen and Moulin Civil, *Cuba sous . . . la Constitución de 1940*.

30. Carreras, *Historia del estado*, 460; Farber, *Revolution and Reaction*, 94.

31. Whitney, "Architect of the Cuban State."

32. Juan Marinello, "Convención Constituyente," *Diario de Sesiones*, vol. 1, no. 1, 1st inaugural sess., February 9, 1940, 13.

33. See de la Fuente, *A Nation for All*, chaps. 5, 6; Fernández Robaina, *El negro en Cuba*.

34. Serviat, *El problema negro*, 130–31.

35. Federación Nacional de Sociedades Cubanas de la Raza de Color, *Manifiesto a la Asamblea Constituyente*.

36. Ibid.

37. Ibid. This document was signed by Pedro Portuondo Calá, delegate, Comité Organizador de la Convención (the convention's organizing committee); Salvador García Agüero, minutes secretary and delegate, province of Havana; Gustavo E. Urrutia, treasurer and national delegate; and Mario Lacret Paisán, president, provincial federation of Oriente. Also signing were José I. Rosell, delegate, province of Oriente; Francisco Guillén, president, provincial federation of Camagüey; Martín Castellanos, delegate, province of Camagüey; Juan Tandrón, president, federation of Santa Clara; Agustín Iznaga, delegate, Santa Clara; Angel Sarracet, president, federation of the

Matanzas; Manuel García Ulloa, delegate, Matanzas; Pedro Rojas, president, federation of Havana; Narciso López, president, federation of Pinar del Río; Otilio Gutierrez, delegate, Pinar del Río; and Pastor de Albear y Friol, technical adviser.

38. See "Pacto de la Unión Revolucionaria y el Partido Comunista," *Mediodía* 90 (October 17, 1938): 10–11.

39. Goluboff, "Thirteenth Amendment"; Serviat, *El problema negro*, chaps. 7, 8.

40. Marinello, "La cuestión racial en la constitución," 12.

41. Roca, "Por la igualdad de todos los cubanos."

42. Cuba, Convención Constituyente, *Diario de Sesiones*, vol. 1, no. 26, 26th sess., April 27, 1940, 21.

43. Jiménez Pastrana, *Salvador García Agüero*.

44. Cuba Convención Constituyente, *Diario de Sesiones*, vol. 1, no. 26, 26th sess., April 27, 1940, 21.

45. Gustavo Martínez to Convención Constituyente (postcard), ANC, Fondo Convención Constituyente, leg. 18, no. 1.

46. Roca, *El pueblo y la nueva constitución*.

47. García Agüero, Convención Constituyente, *Diario de Sesiones*, vol. 1, no. 26, 27–29.

48. J. Scott, *Seeing Like a State*.

49. Whitney, "Architect of the Cuban State"; Farber, *Revolution and Reaction*, 94; Rojas, *Isla sin fin*; Serviat, *El problema negro*; Barreras, *Textos de las constituciones*.

50. Poumier, "La expresión del pensamiento negro."

51. Roca, *El pueblo y la nueva constitución*, 3; Farber, *Revolution and Reaction*; de la Fuente, *A Nation for All*, chap. 6.

52. Graizeau, "Genèse, exégèse et pratique"; Cottrol, "Long Lingering Shadow"; O'Donnell, *Counterpoints*, chap. 7.

53. Andrews, "Black Political Protest." For limited regional black mobilization in 1930s Colombia, see Wade, *Blackness and Race Mixture*, chaps. 7, 8.

EPILOGUE

1. For a sophisticated discussion of these narratives, see Rojas, *Isla sin fin*.

2. Ibid., 76.

3. Farber, *Revolution and Reaction*, chap. 5.

4. Fernández Robaina, *El negro en Cuba*, 149–63; Serviat, *El problema negro*, chap. 8.

:: Bibliography

ARCHIVAL SOURCES

Cuba
Academia de Ciencias, Havana
　　Archivo Histórico del Centro de Estudios de Historia y Organización de la
　　　Ciencia
Archivo Nacional de Cuba, Havana
　　Audiencia de la Habana
　　Fondo Adquisiciones
　　Fondo Convención Constituyente
　　Fondo Donativos y Remisiones
　　Presidios y Cárceles
　　Registro de Asociaciones
　　Secretaría de Gobernación
　　Secretaría de la Presidencia
Archivo Provincial de Cienfuegos
Archivo de la Universidad de la Habana, Havana
　　Colección Museo Montané
　　Fondo Administrativa
　　Fondo Secretaría General
　　Libros Raros
Biblioteca Nacional José Martí, Havana
　　Colección Manuscrita Fernando Ortiz
Instituto de Literatura y Lingüística, Havana
　　Fondo Fernando Ortiz

Spain
Hemeroteca, Madrid

United States
Bancroft Library, University of California at Berkeley
　　August Vollmer Collection
Firestone Library, Princeton University
Latin American Collection, University of Florida, Gainesville
Mudd Library, Yale University

National Archives, Washington, D.C.
  Record Group 59
  Record Group 140
  Record Group 199
  Record Group 350
Schomburg Center for Research in Black Culture, New York City
  Arturo S. Schomburg Papers

NEWSPAPERS AND PERIODICALS

Cuba

Adelante
Anales de la Academia de Ciencias Médicas, Físicas y Naturales
Archivos del Folklore Cubano
Aurora
Azul y Rojo
Bohemia
Cuba Contemporánea
Cuba y América
Derecho y Sociología
Diario de la Familia
Diario de la Marina
El Comercio
El Día
El Mundo
El Popular
Estudios Afrocubanos
La Discusión
La Política Cómica
La Unión Española
Mediodía
Policía Secreta Nacional
Reforma Social
Revista Bimestre Cubana
Revista Cubana
Revista de la Facultad de Letras y Ciencias de la Universidad de la Habana
Vida Nueva

Spain
Higia

United States
Foreign Policy Reports
The Nation

New York Times
Opportunity
Phylon

BOOKS, ARTICLES, PAMPHLETS

Academia de Ciencias Médicas, Físicas y Naturales. *Diego Tamayo: Hombre público.* Havana: Imprenta Fernández y Ca., 1956.

―――. *Homenaje al Dr. Diego Tamayo y Figueredo.* Havana: Imprenta Rambla y Bouza, 1922.

Adams, Mark, ed. *The Wellborn Science: Eugenics in Germany, France, and Brazil.* New York: Oxford University Press, 1990.

Adelman, Jeremy, ed. *Colonial Legacies: The Problem of Persistence in Latin American History.* New York: Routledge, 1999.

―――. "Political Ruptures and Organized Labor: Argentina, Brazil, and Mexico, 1916–1922." *International Labor and Working-Class History* 54 (1998): 103–25.

―――. "Post-Populist Argentina." *New Left Review* 203 (1994): 65–91.

Aguilar, Luis E. *Cuba, 1933: Prologue to Revolution.* Ithaca, N.Y.: Cornell University Press, 1972.

Aguirre, Carlos, and Ricardo Salvatore. *The Birth of the Penitentiary in Latin America: Essays on Criminology, Prison Reform, and Social Control, 1830–1940.* Austin: University of Texas Press, 1996.

Aguirre, Carlos, Gilbert Joseph, and Ricardo Salvatore. *Crime and Punishment in Latin America: Law and Society since Late Colonial Times.* Durham, N.C.: Duke University Press, 2001.

Aguirre, Carlos, and Robert Buffington, eds. *Reconstructing Criminality in Latin America.* Wilmington, Del.: Scholarly Resources, 2000.

Amador, Nicolás. "Eugenica." *Vida Nueva* 2 (February 1914).

Anderson, Benedict. *Imagined Communities: Reflections on the Origins and Spread of Nationalism.* London: Verso Press, 1991.

Andrews, George Reid. "Black Political Protest in São Paulo, 1888–1988." *Journal of Latin American Studies* 24, no. 1 (February 1992): 147–71.

―――. *Blacks and Whites in São Paulo, Brazil, 1888–1988.* Madison: University of Wisconsin Press, 1991.

Anuario de Estudios Cubanos. *La república neocolonial.* Havana: Editorial de Ciencias Sociales, 1973.

Appadurai, Arjun, ed. *The Social Life of Things.* Cambridge: Cambridge University Press, 1988.

Appadurai, Arjun, and James Holston. "Cities and Citizenship." *Public Culture* 8, no. 2 (Winter 1996): 187–204.

Appelbaum, Nancy, Anne Macpherson, and Karin Alejandra Rosemblatt, eds. *Race and Nation in Modern Latin America.* Chapel Hill: University of North Carolina Press, 2003.

Arocha, Jaime. "Inclusion of Afro-Colombians: Unreachable National Goal?" *Latin American Perspectives* 100 (May 1998): 70–89.

Arredondo, Alberto. *El negro en Cuba*. Havana: Editorial Alfa, 1939.

Arteaga, Dr. J. F. "Los Ancianos." *Vida Nueva* 10 (October 1914).

Audivert, Santiago. *Que necesita Cuba?* Havana: Imprenta La Nueva, 1912.

Augier, Angel. *Nicolás Guillén: Notas para un estudio biográfico-crítico.* 2 vols. Las Villas: Universidad Central de Las Villas, 1965.

————, ed. *Nicolás Guillén: Prosa de prisa, 1929–1972.* Havana: Editorial Arte y Literatura, 1975.

Barbarrosa, Enrique. *El proceso de la república.* Havana: Imprenta Militar de Antonio Pérez Sierra, 1911.

Barkan, Elazar. *The Retreat of Scientific Racism.* Cambridge: Cambridge University Press, 1992.

Barkan, Elazar, and Ronald Bush, eds. *Prehistories of the Future: The Primitivist Project and the Culture of Modernism.* Stanford, Calif.: Stanford University Press, 1995.

Barreras, Antonio, ed. *Textos de las constituciones de Cuba, 1812–1940.* Havana: Editorial Minerva, 1940.

Batista, Fulgencio. *The Growth and Decline of the Cuban Republic.* New York: Devin-Adair Co., 1964.

————. *Revolución social o política reformista (once aniversarios).* Havana: Prensa Indoamericana, 1944.

Beals, Carleton. *The Crime of Cuba.* Philadelphia: Lippincott, 1933.

Bederman, Gail. *Manliness and Civilization: A Cultural History of Gender and Race in the United States, 1880–1917.* Chicago: University of Chicago Press, 1995.

Beirne, Piers. "Adolphe Quetelet and the Origins of Positivist Criminology." In Beirne, *Origins and Growth of Criminology*, 101–30.

————, ed. *The Origins and Growth of Criminology: Essays on Intellectual History, 1760–1945.* Brookfield, Vt.: Dartmouth Publishing, 1994.

Benítez-Rojo, Antonio. *The Repeating Island: The Caribbean and the Postmodern Perspective.* Durham, N.C.: Duke University Press, 1992.

Bennett, Tony. *The Birth of the Museum: History, Theory, Politics.* New York: Routledge, 1995.

Berman, Marshall. *All That Is Solid Melts into Air: The Experience of Modernity.* New York: Penguin, 1982.

Borges, Dain. "Healing and Mischief: Witchcraft in Brazilian Law and Literature, 1890–1922." In *Crime and Punishment in Latin America: Law and Society since Late Colonial Times*, edited by Ricardo Salvatore, Carlos Aguirre, and Gilbert Joseph, 181–210. Durham, N.C.: Duke University Press, 2001.

Bremer, Thomas. "The Constitution of Alterity: Fernando Ortiz and the Beginnings of Latin American Ethnography out of the Spirit of Italian Criminology." In *Alternative Cultures in the Caribbean*, edited by Thomas Bremer and Ulrich Fleischmann, 119–29. Frankfurt am Main: Vervuert, 1993.

Bremer, Thomas, and Ulrich Fleischmann, eds. *Alternative Cultures in the Caribbean.* Frankfurt am Main: Vervuert, 1993.

Brereton, Bridget, and Kevin Yelvington, eds. *The Colonial Caribbean in Transition: Essays on Post-Emancipation Social and Cultural History.* Gainesville: University of Florida Press, 1999.

Britton, John A. *Carleton Beals: A Radical Journalist in Latin America*. Albuquerque: University of New Mexico Press, 1987.

Brock, Lisa, and Digna Castañeda Fuertes, eds. *Between Race and Empire: African-Americans and Cubans before the Cuban Revolution*. Philadelphia: Temple University Press, 1998.

Bronfman, Alejandra. "Más allá del color: Clientelismo y conflicto en Cienfuegos, 1912." In *Espacios, silencios y los sentidos de la libertad: Cuba entre 1878 y 1912*, edited by García Martínez, Orlando, Fernando Martínez Heredia, and Rebecca Scott, 285–94. Havana: Ediciones Unión, 2001.

Brooke, John R. *Civil Report of Major-General John R. Brooke, U.S. Army, Military Governor of Cuba*. Washington: Government Printing Office, 1900.

Brown, David. "Toward an Ethnoaesthetics of Santería Ritual Arts: The Practice of Altar-Making and Gift Exchange." In *Santería Aesthetics*, edited by Arturo Lindsay, 77–146. Washington, D.C.: Smithsonian Institution Press, 1996.

Brundage, W. Fitzhugh, ed. *Where These Memories Grow: History, Memory, and Southern Identity*. Chapel Hill: University of North Carolina Press, 2000.

Buffington, Robert. *Criminal and Citizen in Modern Mexico*. Lincoln: University of Nebraska Press, 2000.

Buttari Gaunaurd, J. *Boceto crítico histórico*. Havana: Editorial Lex, 1954.

Cabrera Infante, Guillermo. *Mea Cuba*. Madrid: Plaza Y Janes Editores, 1992.

Cairo Ballester, Ana. *El grupo minorista y su tiempo*. Havana: Editorial de Ciencias Sociales, 1978.

———. *El Movimiento de Veteranos y Patriotas: Apuntes para el estudio ideológico del año 23*. Havana: Editorial Lex, 1954.

———. *La revolución del 30 en la narrativa y el testimonio cubanos*. Havana: Editorial Letras Cubanas, 1993.

Carbonell, Walterio. *Crítica: Como surgió la cultura nacional*. Havana: Ediciones Yaka, 1961.

Carpentier, Alejo. *Ecue-Yamba-O!* 1927. Reprint, Havana: Editorial Arte y Literatura, 1977.

Carr, Barry. "Identity, Class, and Nation: Black Immigrant Workers, Cuban Communism, and the Sugar Insurgency, 1925–1934." *Hispanic American Historical Review* 78, no. 1 (1998): 83–116.

———. "Mill Occupations and Soviets: The Mobilisation of Sugar Workers in Cuba, 1917–1933." *Journal of Latin American Studies* 28, no. 1 (1996): 129–58.

Carr, Raymond. *Modern Spain, 1875–1980*. Oxford: Oxford University Press, 1980.

Carrera y Justiz Francisco. *El municipio y la cuestión de razas*. Havana: Imprenta de Moderna Poesia, 1904.

Carreras, Julio A. *Historia del estado y el derecho en Cuba*. Havana: Editorial Pueblo y Educación, 1983.

Carrillo, Justo. *Cuba, 1933: Students, Yankees, and Soldiers*. Translated by Mario Llerena. Miami: University of Miami Press, 1994.

Carte, Gene, and Elaine Carte. *Police Reform in the United States: The Era of August Vollmer, 1905–1932*. Berkeley: University of California Press, 1975.

Castellanos, Israel. *La Brujería y el ñañiguismo bajo el punto de vista médico-legal*. Havana: Lloredo, 1916.

———. "Confidencias de Israel Castellanos, de la Habana." *Higia* 2 (1917): 307–16.

———. *La delincuencia femenina en Cuba*. Vols. 1–3. Havana: Imprenta Ojeda, 1929.

———. *El pelo en los cubanos*. Havana: Carasa y Ca., 1933.

———. *Un plan para reformar el regimen penal cubano*. Havana: Imprenta La Universal, 1927.

———. La policía técnica." *Policía Secreta Nacional* 1, no. 5 (March 1938): 7–14.

Castellanos, Israel, Raimundo de Castro, Juan Blanco Herrera, and E. Valdes Castillo, eds. *El museo de la catedra de medicina legal de la Universidad de la Habana*. Havana: El Universo, 1930.

Cepeda, Rafael, ed. *Eusebio Hernández: Ciencia y patria*. Havana: Editorial de Ciencias Sociales, 1991.

Céspedes Casado, Emilio. *La cuestión social cubana: Conferencia leida en el instituto Booker T. Washington, la noche del día 21 de Abril de 1906*. Havana: La Propagandista, 1906.

Chakrabarty, Dipesh. "Postcoloniality and the Artifice of History: Who Speaks for 'Indian' Pasts?" *Representations* 37 (Winter 1992): 1–26.

Chamberlin, J. Edward, and Sander L. Gilman, eds. *Degeneration: The Dark Side of Progress*. New York: Columbia University Press, 1985.

Chapman, Charles. *A History of the Cuban Republic: A Study in Hispanic American Politics*. New York: Macmillan, 1927.

Chaterjee, Partha. *The Nation and Its Fragments: Colonial and Postcolonial Histories*. Princeton: Princeton University Press, 1993.

Chávez Alvarez, Ernesto. *El crimen de la niña Cecilia: La brujería en Cuba como fenómeno social, 1902–1925*. Havana: Editorial de Ciencias Sociales, 1991.

Chester, Edmund A. *A Sergeant Named Batista*. New York: Henry Holt and Co., 1954.

Chomsky, Aviva. "The Aftermath of Repression: Race and Nation in Cuba after 1912." *Journal of Iberian and Latin American Studies* 4, no. 2 (1998): 1–40.

Chomsky, Aviva, and Aldo Lauria-Santiago, eds. *Identity and Struggle at the Margins of the Nation-State: The Laboring Peoples of Central America and the Hispanic Caribbean*. Durham, N.C.: Duke University Press, 1998.

Clifford, James. "Objects and Selves." In *Objects and Others: Essays on Museums and Material Culture*, edited by George Stocking Jr., 236–46. Madison: University of Wisconsin Press, 1985.

———. *The Predicament of Culture: Twentieth-Century Ethnography, Literature, and Art*. Cambridge: Harvard University Press, 1988.

Clifford, James, and George E. Marcus, eds. *Writing Culture: The Poetics and Politics of Ethnography*. Berkeley: University of California Press, 1986.

Cohen, James, and Francoise Moulin Civil, eds. *Cuba sous le Régime de la Constitucion de 1940: Politique, pensée critique, litterature*. Paris: L'Harmattan, 1997.

Comaroff, John, and Jean Comaroff. *Ethnography and the Historical Imagination*. Boulder, Colo.: Westview Press, 1992.

Conte, Rafael, and José Capmany. *Guerra de razas: Negros contra blancos en Cuba*. Havana: Imprenta Militar de Antonio Pérez, 1912.

Cook, Mercer. "Urrutia." *Phylon* 4, no. 3 (1943): 221–32.

Cooper, Frederick. "Race, Ideology, and the Perils of Comparative History." *American Historical Review* (1996): 1122–38.

Cooper, Frederick, Thomas Holt, and Rebecca Scott, eds. *Beyond Slavery: Explorations of Race, Labor, and Citizenship*. Chapel Hill: University of North Carolina Press, 2000.

Coronil, Fernando. Introduction to *Cuban Counterpoint* by Fernando Ortiz. Durham, N.C.: Duke University Press, 1995.

Cottrol, Robert J. "The Long Lingering Shadow: Law, Liberalism, and Cultures of Racial Hierarchy and Identity in the Americas." *Tulane Law Review* 76 (2001): 11–80.

Cuba. *Anuario estadístico de la República de Cuba*. Havana: Imprenta El Siglo Veinte, 1915.

———. *Censo de la República de Cuba, 1907*. Washington: Oficina del Censo de los Estados Unidos, 1908.

———. *Census of the Republic of Cuba, 1919*. Havana: Oficina nacional del censo, 1922.

———. Convención Constituyente. *Diario de sesiones de la Convención Constituyente, 1940*.

———. *The Penal Code in Force in Cuba and Porto Rico*. Washington: Government Printing Office, 1901.

———. Secretaría de Justicia. *Memoria de estadística judicial: Quinquenio del 1909 al 1913*. Havana: Imprenta La Mercantil, 1915.

Cunard, Nancy, ed. *Negro Anthology, 1931–1933*. 1934. Reprint, New York: Negro Universities Press, 1969.

Danielson, Ross. *Cuban Medicine*. New Brunswick, N.J.: Transaction Books, 1979.

Darmon, Pierre. *Médecins et assassins à la Belle Epoque: La médicalisation du crime*. Paris: Editions du Seuil, 1989.

de la Fuente, Alejandro. "Myths of Racial Democracy: Cuba, 1900–1912." *Latin American Research Review* 34, no. 3 (1999): 39–73.

———. *A Nation for All: Race, Inequality, and Politics in Twentieth-Century Cuba*. Chapel Hill: University of North Carolina Press, 2001.

———. "Race and Inequality in Cuba, 1899–1981." *Journal of Contemporary History* 30 (1995): 131–68.

———. "Race, National Discourse, and Politics in Cuba: An Overview." *Latin American Perspectives* 25, no. 3 (1998): 43–69.

———. "'With All and for All': Race, Inequality, and Politics in Cuba, 1900–1930." Ph.D. diss., University of Pittsburgh, 1996.

Del Olmo, Rosa. *América Latina y su criminología*. Mexico: Siglo Veintiuno, 1981.

Derby, Lauren H. "The Magic of Modernity: Dictatorship and Civic Culture in the Dominican Republic, 1916–1962." Ph.D. diss., University of Chicago, 1998.

Deschamps Chapeaux, Pedro. *El negro en la economía habanera del siglo XIX*. Havana: Unión de Escritores y Artistas de Cuba, 1971.

———. *Rafael Serra y Montalvo, obrero incansable de nuestra independencia*. Havana: Unión de Escritores y Artistas de Cuba, 1975.

De Solo, Luis. "Conceptos y tendencias del derecho civil moderno." *Derecho y Sociología* 9, no. 1 (1906): 29–37.

De Velasco, Carlos. "Ni la amenaza ni la violencia: La ley." *Cuba Contemporanea* 13, no. 1 (1917): 5–10.

————. "El problema negro." *Cuba Contemporanea* 1:2 (1913): 73–79.

Dollero, Adolfo. *Cultura cubana*. Havana: Imprenta El Siglo XX, 1916.

Domínguez, Jorge. *Cuba: Order and Revolution*. Cambridge: Belknap Press of Harvard University Press, 1978.

————. "Seeking Permission to Build a Nation: Cuban Nationalism and U.S. Response under the First Machado Presidency." *Cuban Studies* 16 (1986): 33–48.

Dubow, Saul. *Scientific Racism in Modern South Africa*. Cambridge: Cambridge University Press, 1995.

Duke, Cathy. "The Idea of Race: The Cultural Impact of American Intervention in Cuba, 1898–1912." In *Politics, Society, and Culture in the Caribbean*, edited by Blanca Silvestrini, 87–109. San Juan: University of Puerto Rico Press, 1983.

Dumoulin, John. *Azúcar y lucha de clases*. Havana: Editorial de Ciencias Sociales, 1980.

Ellis, Keith. "Nicolás Guillén and Langston Hughes: Convergences and Divergences." In *Between Race and Empire: African Americans and Cubans before the Cuban Revolution*, edited by Lisa Brock and Digna Castañeda Fuertes, chap. 7. Philadelphia: Temple University Press, 1998.

Entralgo, Elías. *La liberación étnica cubana*. Havana, 1953.

Fabian, Johannes. *Time and the Other: How Anthropology Makes Its Object*. New York: Columbia University Press, 1983.

Fabre, Genevieve, and Robert O'Meally, eds. *History and Memory in African American Culture*. New York: Oxford University Press, 1994.

Farber, Samuel. *Revolution and Reaction in Cuba, 1933–1960: A Political Sociology from Machado to Castro*. Middletown, Conn.: Wesleyan University Press, 1976.

Fardon, Richard, ed. *Counterworks: Managing the Diversity of Knowledge*. New York: Routledge, 1995.

Federación Nacional de Sociedades Cubanas de la Raza de Color. *Manifiesto a la Asamblea Constituyente*. Havana: Imprenta O'Reilly, 1940.

Fentress, James, and Chris Wickham. *Social Memory*. Cambridge: Blackwell Publishers, 1992.

Fermoselle, Rafael. *The Evolution of the Cuban Military, 1492–1986*. Miami: Ediciones Universal, 1987.

————. *Política y color en Cuba: La Guerrita de 1912*. Montevideo: Editorial Geminis, 1974.

Fernández Robaina, Tomás. *Bibliografía de temas afrocubanos*. Havana: Biblioteca Nacional José Martí, 1985.

————. "Marcus Garvey in Cuba: Urrutia, Cubans and Black Nationalism." In *Between Race and Empire: African-Americans and Cubans before the Cuban Revolution*, edited by Lisa Brock and Digna Castañeda Fuertes, 120–28. Philadelphia: Temple University Press, 1998.

————. *El negro en Cuba, 1902–1958: Apuntes para la historia de la lucha contra la discriminación*. Havana: Editorial de Ciencias Sociales, 1990.

Ferrara, Orestes. *Anuario estadístico de la República de Cuba*. Havana: Imprenta Siglo XX, 1914.

Ferrer, Ada. *Insurgent Cuba: Race, Nation, and Revolution, 1868–1898*. Chapel Hill: University of North Carolina Press, 1999.

————. "Rustic Men, Civilized Nation: Race, Culture, and Contention on the Eve of Cuban Independence." *Hispanic American Historical Review* 78, no. 4 (1998): 663–86.

Ferri, Enrico. *Criminal Sociology*. 1884. Translated by Joseph Kelly and John Lisle. Reprint, Boston: Little, Brown, 1917.

Fields, Barbara. "Ideology and Race in American History." In *Region, Race, and Reconstruction: Essays in Honor of C. Vann Woodward*, edited by J. Morgan Kousser and James McPherson, 143–77. New York: Oxford University Press, 1982.

Figueras, Francisco. *Cuba y su evolución colonial*. Havana: Imprenta Avisador Comercial, 1907.

————. *La intervención y su política*. Havana: Imprenta Avisador Comercial, 1906.

Foreign Policy Association. *Problems of the New Cuba: Report of the Foreign Policy Association*. New York: Foreign Policy Association, 1935.

Fornet, Ambrosio. *En blanco y negro*. Havana: Instituto del Libro, 1967.

————. *El libro en Cuba, siglos 18 y 19*. Havana: Editorial Letras Cubanas, 1994.

Foucault, Michel. *The Order of Things: An Archaeology of the Human Sciences*. 1970. Reprint, New York: Vintage Books, 1994.

Galera, Andrés. *Ciencia y delincuencia: El determinismo antropológico en la España del siglo XIX*. Seville: Consejo Superior de Investigaciones Científicas, 1991.

García-Carranza, Araceli, Norma Suárez Suárez, and Alberto Quesada Morales. *Cronología Fernando Ortiz*. Havana: Fundación Fernando Ortiz, 1996.

García González, Armando, and Raquel Alvarez Peláez. *En busca de la raza perfecta: Eugenesia e higiene en Cuba, 1898–1958*. Madrid: Consejo Superior de Investigaciones Científicas, 1999.

García Martínez, Orlando, Fernando Martínez Heredia, and Rebecca Scott, eds. *Espacios, silencios y los sentidos de la libertad: Cuba entre 1878 y 1912*. Havana: Ediciones Unión, 2001.

Geertz, Clifford. *The Interpretation of Cultures*. New York: Basic Books, 1973.

Gerstle, Gary. "The Protean Character of American Liberalism." *American Historical Review* 99, no. 4 (1994): 1043–72.

Gilly, Adolfo. *El Cardenismo: Una utopia mexicana*. México: Cal y Arena, 1997.

Goluboff, Risa. "The Thirteenth Amendment and the Lost Origins of Civil Rights." *Duke Law Journal* 50 (2000–2001): 1609–85.

Gomes da Cunha, Olívia. *Intenção e Gesto: Pessoa, cor, e a produção cotidiana da (in)diferença no Rio de Janeiro, 1927–1942*. Rio de Janeiro: Arquivo Nacional, 2002.

Gómez, Juan Gualberto. *Preparando la revolución*. Havana: Secretaría de Educación, 1936.

Goody, Jack. *The Expansive Moment: The Rise of Social Anthropology in Britain and Africa, 1918–1970*. Cambridge: Cambridge University Press, 1995.

Gould, Jeffrey. *To Die in This Way: Nicaraguan Indians and the Myth of Mestizaje, 1880–1965*. Durham, N.C.: Duke University Press, 1998.

Gould, Stephen Jay. *The Mismeasure of Man*. New York: Norton, 1981.

Graham, Richard, ed. *The Idea of Race in Latin America, 1870–1940*. Austin: University of Texas Press, 1990.

Graizeau, Nicolas. "Genèse, exégèse et pratique de la Constitución de 1940." In *Cuba sous le régime de la Constitución de 1940: Politique, pensée critique, litterature*, edited by James Cohen and Francoise Moulin Civil. Paris: L'Harmattan, 1997.

Grandin, Greg. *The Blood of Guatemala: A History of Race and Nation*. Durham, N.C.: Duke University Press, 2000.

Greenberg, Stanley, Stanley N. Katz, Melanie Beth Oliviero, and Steven C. Wheatley, eds. *Constitutionalism and Democracy: Transitions in the Contemporary World*. New York: Oxford University Press, 1993.

Grobart, Fabio. "The Cuban Working Class Movement from 1925 to 1933." *Science and Society* 39, no. 1 (1975): 73–103.

Guanche, Jesus. *Componentes étnicos de la nación cubana*. Havana: Ediciones Unión, 1996.

Guerra, Francois-Xavier. *Modernidad e independencias: Ensayos sobre las revoluciones hispánicas*. Mexico: Fondo de Cultura Económica, 1992.

Guerra, Lillian. "From Revolution to Involution in the Early Cuban Republic: Conflicts over Race, Class, and Nation, 1902–1906." In *Race and Nation in Modern Latin America*, edited by Nancy Appelbaum, Anne Macpherson, and Karin Rosemblatt, 132–62. Chapel Hill: University of North Carolina Press, 2003.

Guerra y Sánchez, Ramiro. *Azúcar y población en las Antillas*. Havana: Cultural, 1927.

———. *Un cuarto de siglo de evolución cubana*. Havana: Librería Cervantes, 1924.

Guillén, Nicolás. *Prosa de prisa, 1929–1972*. Edited by Angel Augier. Havana: Editorial Arte y Literatura, 1975.

———. *Songoro Cosongo*. 1931. Reprint, Buenos Aires: Editorial Losada, 1952.

Guridy, Frank. "Racial Knowledge in Cuba: The Making of a Social Fact, 1912–1944." Ph.D. diss, University of Michigan, 2002.

Gutierrez, David. *Walls and Mirrors: Mexican Americans, Mexican Immigrants, and the Politics of Ethnicity*. Berkeley: University of California Press, 1995.

Hale, Charles. "Political and Social Ideas in Latin America, 1870–1930." In *The Cambridge History of Latin America*, vol. 4, edited by Leslie Bethell, 367–441. Cambridge: Cambridge University Press, 1986.

———. *The Transformation of Liberalism in Late-Nineteenth-Century Mexico*. Princeton: Princeton University Press, 1989.

Halperín Donghi, Tulio. *El espejo de la historia*. Buenos Aires: Editorial Sudamericana, 1998.

Hamilton, Nora. *The Limits of State Autonomy: Post-Revolutionary Mexico*. Princeton: Princeton University Press, 1982.

Harrowitz, Nancy. *Antisemitism, Misogyny, and the Logic of Cultural Difference: Césare Lombroso and Matilde Serao*. Lincoln: University of Nebraska Press, 1994.

Helg, Aline. "Black Men, Racial Stereotyping, and Violence in the U.S. South and Cuba at the Turn of the Century." *Comparative Studies in Society and History* 42 (2000): 576–604.

―――. *Our Rightful Share: The Afro-Cuban Struggle for Equality, 1886–1912*. Chapel Hill: University of North Carolina Press, 1995.

―――. "Race in Argentina and Cuba, 1880–1930: Theory, Policies, and Popular Reaction." In *The Idea of Race in Latin America, 1870–1940*, edited by Richard Graham, 37–69. Austin: University of Texas Press, 1990.

Henríquez Ureña, Max. "Problemas de nuestra América: Lecturas de Bunge y Rodó." *Cuba Contemporanea* 15, no. 2 (1917): 97–104.

Hennessy, Alistair, ed. *Intellectuals in the Twentieth Century*. London: Macmillan Press, 1992.

Hernández, Eusebio. *Homicultura*. Havana: Secretaría de Sanidad y Beneficencia, Moderna Poesía, 1911.

Hevia Lanier, Oilda. *El directorio central de las sociedades negras de Cuba, 1886–1894*. Havana: Editorial de Ciencias Sociales, 1996.

Hill, Robert, and Barbara Bair, eds. *Marcus Garvey: Life and Lessons*. Berkeley: University of California Press, 1987.

Hirschman, Albert O. *Exit, Voice, and Loyalty: Responses to Decline in Firms, Organizations, and States*. Cambridge: Harvard University Press, 1970.

Holt, Thomas C. "Marking: Race, Race-Making, and the Writing of History." *American Historical Review* (1995): 1–20.

―――. *The Problem of Race in the Twenty-first Century*. Cambridge: Harvard University Press, 2000.

Horrego Estuch, Leopoldo. *Juan Gualberto Gómez: Un gran inconforme*. Havana: Editorial La Milagrosa, 1954.

―――. *Martín Morúa Delgado: Vida y mensaje*. Havana, 1957.

Howard, Philip. *Changing History: Afro-Cuban Cabildos and Societies of Color in the Nineteenth Century*. Baton Rouge: Louisiana State University Press, 1998.

Huertas, Rafael, and Carmen Ortiz, eds. *Ciencia y Fascismo*. Madrid: Doce Calles, 1998.

Hunt, Lynn. *Politics, Culture, and Class in the French Revolution*. Berkeley: University of California Press, 1984.

Ibarra, Jorge. *Un análisis psicosocial del cubano, 1898–1925*. Havana: Editorial de Ciencias Sociales, 1994.

―――. *Cuba, 1898–1921: Partidos políticos y clases sociales*. Havana: Editorial de Ciencias Sociales, 1992.

―――. "La herencia científica de Fernando Ortiz." *Revista Iberoamericana* 56 (1990): 1339–51.

Ibarzábal, Federico. *Cuentos contemporaneos*. Havana: Editorial Trópico, 1937.

―――. *El problema negro*. Havana: N.p., 1935.

Iglesias, Marial. "José Martí: Mito, legitimación y símbolo: La génesis del mito martiano y la emergencia del nacionalismo republicano en Cuba, 1895–1920." In *Diez nuevas miradas de historia de Cuba*, edited by José Piqueras Arenas, 201–26. Castelló de la Plana: Universitat Jaume I, 1998.

Ingenieros, José. "Las razas en America y las ideas sociológicas de Sarmiento." *Cuba Contemporanea* 10 (1916): 15–36.

Instituto de Historia del Movimiento Comunista y de la Revolución Socialista de Cuba. *El movimiento obrero cubano: Documentos y artículos*. Vol. 2, 1925-35. Havana: Editorial de Ciencias Sociales, 1981.

Iznaga, Diana. *Transculturación en Fernando Ortiz*. Havana: Editorial de Ciencias Sociales, 1989.

James, C. L. R. *The Black Jacobins: Toussaint L'Ouverture and the San Domingo Revolution*. 1938. Reprint, New York: Random House, 1963.

James, Daniel. *Resistance and Integration: Peronism and the Argentine Working Class, 1946–1976*. New York: Cambridge University Press, 1988.

James, Winston. *Holding Aloft the Banner of Ethiopia: Caribbean Radicalism in Early-Twentieth-Century America*. New York: Verso Press, 1998.

Jiménez Pastrana, Juan. *Salvador García Agüero*. Havana: Editorial de Ciencias Sociales, 1985.

Jones, Anna Laura. "Exploding Canons: The Anthropology of Museums." *Annual Reviews in Anthropology* 22 (1993): 201–20.

Joseph, Gilbert M., and Daniel Nugent, eds. *Everyday Forms of State Formation: Revolution and the Negotiation of Rule in Modern Mexico*. Durham, N.C.: Duke University Press, 1994.

Kapcia, Antoni. "The Intellectual in Cuba: The National Popular Tradition." In *Intellectuals in the Twentieth Century*, edited by Alistair Hennessy, 2:58–82. London: Macmillan Press, 1992.

Kelley, Robin D. G. *Race Rebels: Culture, Politics, and the Black Working Class*. New York: Free Press, 1994.

Kevles, Daniel. *In the Name of Eugenics: Genetics and the Uses of Human Heredity*. New York: Knopf, 1985.

Knight, Alan. "Cardenismo: Juggernaut or Jalopy?" *Journal of Latin American Studies* 26 (1994): 73–107.

———. "Populism and Neo-Populism in Latin America, Especially Mexico." *Journal of Latin American Studies* 30, no. 2 (1998): 223–48.

———. "Racism, Revolution, and *Indigenismo*: Mexico, 1910–1940." In *The Idea of Race in Latin America, 1870–1940*, edited by Richard Graham. Austin: University of Texas Press, 1990.

Kopytoff, Igor. "The Cultural Biography of Things: Commoditization as Process." In *The Social Life of Things*, edited by Arjun Appadurai, 64–91. Cambridge: Cambridge University Press, 1988.

Kuklick, Henrika. *The Savage Within: The Social History of British Anthropology, 1885–1945*. Cambridge: Cambridge University Press, 1991.

Kutzinski, Vera. *Sugar's Secrets: Race and the Erotics of Cuban Nationalism*. Charlottesville: University of Virginia Press, 1993.

Lachatañeré, Romulo. "El sistema religioso de los Lucumís y otras influencias Africanas en Cuba"—Part 1. *Estudios Afrocubanos* 3 (1939): 28–84.

———. "El sistema religioso de los Lucumís y otras influencias Africanas en Cuba"—Part 2. *Estudios Afrocubanos* 4 (1940): 27–38.

Lafuente, A., A. Elena, and M. L. Ortega, eds. *Mundialización de la ciencia y cultura nacional*. Aranjuez, Spain: Doce Calles, 1993.

Lancis Sánchez, Francisco. *Estudios históricos y medicolegales: Cuadernos de la Salud Pública*. Havana: Centro Nacional de Información de Ciencias Medicas, 1991.

Lears, T. J. Jackson. "The Concept of Cultural Hegemony: Problems and Possibilities." *American Historical Review* 90, no. 3 (1985): 567–93.

Legêne, Susan. "From Brooms to Obeah and Back: Fetish Conversion and Border Crossings in Nineteenth-Century Suriname." In *Border Fetishisms: Material Objects in Unstable Spaces*, edited by Patricia Spyer, 35–59. New York: Routledge, 1998.

LeGoff, Jacques. *History and Memory*. New York: Columbia University Press, 1992.

León Rosabal, Blancamar. *La voz del Mambí: Imagen y mito*. Havana: Editorial de Ciencias Sociales, 1997.

LeRiverend, Julio. *La República: Dependencia y revolución*. Havana: Instituto del Libro, 1969.

Lindsay, Arturo, ed. *Santería Aesthetics*. Washington, D.C.: Smithsonian Institution Press, 1996.

Linke, Uli. "Folklore, Anthropology, and the Government of Social Life." *Comparative Studies in Society and History* 32, no. 1 (January 1990): 117–48.

Lombroso, Césare. *L'Homme Criminel*. Paris: Alcan, 1887.

Lombroso, Gina, ed. *Criminal Man according to the Classification of Césare Lombroso*. New York: Putnam, 1911.

López Lemus, Virgilio, ed. *Entrevistas: Alejo Carpentier*. Havana: Editorial Letras Cubanas, 1985.

MacGaffey, Wyatt. "The Eyes of Understanding: Kongo Minkisi." In *Astonishment and Power: Kongo Minkisi and the Art of Renée Stout*, edited by Wyatt MacGaffey and Michael Harris, 21–103. Washington, D.C.: Smithsonian Institution Press, 1993.

MacGaffey, Wyatt, and Michael Harris, eds. *Astonishment and Power: Kongo Minkisi and the Art of Renée Stout*. Washington, D.C.: Smithsonian Institution Press, 1993.

Machado y Morales, Gerardo. *Declaraciones del General Machado y Morales*. Havana: Rambla y Bouza, 1928.

———. *Mensaje del Presidente Gerardo Machado y Morales al Congreso de la República de Cuba*. Havana: Rambla, Bouza y Ca., 1928.

———. *Ocho años de lucha*. Miami: Ediciones Históricas Cubanas, 1982.

Mañalich, Octavio. *La homicultura: Breves consideraciones sobre la ciencia de los maestros Pinard-Hernández*. Havana: Imprenta Cuba Pedagógica, 1915.

Mannheim, Hermann, ed. *Pioneers in Criminology*. Montclair, Calif.: Patterson Smith, 1972.

Marinello, Juan. "Carta a un trinitario airado." *Bohemia* 26, no. 7 (February 25, 1934): 24.

———. "Linch en Trinidad." *Bohemia* 26, no. 5 (February 4, 1934): 36.

Marshall, T. H. *Citizenship and Social Class and Other Essays*. Cambridge: Cambridge University Press, 1950.

Martí, José. *Obras completas*. 27 vols. Havana: Editorial Nacional de Cuba, 1963.

Martínez, Juan. *Cuban Art and National Identity: The Vanguardia Painters, 1927–1950*. Gainesville: University of Florida Press, 1994.

Martínez-Alier, Verena. *Marriage, Class, and Colour in Nineteenth-Century Cuba: A Study of Racial Attitudes and Sexual Values in a Slave Society*. 2nd ed. Ann Arbor: University of Michigan Press, 1989.

Martínez Furé, Rogelio. *Diálogos imaginarios*. Havana: Editorial Letras Cubanas, 1997.

Martínez Heredia, Fernando. "El problemático nacionalismo de la primera República." *Temas* 24–25 (January–June 2001): 34–44.

Marx, Anthony. *Making Race and Nation*. Cambridge: Cambridge University Press, 1998.

McCleod, Marc. "Undesirable Aliens: Haitians and British West Indies Immigrant Workers in Cuba." Ph.D. diss., University of Texas at Austin, 2000.

———. "Undesirable Aliens: Race, Ethnicity, and Nationalism in the Comparison of Haitian and British West Indian Immigrant Workers in Cuba, 1912–1939." *Journal of Modern History* 31, no. 3 (Spring 1998): 599–623.

Merryman, John Henry. *The Civil Law Tradition: An Introduction to the Legal Systems of Western Europe and Latin America*. Stanford, Calif.: Stanford University Press, 1985.

Mestre, Arístides. "Brujería y criminalidad en Cuba." *Revista de la Facultad de Letras y Ciencias* 33 (1923): 307–24.

———. "Las leyes de herencia y la biología aplicada." *Revista de la Facultad de Letras y Ciencias* 28 (1918): 20–35.

———. *Montané en la antropología cubana*. Havana: Imprenta La Propagandista, 1938.

———. *La política moderna y la ciencia antropológica: El problema de la colonización*. Discurso leido en la sesión solemne de la sociedad antropológica, 7 octubre, 1887 y publicada en la "Revista Cubana." Havana: Soler, Alvarez y Cia., 1887.

Mestre y Amabile, Vicente. *Cuba: Un año de república*. Paris, 1903.

Montalvo, J. R., Carlos de la Torre, and Luis Montané. *El craneo de Maceo: Estudio antropológico*. Havana: Imprenta Militar, 1900.

Montané, Louis. "Rapport sur l'état des sciences anthropologiques a Cuba." *Bulletins et Memoirs de la Societe d'Anthropologie de Paris* 10, nos. 4–5 (1909): 370–75.

Moore, Robin D. *Nationalizing Blackness: Afrocubanismo and Artistic Revolution in Havana, 1920–1940*. Pittsburgh: University of Pittsburgh Press, 1997.

Morejón, Nancy. *Nación y mestizaje en Nicolás Guillén*. Havana: Unión de Escritores y Artistas de Cuba, 1982.

Moreno Fraginals, Manuel. *La historia como arma y otros estudios sobre esclavos, ingenios y plantaciones*. Barcelona: Editorial Crítica, 1983.

Morris, Rosalind. "Anthropology in the Body Shop: Lords of the Garden, Cannibalism, and the Consuming Desires of Televisual Anthropology." *American Anthropologist* 98, no. 1 (1996): 137–50.

Mustelier, Gustavo. *La extinción del negro: Apuntes político-sociales*. Havana: Imprenta Rambla Bouza y Ca., 1912.

Naranjo Orovio, Consuelo, and Armando García González. *Medicina y racismo en Cuba: La ciencia ante la inmigración canaria en el siglo XX*. Taller de Historia. Tenerife, Canary Islands: Centro de la Cultura Popular Canaria, 1996.

Naranjo Orovio, Consuelo, and Miguel Angel Puig-Samper. "Delincuencia y racismo en Cuba: Israel Castellanos versus Fernando Ortiz." In *Ciencia y fascismo*, edited by Rafael Huertas and Carmen Ortiz, 11–23. Madrid: Doce Calles, 1998.

Naranjo Orovio, Consuelo, and Miguel Angel Puig-Samper. "Pensamiento

científico y revolución en Cuba a finales del siglo XIX en la Revista Cubana."
Ibero-Americana Pregensia 32 (1998): 97–110.

Naranjo Orovio, Consuelo, and Mallo Gutierrez, Tomás, eds. *Cuba: La perla de las Antillas, Actas de las I Jornadas sobre "Cuba y su Historia."* Aranjuez, Spain: Doce Calles, 1994.

Naranjo Orovio, Consuelo, Miguel Angel Puig-Samper, and Luis Miguel García Mora, eds. *La nación soñada: Cuba, Puerto Rico y Filipinas ante el 98.* Aranjuez: Doce Calles, 1996.

Nirenberg, David. *Communities of Violence: Persecution of Minorities in the Middle Ages.* Princeton: Princeton University Press, 1996.

Novas Calvo, Lino. *El negrero.* 1932. Reprint, Buenos Aires: Espasa-Calpe, 1944.

Nye, Robert A. *Crime, Madness, and Politics in Modern France: The Medical Concept of National Decline.* Princeton: Princeton University Press, 1984.

———. "Sociology and Degeneration: The Irony of Progress." In Edward Chamberlin and Sander Gilman, *Degeneration: The Dark Side of Progress,* 49–71. New York: Columbia University Press, 1985.

O'Donnell, Guillermo. *Counterpoints: Selected Essays in Authoritarianism and Democratization.* Notre Dame, Ind.: University of Notre Dame Press, 1999.

Olwig, Karen Fog, and Kirsten Hastrup, eds. *Siting Culture: The Shifting Anthropological Object.* New York: Routledge, 1997.

Omi, Michael, and Howard Winant. *Racial Formation in the United States from the 1960's to the 1990's.* New York: Routledge, 1994.

Ortiz, Fernando. "Brujos o santeros," *Estudios Afrocubanos* 3 (1939): 85–90.

———. *Los cabildos y la fiesta afrocubanos del Día de Reyes.* 1921. Reprint, Havana: Editorial de Ciencias Sociales, 1992.

———. *Cuban Counterpoint.* 1940. Reprint, Durham, N.C.: Duke University Press, 1995.

———. *La decadencia cubana.* Havana: Imprenta y Papelería "La Universal," 1924.

———. *Entre cubanos: Psicología tropical.* 1913. Reprint, Havana: Editorial de Ciencias Sociales, 1987.

———. "La fiesta afrocubana del 'Día de Reyes.'" *Archivos del Folklore Cubano* 1, no. 2 (April 1924): 146–65; 1, no. 3 (1924): 228–43; 1, no. 4 (June 1925): 340–55.

———. *La hampa afro-cubana: Los negros brujos (apuntes para un estudio de etnología criminal).* 1906. Reprint, Madrid: Editorial América, 1917.

———. *Martí y las razas.* Havana: Comisión nacional organizadora de los actos y ediciones del centenario y del monumento de Martí, 1953.

———. *Los negros curros.* Havana: Editorial de Ciencias Sociales, 1986.

———. "Niños y Salvajes," in *Azul y Rojo* 2, no. 1 (January 1903).

———. "Origen de los Afro-Cubanos." *Cuba Contemporanea* 11 (1916): 213–39.

———. *Proyecto de Código Criminal Cubano.* Havana: Comisión Nacional Codificadora, 1926.

———. *La reconquista de América.* Paris: P. Ollendorf, 1911.

———. *La secta conga de los "Matiabos" de Cuba.* Mexico: Universidad Autónoma de Mexico, 1956.

———. "Tarjetas postales y la criminología." *Azul y Rojo* 1, no. 10 (October 1902): 4–5.

Ortiz, Fernando, Ramón Vasconcelos, et al. "Las comparsas populares del Carnaval Habanero." *Estudios Afrocubanos* 5 (1945–46): 130–47.

Orum, Thomas. "The Politics of Color: The Racial Dimension of Cuban Politics during the Early Republican Years, 1900–1912." Ph.D. diss., New York University, 1975.

Palmié, Stephan. "The Color of the Gods: Notes on a Question Better Left Unasked." In *Transnational America: The Fading of Borders in the Western Hemisphere*, edited by Berndt Ostendorf, 163–75. Heidelberg: Universitätsverlag C. Winter, 2002.

———. "Fernando Ortiz and the Cooking of History." *Ibero-Amerikanisches Archiv* 24 (1998): 1–21.

———. *Wizards and Scientists: Explorations in Afro-Cuban Modernity and Tradition*. Durham, N.C.: Duke University Press, 2002.

Pasquino, Pasquale. "Criminology: The Birth of a Special Savior." In *Ideology and Consciousness*, 131–46. In *The Origins and Growth of Criminology: Essays on Intellectual History, 1760–1945*, edited by Piers Beirne. Brookfield, Vt.: Dartmouth Publishing, 1994.

Patriarca, Silvana. *Numbers and Nationhood: Writing Statistics in Nineteenth-Century Italy*. New York: Cambridge University Press, 1996.

Peard, Julyan G. *Race, Place, and Medicine: The Idea of the Tropics in Nineteenth-Century Brazilian Medicine*. Durham: Duke University Press, 1999.

Pels, Peter, and Oscar Salemink, eds. *Colonial Subjects: Essays on the Practical History of Anthropology*. Ann Arbor: University of Michigan Press, 1999.

Pereda, Diego de, ed. *El nuevo pensamiento político de Cuba*. Havana: Editorial Lex, 1943.

Pérez, Pelayo. "El peligro amarillo y el peligro negro." *Cuba Contemporanea* 9 (1915): 250–259.

Pérez, Louis A., Jr. *Army Politics in Cuba, 1898–1958*. Pittsburgh: University of Pittsburgh Press, 1976.

———. *Cuba between Empires, 1878–1902*. Pittsburgh: University of Pittsburgh Press, 1983.

———. *Cuba under the Platt Amendment, 1902–1934*. Pittsburgh: University of Pittsburgh Press, 1986.

———. *Cuba and the United States: Ties of Singular Intimacy*. Athens: University of Georgia Press, 1990.

———. *Essays on Cuban History: Historiography and Research*. Gainesville: University Press of Florida, 1995.

———. *Intervention, Revolution, and Politics in Cuba, 1913–1921*. Pittsburgh: University of Pittsburgh Press, 1978.

———. *On Becoming Cuban: Identity, Nationality, and Culture*. Chapel Hill: University of North Carolina Press, 1999.

———. "Politics, Peasants, and People of Color: The 1912 'Race War' Reconsidered." *Hispanic American Historical Review* 66, no. 3 (1986): 509–39.

Pérez Sarduy, Pedro, and Jean Stubbs, eds. *Afro-Cuban Voices: On Race and Identity in Contemporary Cuba*. Gainesville: University Press of Florida, 2000.

Pérez-Stable, Marifeli. *The Cuban Revolution: Origins, Course, and Legacy*. New York: Oxford University Press, 1993.

Peset, José Luis, and Mariano Peset. *Lombroso y la escuela postivista*. Madrid: Consejo Superior de Investigaciones Científicas, 1975.

Phillips, Ruby Hart. *Cuba: Island of Paradox*. New York: McDowell, Obolensky, Inc., 1962.

Pick, Daniel. "The Faces of Anarchy: Lombroso and the Politics of Criminal Science in Post-Unification Italy." *History Workshop Journal* 21 (1986): 60–86.

———. *The Faces of Degeneration: A European Disorder, 1848–1918*. Cambridge: Cambridge University Press, 1989.

Pietz, William. "The Problem of the Fetish, I." *Res* 9 (Spring 1985): 5–17.

———. "The Problem of the Fetish, II." *Res* 13 (Spring 1987): 23–45.

———. "The Problem of the Fetish, IIIa." *Res* 16 (Autumn 1998): 105–23.

Piqueras Arenas, José, ed. *Diez nuevas miradas de historia de Cuba*. Castelló de la Plana: Universitat Jaume I, 1998.

Portuondo Linares, Serafín. *Los independientes de color*. Havana: Editorial Librería Selecta, 1950. Reprint, with a prologue by Fernando Martínez Heredia (Havana: Editorial Caminos, 2002).

Poumier, Maria. "La expresión del pensamiento negro en Cuba bajo la Constitución de 1940." In *Cuba sous le régime de la Constitución de 1940: Politique, pensée critique, litterature*, edited by James Cohen and Francoise Moulin Civil. Paris: L'Harmattan, 1997.

Poveda Ferrer, Simeon. *Nydia y Fidel: Novela cubana*. Havana: Imprenta La Prueba, 1920.

Primera Conferencia Panamericana de Eugenesia y Homicultura de las Repúblicas Americanas. *Actas de la primera conferencia Panamericana de Eugenesia y Homicultura de las Repúblicas Americanas*. Havana, 1928.

Pruna, Pedro. *Darwinismo y sociedad en Cuba, siglo XIX*. Madrid: Consejo Superior de Investigaciones Científicas, 1984.

Quiza Moreno, Ricardo. "Fernando Ortiz y su *hampa afrocubana*." In *Diez nuevas miradas de historia de Cuba*, edited by José Piqueras Arenas, 227–45. Castelló de la Plana: Universitat Jaume I, 1998.

Rama, Angel. *The Lettered City*. Translated by John Chasteen. Durham, N.C.: Duke University Press, 1996.

Ramos, Domingo F. "Algo sobre la homicultura: La genetica y la embriología experimentales en relación con la medicina." *Vida Nueva* 5 (May 1916).

———. "Homiculture in Its Relation to Eugenics in Cuba." In *Eugenics in Race and State: Scientific Papers of the Second International Congress of Eugenics*, 2:432–34. Baltimore: Williams and Wilkins Co., 1923.

Ramos, José Antonio. *Entreactos*. Havana: Librería Cervantes, 1913.

Rexach, Rosario. "La segunda generación republicana en Cuba y sus figuras principales." *Revista Iberoamericana* 152–53 (July–December 1990): 1291–1311.

Ricardo, José G. *La imprenta en Cuba*. Havana: Editorial Letras Cubanas, 1989.

Richardson, Michael, ed. *Refusal of the Shadow: Surrealism and the Caribbean*. New York: Verso Press, 1996.

Ripoll, Carlos. *La generación del 23 en Cuba y otros apuntes sobre el vanguardismo*. New York: Las Américas, 1986.

Rivero de la Calle, Manuel, ed. *Actas: Sociedad antropológica de la isla de Cuba*. Havana: Comisión Nacional Cubana de la Unesco, 1966.

———. "Primer centenario de la fundación de la Sociedad Antropológica de la isla de Cuba." Paper presented at the Inauguración de la exposición dedicada a la Sociedad Antropológica de la Isla de Cuba, Havana, 1977.

Robreño, Eduardo, ed. *Teatro Alhambra: Antología*. Havana: Editorial Letras Cubanas, 1979.

Roca, Blas Calderío. *Por la igualdad de todos los cubanos*. Havana: Ediciones Sociales, 1939.

———. *El pueblo y la nueva constitución*. Havana: Ediciones Sociales, 1940.

Roche y Monteagudo, Rafael. *La policía y sus misterios en Cuba*. 1908. Reprint, Havana: La Moderna Poesía, 1925.

Rodgers, Daniel T. *Atlantic Crossings: Social Politics in a Progressive Age*. Cambridge: Harvard University Press, 1998.

———. "In Search of Progressivism." *Reviews in American History* 10 (1982): 113–32.

Roig de Leuchsenring, Emilio. "Las comparsas carnavalescas de la Habana en 1937." *Estudios Afrocubanos* 5 (1945–46): 148–72.

———. *Males y vicios de Cuba republicana, sus causas y sus remedios*. Havana: Oficina del Historiador de la Ciudad, 1959.

———. *Médicos y medicina en Cuba: Historia, biografía, costumbrismo*. Havana: Museo Histórico de las Ciencias Médicas "Carlos J Finlay," 1965.

Rojas, Rafael. *Isla sin fin: Contribución a la crítica del nacionalismo cubano*. Miami: Ediciones Universal, 1998.

Román, Reinaldo. "Conjuring Progress and Divinity: Religion and Conflict in Cuba and Puerto Rico, 1899–1956." Ph.D. diss., University of California at Los Angeles, 2000.

Roseberry, William. *Anthropologies and Histories: Essays in Culture, History, and Political Economy*. New Brunswick, N.J.: Rutgers University Press, 1989.

Rosell, Mirta, ed. *Luchas obreras contra Machado*. Havana: Editorial de Ciencias Sociales, 1973.

Rosenberg, Charles. "Eugenics in Race and State." Paper presented at the Second International Congress on Eugenics, New York, 1921.

Ruíz Funes, Mariano. *Delito y libertad: Ensayos*. Madrid: Javier Morata, 1930.

Sabato, Hilda. "Citizenship, Political Participation, and the Formation of the Public Sphere in Buenos Aires, 1850's–1880's." *Past and Present* 136 (August 1992): 139–63.

Sánchez Martínez, Luis. *Guía del policía cubano*. Havana: Imprenta Comas y Lopez, 1914.

Sarmiento, Domingo F. *Conflicto y armonía de las razas en America*. Buenos Aires: La Cultura Argentina, 1915.

Schneider, William. *Quantity and Quality: The Quest for Biological Regeneration in Twentieth-Century France*. New York: Cambridge University Press, 1990.

Schorske, Carl E. "History and the Study of Culture." *New Literary History* 21, no. 2 (1990): 407–20.

Schwarcz, Lilia Moritz. *The Spectacle of the Races: Scientists, Institutions, and the Race Question in Brazil, 1870–1930.* Translated by Leland Guyer. New York: Hill and Wang, 1999.

Schwarz, Rosalie. "Cuba's Roaring Twenties: Race Consciousness and the Column 'Ideales de una Raza.'" In *Between Race and Empire: African-Americans and Cubans before the Cuban Revolution,* edited by Lisa Brock and Digna Castañeda Fuertes, 104–19. Philadelphia: Temple University Press, 1998.

———. *Pleasure Island: Tourism and Temptation in Cuba.* Lincoln: University of Nebraska Press, 1997.

Scott, James. *Seeing Like a State: How Certain Schemes to Improve the Human Condition Have Failed.* New Haven: Yale University Press, 1998.

Scott, Rebecca J. "Cuba: Questions sociales, raciales et politiques d'une transition à l'autre." *Problèmes d'Amerique Latine* 17 (April–June 1995): 3–16.

———. "'The Lower Class of Whites' and 'The Negro Element': Race, Social Identity, and Politics in Central Cuba, 1899–1909." In *La nación soñada: Cuba, Puerto Rico y Filipinas ante el 98,* edited by Consuelo Naranjo Orovio, Miguel Angel Puig-Samper, and Luis Miguel García Mora, 179–91. Aranjuez: Doce Calles, 1996.

———. "The Provincial Archive as a Place of Memory: Confronting Oral and Written Sources on the Role of Former Slaves in the Cuban War of Independence (1895–1898)." *New West Indian Guide* 76, nos. 3–4 (2002): 191–209.

———. "Race, Labor, and Citizenship in Cuba: A View from the Sugar District of Cienfuegos, 1886–1909." *Hispanic American Historical Review* 78, no. 4 (1998): 687–728.

———. "Reclaiming Gregoria's Mule: The Meanings of Freedom in the Arimao and Caunao Valleys, Cienfuegos, Cuba, 1880–1899." *Past and Present* 170 (February 2001): 181–216.

———. *Slave Emancipation in Cuba: The Transition to Free Labor, 1860–1899.* Princeton: Princeton University Press, 1985.

Scott, Rebecca J., and Michael Zeuske. "Property in Writing, Property on the Ground: Pigs, Horses, Land, and Citizenship in the Aftermath of Slavery, Cuba, 1880–1909." *Comparative Studies in Society and History* 44, no. 4 (2002): 669–99.

Serra y Montalvo, Rafael. *Para blancos y negros: Ensayos políticos, sociales y económicos.* Havana: Imprenta "El Score," 1907.

Serviat, Pedro. *El problema negro en Cuba y su solución definitiva.* Havana: Editora Política, 1986.

Shannon, Magdaline. *Jean Price-Mars, the Haitian Elite, and the American Occupation, 1915–1935.* New York: St. Martin's Press, 1996.

Sixto de Sola, José. "El acercamiento intelectual de America: 'El hombre mediocre' de José Ingenieros." *Cuba Contemporanea* 10 (1916): 193–210.

Skidmore, Thomas. *Black into White: Race and Nationality in Brazilian Thought.* 2nd ed. Durham, N.C.: Duke University Press, 1993.

Smorkaloff, Pamela Maria. *Readers and Writers in Cuba: A Social History of Print Culture, 1830's–1990's.* New York: Garland Publishing, 1997.

Somers, Margaret. "What's Political or Cultural about Political Culture and the Public Sphere? Toward an Historical Sociology of Concept Formation." *Sociological Theory* 13, no. 2 (1995): 113–42.

Sosa Rodriguez, Enrique. *Los Ñáñigos*. Havana: Casa de las Américas, 1982.

Soto, Lionel. *La revolución del 33*. 3 vols. Havana: Editorial de Ciencias Sociales, 1977.

Spain. Ministerio de Ultramar. *Spanish Rule in Cuba: Laws Governing the Island: Review published by the Colonial Office in Madrid, with Data and Statistics Compiled from Official Records*. Authorized translation with additional notes. New York, 1896.

Spyer, Patricia, ed. *Border Fetishisms: Material Objects in Unstable Spaces*. New York: Routledge, 1998.

Starobinski, Jean. *Blessings in Disguise, or The Morality of Evil*. Cambridge: Harvard University Press, 1993.

Steinhardt, Dr. Irving. "La madre debe ser criandera." *Vida Nueva* 9 (September 1910).

Stepan, Nancy Leys. *"The Hour of Eugenics": Race, Gender, and Nation in Latin America*. Ithaca, N.Y.: Cornell University Press, 1991.

Stewart, Susan. *On Longing: Narratives of the Miniature, the Gigantic, the Souvenir, the Collection*. Baltimore: Johns Hopkins University Press, 1984.

Stewart, T. D., ed. *Hrdlicka's Practical Anthropometry*. 4th ed. Philadelphia: Wistar Institute of Anatomy and Biology, 1952.

Stocking, George W., Jr. *After Tylor: British Social Anthropology 1888–1951*. Madison: University of Wisconsin Press, 1995.

———. *Race, Culture, and Evolution: Essays in the History of Anthropology*. Chicago: University of Chicago Press, 1982.

———, ed. *The Ethnographer's Magic and Other Essays in the History of Anthropology*. Madison: University of Wisconsin Press, 1992.

———, ed. *Objects and Others: Essays on Museums and Material Culture*. Madison: University of Wisconsin Press, 1985.

———. "Paradigmatic Traditions in the History of Anthropology." In *The Ethnographers' Magic and Other Essays in the History of Anthropology*, edited by George W. Stocking Jr., 342–61. Madison: University of Wisconsin Press, 1992.

———, ed. *Romantic Motives: Essays on Romantic Sensibility*. Madison: University of Wisconsin Press, 1989.

Stoner, K. Lynn. *From the House to the Streets: The Cuban Woman's Movement for Legal Reform, 1898–1940*. Durham, N.C.: Duke University Press, 1991.

Stubbs, Jean. *Tobacco on the Periphery: A Case Study in Cuban Labour History, 1860–1958*. Cambridge: Cambridge University Press, 1985.

Suárez Díaz, Ana, ed. *Juan Marinello: Cuba: Cultura*. Havana: Editorial Letras Cubanas, 1989.

Tabares del Real, José. *La revolución del 30: Sus dos ultimos años*. Havana: Editorial de Ciencias Sociales, 1973.

Thomas, Hugh. *Cuba: The Pursuit of Freedom*. New York: Harper and Row, 1971.

Thomas, Nicholas. *Entangled Objects: Exchange, Material Culture, and Colonialism in the Pacific*. Cambridge: Harvard University Press, 1991.

Thompson, Charles A. "The Cuban Revolution: Reform and Reaction." *Foreign Policy Reports* 11, no. 22 (January 1, 1936): 262–76.

Tilly, Charles. *Big Structures, Large Processes, Huge Comparisons*. New York: Russell Sage, 1984.

———. "Citizenship, Identity, and Social History." *International Review of Social History* 40, supp. 3 (1995): 1–17.

Tocqueville, Alexis de. *Democracy in America*. 2 vols. 1835. Reprint, New York: Vintage Press, 1990.

Trelles y Govín, Carlos M. "Bibliografía de autores de la raza de color de Cuba." *Cuba Contemporanea* 43 (1927): 30–78.

Trouillot, Michel-Rolph. *Haiti: State against Nation: The Origins and Legacy of Duvalierism*. New York: Monthly Review Press, 1990.

Trujillo, José. *Los criminales de Cuba*. Barcelona, 1882.

Tucker, William H. *The Science and Politics of Racial Research*. Chicago: University of Illinois Press, 1994.

Turits, Richard. "The Foundations of Despotism: Agrarian Reform, Rural Transformation, and Peasant-State Compromise in Trujillo's Dominican Republic, 1930–1944." In *Identity and Struggle at the Margins of the Nation-State: The Laboring Peoples of Central America and the Hispanic Caribbean*, edited by Aviva Chomsky and Aldo Lauria-Santiago, 292–334. Durham, N.C.: Duke University Press, 1998.

University of Havana. *Memorias anuarios, 1901–1940*. Havana: Imprenta Avisador Comercial, 1901–40.

Uribe, Maria Victoria, and Eduardo Restrepo, eds. *Antropología en la modernidad: Identidades, etnicidades y movimientos sociales en Colombia*. Bogota: Instituto Colombiano de Antropología, 1997.

Urrutia, Gustavo E. *Puntos de vista del nuevo negro*. Havana: Imprenta El Score, 1937.

———. "Racial Prejudice in Cuba: How It Compares to That of the North Americans." In *Negro Anthology*, edited by Nancy Cunard, 473–74.

Varona, Enrique José. "La Reconquista." *Cuba Contemporanea* 9 (1915): 32–38.

Vasconcelos, José. *La raza cósmica*. 1925. Reprint, Baltimore: Johns Hopkins University Press, 1997.

Villoldo, Julio. "El lynchamiento, social y juridicamente considerado." *Cuba Contemporanea* 21, no. 81 (1919): 5–19.

Wade, Peter. *Blackness and Race Mixture: The Dynamics of Racial Identity in Colombia*. Baltimore: Johns Hopkins University Press, 1993.

———. *Race and Ethnicity in Latin America*. London: Pluto Press, 1997.

———. "'Race,' Nature, and Culture." *Man* 29 (1993): 17–34.

———. *Race, Nature, and Culture: An Anthropological Perspective*. London: Pluto Press, 2002.

Weinstein, Barbara. *For Social Peace in Brazil: Industrialists and the Remaking of the Working Class in São Paulo, 1920–1940*. Chapel Hill: University of North Carolina Press, 1996.

———. "Racializing Regional Difference: São Paulo versus Brazil, 1932." In *Race and Nation in Modern Latin America*, edited by Nancy Appelbaum, Anne

MacPherson, and Karin Rosemblatt, 237–62. Chapel Hill: University of North Carolina Press, 2003.

Whitney, Robert. "The Architect of the Cuban State: Fulgencio Batista and Populism in Cuba, 1937–1940." *Journal of Latin American Studies* 32, no. 2 (2000): 435–59.

———. *State and Revolution in Cuba: Mass Mobilization and Political Change*. Chapel Hill: University of North Carolina Press, 2001.

Whitten, Norman, Jr., and Arlene Torres, eds. *Blackness in Latin America and the Caribbean: Social Dynamics and Cultural Transformations*. Bloomington: University of Indiana Press, 1998.

Williams, Daryle. *Culture Wars in Brazil: The First Vargas Regime, 1930–1945*. Durham, N.C.: Duke University Press, 2001.

Williams, Elizabeth. "Art and Artifact at the Trocadero: Ars Americana and the Primitivist Revolution." In *Objects and Others: Essays on Museums and Material Culture*, edited by George W. Stocking Jr., 146–66. Madison: University of Wisconsin Press, 1985.

Yelvington, Kevin. "The War in Ethiopia and Trinidad, 1935–1936." In *The Colonial Caribbean in Transition: Essays on Post-Emancipation Social and Cultural History*, edited by Bridget Brereton and Kevin Yelvington. Gainesville: University of Florida Press, 1999.

Yglesia Martínez, Teresita. *Cuba: Primera república, segunda intervención*. Havana: Editorial de Ciencias Sociales, 1976.

Zeuske, Michael. "The *Cimarrón* in the Archives: A Re-Reading of Miguel Barnet's Biography of Esteban Montejo." *New West Indian Guide* 71, nos. 3–4 (1997): 265–79.

———. "'Los negros hicimos la independencia': Aspectos de la movilización afrocubana en un hinterland cubano: Cienfuegos entre colonia y república." In *Espacios, silencios y los sentidos de la libertad: Cuba entre 1878 y 1912*, edited by Orlando García Martínez, Fernando Martínez Heredia, and Rebecca J. Scott, 193–234. Havana: Ediciones Unión, 2001.

Zimmermann, Eduardo A. *Los liberales reformistas: La cuestión social en la Argentina, 1890–1916*. Buenos Aires: Editorial Sudamericana, 1995.

———. "Racial Ideas and Social Reform: Argentina, 1890–1916." *Hispanic American Historical Review* 72, no. 1 (1992): 23–46.

———. "Raza, medicina y reforma social en la Argentina, 1890–1920." In *Mundialización de la ciencia y cultura nacional*, edited by A. Lafuente, A. Elena, and M. L. Ortega, 573–85. Aranjuez, Spain: Doce Calles, 1993.

:: Index

Camagüey, 82, 156

Campos Marquetti, Generoso, 11, 85, 95, 157

Capestany, Manuel, 135, 136

Cárdenas, Lázaro, 172

Carrera y Justiz, Francisco, 41, 42, 119

Castellanos, Alberto, 85

Castellanos, Israel, 62–64, 93, 126–33

Cebreco, Agustín, 85

Cecilia (kidnapped child), 99, 100

Celia (kidnapped child), 38

Céspedes, Miguel Angel, 136, 144, 154, 169

Céspedes Casado, Emilio, 42

Chapman, Charles, 104

Chávez Alvarez, Ernesto, 53

Cienfuegos, 142

Citizenship: and Directorio de las Sociedades de Color, 10; and military participation, 11–12, 68, 71, 75–77; and civic virtue, 12, 68, 162; and Rafael Serra, 70–75; and the PIC, 77; and sociedades de color, 88–93, 140–44; and Urrutia, 144–47; and comparsas, 161, 171

Clientelism, 75, 76–77

Clifford, James, 19, 112

Club Atenas, 89, 102–4, 115–16, 135, 140, 154, 156, 157, 170, 174

Cold Spring Harbor Eugenics Office, 120

Comercio, El, 52

Comité de Acción de Veteranos y Sociedades de la Raza de Color, 11

Comité por los Derechos del Negro, 157, 172, 175

Communism, 152–53, 172

Communist Party of Cuba. See Partido Comunista de Cuba

Comparsas, 22, 159–61, 164, 168–71

Confederación Nacional Obrera de Cuba (CNOC), 105, 108, 154–55

Conservative Party, 74, 85

Constitution: of 1901, 2, 23–24, 57, 73, 90, 161, 173, 178; of 1940, 14, 162, 165, 179–81, 184; colonial, 23

Constitutional convention of 1940, 162, 171–78

Convención de Sociedades Negras, 166, 167

Cook, Mercer, 145

Cosculluela, Antonio, 114

Craneo de Maceo: Estudio antropológico, El, 1

Crime of Cuba, The, 151

Criminology, 13–14, 38, 50, 109, 111, 124–34, 139

Cuban Anthropological Society, 28, 30

Cuban Association of Sugar Manufacturers, 163

Cuba y América, 60

Cuesta, Ramiro, 81, 85, 145

Dance of the Millions, 104, 123

Darwin, Charles, 29, 30

Davenport, Charles, 120–23

De la Concepción Valdés, Gabriel ("Plácido"), 167

De la Cuesta, Federico, 157

De la Fuente, Alejandro, 4–5, 39, 68, 91, 137

De la Torre, Carlos, 114

Delgado, Manuel, 85, 136

Demócrata República, 172

Derecho y Sociología, 60, 61

Deschamps Chapeaux, Pedro, 69

De Tocqueville, Alexis, 4

Día, El, 39, 95, 99, 101

Día de Reyes, 22

Diario de la Familia, 52

Diario de la Marina, 44, 116, 140, 144, 145, 170

Dickinson Abreu, Antolín, 154

Dolz, Maria Luisa, 119

Domínguez, Jorge, 67, 108

D'Ou, Lino, 85, 95, 149

Du Bois, W. E. B., 67, 145, 167

Duque, Matías, 141

El Gabriel, 37

Estenoz, Evaristo, 68, 69, 77, 81–82, 85

Larrinaga, Angel, 54
Latapier, Juan, 56, 58, 96
Latin America: and colonial legacies, 2; and liberalism, 3; in social scientific journals, 61; and eugenics, 121–23; and role of the state in 1930s, 164; and popular mobilization, 180
La Unión Española, 52
Law: legal system in republic, 23–25; and illicit association, 56–57; and ban on discrimination, 179–81, 184. *See also* Constitution
Légitime Défense, 153
Liberalism, 3, 23
Liberal Party, 33, 67, 74, 85, 104, 107, 149, 172
Liga Nacional de Homicultura, 119
Lombard, Aquilino, 140–41, 154–55, 157
Lombrosian theory, 29–31, 46, 52, 62–63, 133. *See also* Lombroso, Césare
Lombroso, Césare, 13, 30–31, 34, 46, 52, 59, 61, 62. *See also* Lombrosian theory
Los negros brujos, 48–51, 95; reviews of, 51–53
Los negros curros, 112–13
Lynching, 99–101; critique of, 102–4

Maceo, Antonio, 1, 79, 167
Machado y Morales, Gerardo: and reformist agenda, 107–8; support of scientific activity, 109, 117, 121, 134; and Sociedad del Folklore Cubano, 114; and criminology, 124; support of sociedades de color, 135–39, 140; and revolution of 1933, 155–58; and constitutional reform of 1928, 164
Mañach, Jorge, 172
Mañalich, Octavio, 120
Mansip, Estanislao, 20, 156
Mariel, 99
Marinello, Juan, 114, 153, 157, 166, 168, 172, 174, 175
Marshall, T. H., 161
Martí, José, 2, 70, 71, 73, 82, 183
Martínez, Juan, 157
Martínez, Sánchez, 24

Martínez Ortiz, Rafael, 121–22
Martínez Villena, Rubén, 114
Marxism, 152–53
Matanzas, 70, 99, 100, 101, 103, 117
Mediodía, 149
Mella, Julio Antonio, 105, 118, 149
Menocal, Mario, 61, 172
Mestizaje, 121–22, 128–31, 133, 138, 148–52, 178
Mestre, Arístides, 28–29, 60, 120
Mexico, 164, 172, 180
Miscegenation. *See* Mestizaje
Model Prison, 124, 128
Moderate Party, 74
Molina, Victor, 38, 45
Montané, Luis, 7, 28, 30–31, 38, 53, 58–60
Monteagudo, José Jesus, 86
Moore, Robin, 22
Morúa Amendment, 77, 79, 81, 84
Morúa Delgado, Martín, 68, 70, 77, 136, 141, 167
Motherhood Competitions, 119
Mundo, El, 37, 44, 45, 51, 53, 78, 84
Museo Antropológico Montané (Museum of Anthropology), 9, 12, 18, 28, 30–32, 38, 72

Ñáñigos, 18, 20–21, 23–25, 31, 32, 39; in the press, 43; legal definition of, 54–56; and Israel Castellanos, 63, 128
National Association for the Advancement of Colored People (NAACP), 145, 153
National identity: and anxieties about civilization, 39, 41; and social science, 61–62; and constitution of 1940, 184
Nationalism, 1, 18, 34; and anti-imperialism, 104–5; and Machado, 107–8, 124; and eugenics, 119, 121–22
National Motherhood, Homiculture, and Eugenic Reproduction Competitions, 119
Navarrete, Raúl, 137
Négritude, 152
Negro World, 152
New Deal, 164